Geoff Andrews is a writer and historian who specialises in the history of political ideas and movements. His previous books include *The Slow Food Story: Politics and Pleasure*; *Not a Normal Country: Italy After Berlusconi* and *Endgames and New Times: The Final Years of British Communism*. He is Senior Lecturer in Politics at The Open University.

'This quite unapologetic and exciting biography rescues James Klugmann from the condescension of posterity and from those of us who regarded him (mistakenly) as simply a dull British communist apparatchik. By strongly contextualising Klugmann's life, Geoff Andrews gives us a fuller picture of the man, an unswerving communist, a friend of the Cambridge spies, a recruit of Soviet intelligence, a senior SOE operative (under the nose of MI5), a great supporter of Tito before joining in Stalin's fatwa, and, yes, also an ultra-loyalist communist hack.'

Donald Sassoon, author of *One Hundred Years of Socialism*

'Klugmann developed from the brilliant Cambridge undergraduate and student communist into a Stalinist intellectual, willing to denounce his former wartime comrades in the Yugoslav Communist Party. He can be an elusive quarry, and Geoff Andrews has done a fine job in piecing together the story. This fascinating biography illuminates the world of the mid-twentieth-century communist intellectuals: the idealism that motivated them, and the choices that they had to make.'

Tom Buchanan, Professor of Modern British and European History, University of Oxford

THE SHADOW MAN

At the **Heart** of the
Cambridge Spy Circle

GEOFF ANDREWS

I.B. TAURIS

LONDON · NEW YORK

Published in 2015 by
I.B.Tauris & Co. Ltd
London • New York
www.ibtauris.com

ISBN: 978 1 78453 166 9
eISBN: 978 0 85773 956 8

A full CIP record for this book is available from the British Library
A full CIP record is available from the Library of Congress

Library of Congress Catalog Card Number: available

Typeset by JCS Publishing Services Ltd, www.jcs-publishing.co.uk
Printed and bound by ScandBook AB, Sweden

Contents

Illustrations

Acknowledgements

The book draws on James Klugmann's own extensive archive and papers, housed in the Marx Memorial Library, the Labour History Archive and Study Centre at the People's History Museum in Manchester, the School of Slavonic and East European Studies at University College, London and the Klugmann Collection at the University of Sheffield. I would like to thank Alan Powderly at the Marx Memorial Library for his help while he was cataloguing the Klugmann papers and subsequently Meirian Jump for permission to use photographs. Darren Treadwell at the Labour History Archive and Study Centre, at the People's History Museum in Manchester, has been very kind in arranging access to Klugmann material, held in its CPGB Archive, on several visits. The Eva Tas papers at the Social History Institute in Amsterdam provided an another important collection which detailed Klugmann's RME years in Paris, and I am grateful for the help from archivists during my visit.

I would like to thank Mike Fitzmaurice of The Hall School, Hampstead for making the school's archive available and arranging a visit to the school, as well as the permission to use James Klugmann's poem 'On the Lower Fourth Debating Society'. Liz Larby at the Gresham's School archive answered many queries and Simon Kinder, the school's history tutor, has been generous with his time and in sharing his own thoughts on James Klugmann and his Gresham's cohort. I am indebted to Jonathan Smith, archivist at Trinity College, Cambridge, which holds the papers of several of Klugmann's contemporaries. Hannah Westall, archivist at Girton College, Cambridge, was very helpful in locating material on Kitty Klugmann.

Archivists at the Institute of Education and Goldsmith's College helped with the Brian Simon and Margot Heinemann collections, and thanks are also due to the librarians at The National Archives in Kew, the British Library, the Imperial War Museum, and the Bodleian Library, Oxford, for answering many queries.

I am grateful to Roderick Bailey for reading earlier draft chapters on Klugmann's SOE years. I would also like to thank Roderick Floud and Nicholas Deakin for inviting me to contribute to the Gresham College series 'Middle Class

Recruits to Communism in the 1930s' and to the Floud family for permission to use photographs from the China delegation in 1938. It has been a pleasure to talk about the politics of the 1930s with Jane Bernal and to hear more about her research on the life of her mother, Margot Heinemann.

I am grateful to the following for granting me interviews: Tom Bell, Joan Bellamy, the late Michael Barratt Brown, Mike Carter, the late Pete Carter, Henry Cook, the late John Earle, Roderick Floud, Renzo Galeotti, Julian Tudor Hart, the late Eric Hobsbawm, Martin Jacques, the late Grahame Locke, Linda Rene-Martin, Andreas Michaelides, Canon Paul Oestreicher, James Pettifer, Stephen Sedley, Michael Seifert, Jeff Skelley, Peter Stansky, Wolf Suschitzky and Conrad Wood.

The initial stages of my research benefited from the support of the Barry Amiel and Norman Melburn Trust. The Open University's Politics Department helped fund travel and archive visits as the book progressed.

The following provided various forms of help or suggestions: Sabrina Aaronovitch, Sasha Abramsky, Leighton Andrews, Sarah Benton, Tony Britten, David Burke, Peter J. Conradi, Sally Davison, Nicholas Deakin, Pat Devine, Mike Elliott, Hywel Francis, Juliet Gardiner, Gayle Gow, Nicholas Jacobs, Martin Kettle, Francis King, Andrew Lownie, David Margolies, Kevin Morgan, David Purdy, David Selbourne, Willie Thompson, Jason Toynbee and Richard Waterborn.

At I.B.Tauris, I would like to thank Jo Godfrey for her editorial input and for encouraging the book in its various stages and Jessica Cuthbert-Smith for copy-editing. Finally, Anita Sandhu thought James Klugmann 'an interesting character' from early on and has helped in many ways.

Geoff Andrews
Oxford

Note on Intelligence Sources

The release of James Klugmann's Security Service (MI5) files in 2002 has been invaluable in the research for this book, but some further explanation on the use of material from Security Service archives is necessary. MI5 files, including Klugmann's personal files used here, can be incomplete and held back without explanation. Material is normally only released after 50 years and the files themselves are only released after the death of the subject. This means we do not know what other material was held by MI5 on Klugmann beyond the early 1950s. (The relevant Special Operations Executive (SOE) files were released in 1997, though earlier War Office material alluded to some SOE activities). Although Klugmann's influence in the leadership of the Communist Party of Great Britain (often referred to in the following pages as 'the Party' or CPGB) waned from the 1960s, MI5 renewed its interest in him following the public exposure of Kim Philby, their interrogation of Bernard Floud and the interrogation and subsequent negotiations with John Cairncross. Therefore the use of memoirs from both 'sides' – Anthony Blunt's 'Autobiographical Memoir' held at the British Library and Guy Liddell's diaries at The National Archives, for example – interviews and secondary sources were important in building a wider picture of Klugmann's espionage links, assumptions about his role, together with his own fears and actions.

Much of the relevant material from the KGB and Soviet Intelligence archive in Moscow has either not been available for researchers or subject to restricted or intermittent access. I am grateful therefore for the pioneering work carried out by Nigel West with the help of Oleg Tsarev in making public details of KGB/NKVD files held on British agents, which provided evidence of James Klugmann's recruitment by Soviet intelligence and the role he played in the subsequent recruitment of John Cairncross. The material also provides insight on the role of NKVD controller Arnold Deutsch – 'Otto' – and his estimation of Klugmann's work and potential. Christopher Andrew's work in making public material collected by Vasili Mitrokhin, a former employee of the KGB's foreign intelligence archives, has been very helpful too in this regard. The activities of the NKVD, the People's Commissariat for Internal Affairs responsible for state security and espionage in the 1930s, were later incorporated into the KGB from 1954.

Notwithstanding the caution needing to be applied in the use of security and intelligence archives, if used judiciously and with context they can be a rich and fertile source for researchers. In the case of James Klugmann, they provide a range of insight into different parts of his life during the Cold War period. The files contain material from telephone checks on his home and at the Communist Party's King Street, Covent Garden offices in central London – as well as transcripts from meetings picked up by hidden microphones placed in the King Street meetings room – copies of mail obtained by Home Office warrant; Special Branch reports written up from public meetings attended by their officers and details of observation provided by MI5 'watchers'. The first serious interest taken by MI5 in Klugmann's activities occurred during the student delegation he led to China in 1938. Thereafter, the file includes correspondence related to his controversial role in the Special Operations Executive during World War II – including a long and particularly revealing debriefing with CPGB official Bob Stewart that MI5 recorded in August 1945 and the frank exchanges between MI5 and his SOE superiors – and subsequently during the Cold War when he was regarded as a security threat. The disappearance of Guy Burgess and Donald Maclean sparked increased MI5 surveillance, as did other developments concerning the Cambridge spy circle, while his work on behalf of the Party, as its expert on Yugoslavia and Eastern Europe, in contacts with Eastern European embassies, and in his other work in the leadership of the Party, was regularly monitored.

Prologue

On an early spring evening in 1937, two university friends met at the entrance to Regent's Park in London. They were among the most brilliant linguists of their generation and had recently left Cambridge with outstanding prospects. They shared common interests in French and German literature which had sustained their friendship after university. Their left-wing politics had further brought them together in the resistance to the rise of Nazism in Germany, and at a time of acute international political crisis they were both committed to the anti-fascist movement.

John Cairncross was Scottish, slim and engaging, if a little taciturn. He had just taken up a post at the Foreign Office. He was 23 years old. His friend James Klugmann was shorter, Jewish and slightly chubby. He was over on a brief visit from Paris, where he was researching French literature and working for an international student association. He was 25 years old.

On this particular spring evening, as they made their way towards a more secluded part of the park, Klugmann's demure wit, avuncular personality and political enthusiasms were absent. An awkward few minutes of uneasy pleasantries came to an end as another figure stepped forward from the trees and Klugmann, after introducing him to his younger friend, promptly made his excuses and slipped away into the shadows. Cairncross and Klugmann would not meet again for 30 years, both their friendship and their own futures tainted by the consequences of those few minutes in Regent's Park. The visitor was Arnold Deutsch, introduced by his code name 'Otto', who in the same park three years earlier had recruited Kim Philby to Soviet intelligence.

For Cairncross, whose attraction to communism did not last beyond Cambridge and who had never taken out a Party membership card, the meeting meant the beginning of an espionage career he had not sought and did not expect to be thrust upon him. For Klugmann, another reluctant spy, who had already decided to dedicate his life to communism, this untimely and distasteful rendezvous had been ordered by the British Communist Party leadership. His friendship with Cairncross and his growing reputation in the communist movement – it was the Communist International (Comintern) in Moscow which funded his role as leader of the World Student Association – meant that he was the only one who could deliver the young Foreign Office official to Soviet intelligence.

Klugmann and Cairncross were of a political generation that had an unrivalled certainty about the impending international crisis facing the world and the necessary sacrifices needed in order to change it. They and many like them had little faith in Britain's old and decaying order and were contemptuous of its feeble opposition to the rise of Nazism, while at the same time they were inspired by growing internationalism in Spain, France and elsewhere.

Indeed, it was through their dedication to the cause of international anti-fascism that these men justified the main acts of 'treachery' for which they have subsequently been condemned. In Cairncross's case, this amounted to passing Enigma decrypts of German military activities to Russia in the lead-up to the battle of Kursk in 1943: the most significant of a range of secret documents he gave to the Soviets. For Klugmann, it was the manipulation of documents to exaggerate Yugoslav partisan strengths in order to win Allied support in the same period.

Conventional accounts of the Cambridge spy circle often depreciate the historical context, the motives behind their actions and the scale of the international crisis, in favour of more sensationalist accounts of treachery and betrayal, personality traits and sexual deviance – 'Spies, Lies, Buggery and Betrayal', as the subtitle of one such work put it. In the race to name the 'fourth man' or 'fifth man' – both labels were attributed to Cairncross and Klugmann at different times – contexts and complexities were the first casualties. James Klugmann's role, for example, as the 'shadowy' figure in the background, is normally attributed to a dual personality. The amiable intellectual, whose gentle elucidation of the Marxist tenets and prognosis of the inevitability of revolution were delivered in soft words to innocent acolytes, had a 'sinister' darker side, in the view of Chapman Pincher and others.

Many labour and left historians, however, have largely treated the whole question of Soviet espionage with either contempt or ambivalence. For some, the very suggestion that James Klugmann, a much-loved figure in the Party, could be involved in espionage was an insult and the outcome of conspiracy theories. For others, the whole business of espionage was too sensitive for serious examination. With the exception of the work of the historians Victor Kiernan and Eric Hobsbawm, two of Klugmann's Cambridge near contemporaries, there has been little attempt to explain the political allegiances of the 1930s which gave rise to the choices, compromises and constraints of those who found themselves in his position. Here too, the wider context of Klugmann's remarkable life has remained closed. It is an irony that Klugmann was someone who epitomised for a brief period in his middle age the features of the classic Cold War intellectual, yet his own story has been suppressed by Cold War assumptions.

Following the wider availability of archives and the erosion of Cold War polarities, it is no longer possible to omit the question of espionage from the wider history of that period. Rather, the commitments, sacrifices, international contexts and ultimately consequences faced by Klugmann's generation of communists need more exploration. His was a twentieth-century political life shaped in many ways by the hopes and fears of the 1930s, and one which helps illuminate the defining moments in the wider history of the left.

A brilliant pupil who excelled at an early age and won all the prizes at Gresham's School, an outstanding Cambridge student destined – according to his professors and peers – for an academic career, Klugmann eschewed personal ambitions and put his immense intellectual talents at the service of the Communist Party. This was not a unique decision, given the ultimate sacrifices made by his close friends John Cornford and David Guest who died in the Spanish Civil War. However, for him it meant a lifelong commitment as a communist intellectual. At its peak it took him from talent-spotting at Cambridge to leading the international student movement in Paris and a unique role in the Special Operations Executive (SOE) with its origins in the 'boat university' he set up en route to Cairo and culminated with his sermons to exiled Croatian communists as they prepared for dangerous assignments. He was a brilliant teacher, and a lucid and eloquent exponent of Marxism and the Communist Party's policy; the hopes he invested in the future drove his lecturing, writing and research.

As the leading communist student of his generation Klugmann found himself both intellectual mentor to his Cambridge comrades and sought after by the Comintern. It was the combination of these two realities, at a time of more tenuous political loyalties, that dragged him briefly – and reluctantly – into the espionage world, an experience that would haunt him for the rest of his life.

His commitment came with severe costs for his personal and political allegiances. As a 'Cold War' intellectual whose loyalties to Moscow shaped many of his political judgements in the early 1950s, he was obliged to meet intelligence agents and Eastern European embassy officials at the time he himself was being pursued by British intelligence, following the disappearance of his friends Guy Burgess and Donald Maclean. In 1956, a year of turbulent and tumultuous events in the communist world, he was found wanting by those who had considered him their 'intellectual guru' in earlier years and now looked to him for leadership. Instead, he put his loyalty to the Party before his better judgement and for a while reverted to what for him was the unenviable role of the Communist Party functionary. The expert on Yugoslav communism and friend of Tito and the partisans was required by his party – under pressure from Moscow – to denounce his former ally, which he achieved through a very disingenuous work, *From Trotsky to Tito*.

His intellectual insecurity was also shaped by internal private conflicts. Released from some of the immediate duties of a Party functionary, he spent much of the last two decades of his life organising the Marxist–Christian dialogue, editing *Marxism Today* and writing the first two volumes of the official history of the Communist Party. The Marxist–Christian dialogue, which developed into a prominent public debate covering many meetings and publications, was also, in retrospect, an act of catharsis and reparation on his part. It enabled him to rediscover the humanism which had brought him to communism in the first place, and privately to reassess his earlier actions.

Klugmann could not, however, realise his earlier intellectual promise, and his well-researched volumes of the Party's early history tell us more about his later life as a Party functionary, as he avoided the contentious areas. Although he had spent two decades on the work, it is now difficult to believe that he would have been able to complete the subsequent volumes which concerned the years he was himself in the Party. His own story reflects the wider hopes and fears of the Party to which he had dedicated his life. As a communist intellectual who had been a leading participant in some of its most defining and difficult moments, he was ultimately unable to extract himself from these conflicts of loyalties.

Ultimately, it was his loyalty to the Party, as a 'good Jesuit' who espoused the cause to all who would listen but whose vows of obedience curtailed his intellectual energies, that compounded his wider dilemmas. A deeply private man, modest and quiet by nature, Klugmann's Party became his family and communism his religion. Estranged from most of his relatives –though influenced by his elder sister Kitty, who became a communist before him – his devotion to the cause took precedence over his private life. His own sexuality – he was thought by most to be homosexual without anyone knowing of any relationships – was repressed at an early stage, seemingly because of his fear of the implications it would have for the Party's image. His Jewish identity was also subordinate to the Party line, which put all human emancipation first and retained the illusion, long after critics had exposed it to be otherwise, that the Jewish community was prospering in the Soviet Union. Even his love of book-collecting, his only other passion beyond the Party, was itself, as he told a BBC Radio 4 interviewer near the end of his life, driven by his desire to serve the working-class movement.

These hopes and fears partly explain the wider mystery of Klugmann's life. The intensity, courage and spirit of adventure that marked his early years as a revolutionary contrasted sharply with the compromised, timid and often lonely figure he appeared to be later. No wonder that many later communists reduced his significance to that of the editor of *Marxism Today* and as the Party's official historian. Even his entry in the Dictionary of National Biography, written by one of his Cambridge contemporaries, erroneously attributes him with two older brothers. 'What did one know about him?' Eric Hobsbawm, who knew him better than most, has written. 'He gave nothing away.'[1]

1

Hampstead: Bourgeois Beginnings

James Klugmann's impeccable bourgeois background has been remarked on by several commentators attentive to the ironies in the origins of communist intellectuals. He himself often seemed apologetic about his prosperous family circumstances when in the company of fellow communists. Yet, his affluent Jewish background in Hampstead belies the resolute determination of his father to be accepted by the British liberal establishment. Samuel Klugmann was born in 1868 in Wiesenbronn, Bavaria, the son of Nathan and Caroline Klugmann, from a family of merchants. Samuel followed his elder brother Felix to Britain in 1891 to help establish the family business, finding residence initially at St George's, in Bloomsbury, London, where he first lived as a boarder while waiting for his naturalisation certificate. Finally, in June 1894 he was given the news that he was now a naturalised Briton, by which time he was a resident in Richmond, south-west London. After naturalisation he and his brother Felix established Klugmann and Co., 'Rope and Twine Merchants', in Basinghall Street in the City of London. His pledge to the then home secretary, Herbert Henry Asquith, to 'be faithful and bear true allegiance to Her Majesty Queen Victoria, her heirs and successors, according to law' may have amused his son later. However, Samuel's allegiance to Asquith's liberalism would become a serious one, enabling him to embrace the values of his adopted country and influence the upbringing of his family, including the choices he made on their behalf.

We do not know when Samuel first met Anna Browne ('Cissie') Rosenheim, James Klugmann's mother, but it is likely that their families knew each other through prosperous German Jewish business circles. It was certainly a good marriage for Samuel. Cissie was part of the large and expansive Rosenheim family with its modern origins in the wine merchants established by Loeb Rosenheim in Heidingsfeld, in the late eighteenth century. Her more recent relatives had left Würzburg in the mid-nineteenth century so that by the time she was born in 1884, the only girl of the Rosenheim's four children, her family was already settled in the Belsize Park area of Hampstead, north-west London. Her father William, together with one of his brothers, Theodore, had set up a tea and coffee trading business, with investments in Foochow Teas in China, while his other two brothers continued in the wine trade. The family household in 8 Belsize Grove, where she was brought up, was large: in addition to the four children, the family employed three servants.

Samuel and Cissie were married at St John's Wood Synagogue in October 1904, an orthodox place of worship with liberal inclinations, and moved into 27 Lancaster Road, Belsize Park, shortly after. Lancaster Road had been developed in the 1870s and its large houses were ideal for prosperous businessmen and their house-proud spouses. Samuel's brother Felix, who was head of the family firm, and his wife Eugenie ('Jenny') were their next-door neighbours at number 25 and Jenny's mother, Mrs Bechman, was on the other side at number 29. Both Felix and Samuel were able to employ three servants and to stock their large drawing rooms with lavish 'Germanic' furnishings. Other members of the Rosenheim family had houses in Belsize Grove and Belsize Park Gardens, and it must have been a very comfortable environment to bring up children, enhanced by a close-knit family and a thriving Jewish community.

For Samuel Klugmann, it provided the opportunity to integrate seamlessly into the middle-class world. It was very distant from the experiences of working-class Jews growing up in the harsh conditions of London's East End, just a few miles away. Anti-fascist activism there in the 1930s would become one of the Communist Party's main causes, and its leading cadres some of Klugmann's closest friends. The nearest contact the Klugmanns and Rosenheims had with East End Jews would have been through the work of the Sick Room Help Society in supporting the welfare of the 'East End poor', to which the Klugmann and Rosenheim wives contributed. Family life would have had little need to go much beyond Belsize Park, save for occasional holidays to relatives in Germany. The community was flourishing by the time Kitty Karoline, James's elder sister, was born in 1908. She already had two older cousins next door – Frank Norman and John Donald – and other relatives nearby. The expansion of the area had brought new houses for successful businessmen and the Belsize Park underground station had been built the year before to take its inhabitants to the West End, while the John Barnes department store on nearby Finchley Road would also cater for the needs of the rising middle classes. By the time Norman John Klugmann was born in 1912, the family was well established and Samuel Klugmann must have been content with his hard-earned position. He seems to have become 'James' at some point during his time at Gresham's School, but he was 'Norman' to his family through much of his childhood, the name fitting comfortably with the Klugmanns' pursuit of anglicised respectability.

Prosperous cigar-smoking businessmen, however, were not the only sign of up-and-coming Hampstead at this time. Their neighbours included composers and writers, doctors, booksellers and architects, with even some early signs of bohemia. Nestled between the Rosenheim aunts, uncles and cousins at 18, 68, and 72 Belsize Park Gardens nearby – Klugmann's grandmother Martha would later move to number 89 – Lytton Strachey's family made their home in two separate houses, moving first in 1907 to number 67, a 'spacious, dilapidated house', and later to number 6.[1] Though Strachey was initially excited by his new 'bijou' Hampstead residence, he soon grew restless with the 'ghastly solitude' of Belsize Park Gardens and its 'hole-and-corner, one-place-at-table-laid-for-six life'.[2] Instead he sought frequent 'psychological escapes' to town to meet Ottoline Morrell, John Maynard Keynes and his cousin, and sometime lover, the artist Duncan Grant, in what became some of the defining moments in the history of the Bloomsbury group.[3]

This early bohemianism in Edwardian Hampstead was some way from the more politically committed writers, exiled communists and Jewish refugees who would congregate there in the 1930s, never mind the Belsize Park communists of the 1940s and 1950s who were a big influence on the left-wing historian Raphael Samuel. But it did offer new attitudes and outlooks for those who were open to them, and intellectuals, particularly in Hampstead's northern parts, were growing in number and influence. James Klugmann would find another way of 'cutting free' from both the restraints of bourgeois Hampstead and family pressures, but for his father, in the years before and after World War I, assimilation into the respectable world of the British middle class was of paramount importance. There was still a sense of fear and insecurity for Jews recently arrived in Britain. A cousin of Klugmann's mother anglicised his name – not an uncommon practice at the time – from Rosenheim to Ross in order to join the Royal Welsh Fusiliers in 1914. Later, his aunt 'Jenny' Klugmann (wife of Felix) and her sons would change their name by deed poll, removing the final 'n' from their surnames as World War II approached. A visitor to the Klugmanns', just after World War I, recalled a household 'barred against intruders more rigorously than any house I had ever known'.[4]

Nevertheless, Samuel Klugmann's politics were liberal by inclination. He voted for the British Liberal Party nearly all his life, only altering his choice in the fateful 1931 election in which the Labour Party suffered its worst ever electoral performance but its former leader Ramsay MacDonald, backed by the overwhelming Conservative majority, remained prime minister of the National Government. In 1931 Samuel Klugmann voted Labour for the one and only time. ('It did him no good', his son later remarked.) His liberalism was rooted in the idea of self-improvement and individual responsibility, of wanting to get on and improve yourself while providing for your family. Although his liberalism would not have encompassed Lytton Strachey's bohemianism, Samuel Klugmann was clearly open to new ideas and saw the extension of knowledge as the key to the successful futures for his two children. At the same time, it was a liberalism which sought a wider civic duty, to use the advantages of privilege to aid the common good. In all of these values, education was taken very seriously. He could not have envisaged the impact that education and the opening up of new horizons would have for the futures of his children.

The Klugmanns did not have to look beyond the Belsize Park enclave for the kind of progressive liberal education they were seeking, though in Kitty's case it almost arrived by accident. After an early kindergarten, divided informally between parents in the surrounding streets, as was the custom at the time, in 1916 Kitty Klugmann enrolled at a school at the end of Lancaster Road, only a few minutes' walk away. Kingsley School, at 46 Belsize Park, had been established in 1890 'For the Daughters of Gentlemen and Doctors', which would surely have impressed Samuel Klugmann. The year before Kitty enrolled at the school, it had been taken over by four women; the philosopher Susan Stebbing, her sister Helen and two colleagues, Hilda Gavin, her former Girton College contemporary, and her friend Vivian Shepherd. The women lived together in Kingsley Lodge at number 26 Belsize Park, with Gavin taking on the role of headmistress, Shepherd teaching Maths and Music, Susan Stebbing teaching two courses in Logic and Ethics and Principles of Criticism, and Helen Stebbing taking classes on Art and Sewing. At the time, Susan Stebbing was also teaching Philosophy at Bedford College, at the beginning of a career which would see her become the first British woman Professor of Philosophy. In the austere years of World War I and at the moment of the women's suffrage movement, she was committed to providing a broad-based education for girls who were serious about studying, even if it meant breaking with some taboos and conventions.

It was not a large school and could not compete with its more established and prestigious neighbour, South Hampstead School for Girls, in meeting the aspirations of ambitious Hampstead parents (and where Margot Heinemann, who would become one of Klugmann's closest friends, was briefly a pupil), but it made up for it through its greater social mix and founding ethos, both of which elicited from the girls a strong loyalty and identity. About 100 pupils, mostly day boarders (and approximately one third from Jewish backgrounds), dressed in their maroon and white blazers, packed into number 46 each day for their lessons. Linda Rittenberg, a former Kingsley pupil, who started at the school just as Kitty was leaving, recalled the

> smelly plimsolls in the basement cloakroom mixing with delicious odours from the 'domestic science' class in the kitchen area [...] Then up through numerous levels, coal-burning classrooms, sulphurous smells on the top-floor where chemistry consisted of bunsen burners, pipettes, scales and flasks under a secure slate roof, so everyone hoped, and where the atom was still an invisible particle, or so we were told.[5]

It was Susan Stebbing's classes which caught the imagination and would have a lasting influence on Kitty, providing her with the tools to look at the world with a critical eye. It was under Stebbing's influence that she went on to study Philosophy (Moral Sciences) at Girton College, Cambridge, while at the same time it opened up wider horizons. 'Hers was a rigorous introduction to logic, ethics, principles of criticism, and clear thinking,' Linda Rittenberg remembered. 'She taught us *how* to think, not *what* to think.'[6]

Linda Rittenberg's mother was not happy with her daughter studying Logic, which she thought would make her too argumentative and scare off potential suitors, and it is possible that Cissie Klugmann, had she ventured out of her domestic and community obligations, would have responded similarly; the need to find a good marriage for their daughters was still high in the aspirations of the wives of Jewish businessmen. Cissie Klugmann was a caring, perhaps doting mother who would grow to be proud of her two children's academic success in the years that followed, without beginning to understand much about their politics.

Stebbing's classes were challenging: debunking myths and demanding facts in support of arguments and cutting through the rhetoric of politicians and newspaper columnists to bring world affairs to the girls' attention. She would later argue in her classic book on philosophy, *Thinking to Some Purpose*, that electors needed to be able to evaluate evidence before making political choices. The problem with many politicians, she argued, was that they used the methods of 'rational persuasion', 'with a client or policy to defend [...] seeking to make a favourable impression', rather than 'rational argument' based on facts.[7]

It is likely that some of the examples she draws on in her writing may first have been discussed with her girls at Kingsley. The assumption held by some that 'all pacifists are cowardly', a recurring debate during Kitty's first years at the school, could easily be challenged, Stebbing pointed out, by 'much evidence to the contrary'; the testimonies of many conscientious objectors suggested that they were acting out of principle.[8] Kitty's last year at the school was 1926, the year of the General Strike, and Stebbing, whose sympathies lay broadly with the strikers, was not impressed with the newspapers' view that the strike was 'aimed at the whole community' and threatened 'the liberties of the people of these islands'. Her response would have stirred Kitty. 'Are not the strikers, we may well ask, to be included among the people of these islands? Do they not belong to the "community"?'[9]

Kingsley pupils were not given a narrow or dogmatic political education. Rather, it was a small school with high principles, and with the shadow of World War I hanging over Kitty's Kingsley years, pupils were introduced to the League of Nations, asked to evaluate the prospects for peace, acquainted with women's suffrage and offered a critical history of the empire. There was much fun too, with hobbies, clubs and sports available despite the cramped surroundings. They were encouraged to look beyond their immediate environment and were taken on visits to art galleries, as well as summer camps in Gloucestershire and Cornwall. Later, as the threat of fascism increased, Stebbing and her colleagues provided homes and education for refugees fleeing Nazism. Stebbing did not always suffer fools gladly, occasionally dismissing her more trying pupils as 'mindless blobs of protoplasm'; she was unimpressed by cinema and the emerging mass culture and saw important civic and democratic values threatened by superficiality. She had a particular disdain for Selfridges' claim that it was 'the finest store ever dedicated to the service of man'.[10]

This critical outlook towards the modern world had a lasting influence on Kitty. The breadth of experience she enjoyed at Kingsley opened her eyes to many new passions, including art, literature and history. It also introduced her in a roundabout way to communism. Felicia Browne, a few years ahead of Kitty, was a talented art student who would later join the Communist Party and go to fight on the Republican side in the Spanish Civil War, where she would be the first British casualty, in August 1936. In a small school it was likely that the two girls knew each other, with avant-garde art being another of Kitty's early interests, and they may well have shared interests under the watchful attention of art teacher Helen Stebbing. More direct influence came from another of her teachers, Miss Beauchamp. Already a communist by this point, Kay Beauchamp, who would later be jailed for her beliefs and then rise to be a leading figure in the Communist Party's International Department, taught history, including the history of the empire. On Kitty's death, nearly 50 years later, Beauchamp would tell James Klugmann that Kitty had said that it was her Kingsley classes that set her on the road to communism. In the short term, however, it was philosophy that was Kitty's abiding passion, and after excellent examination results she won a scholarship to Stebbing's old Cambridge college, Girton, to read Moral Sciences. This was not a regular occurrence at Kingsley and the whole school cheered at the news.

Directly opposite Kingsley School, on the corner of Buckland Crescent, was a flourishing boys' prep school which was to provide Norman Klugmann with his first taste of education. It was not only the location of The Hall that must have appealed to Samuel Klugmann. The Hall has its origins in the Belsize School set up in 1889 by F.J. Wrottersley, an assistant clergyman in nearby Hampstead churches, who was looking for somewhere to educate his three sons according to his high 'classicist' principles and educational philosophy. Though his sons' education prospered, numbers at his school remained tiny and when he sold up in 1898 the school was purchased by another clergyman – and another classicist – the Reverend Douglas Hamilton Marshall, whose strict Victorian ethos ensured effective teaching and organisation and rising numbers, which enabled the school to expand to new premises in nearby Crossfield Road in 1905, when it took its new name. Marshall left in 1909 to start a prep school in Brighton, but the arrival of his successor, E.H. Montauban, formerly headmaster of a school in Ramsgate, marked a decisive moment in the school's history. Montauban ('Monty'), a devoted and popular, if unorthodox teacher, expanded the school buildings and playing fields, including the site in Buckland Crescent and presided over the school during World War I, even offering temporary war-time accommodation at his place in Caversham, in Berkshire. An inspirational educationalist, he gave up the headship in 1919 (though he continued teaching at the junior school until 1923) to help found Stowe School, in Buckinghamshire.[11]

By the time that Norman Klugmann joined the school in 1919, its reputation as a modern liberal establishment had risen among the aspirant well-to-do Hampstead parents. The new headmaster, Robin Gladstone, ran the school with his sister and was joined in partnership by his uncle, Gerard Wathen, in 1924. They brought further reorganisation and expansion, with sport, literary and cultural activities given strong prominence. The seven years Klugmann spent at The Hall were happy ones, marked by his outstanding academic potential together with the development of his personality as a clever, playful, modest and genial friend.

The school had a high intake of Jewish pupils and was seen as exceptionally tolerant in attitudes, ethos and teaching methods. Robin Gladstone, a very large man with a loud voice, 'whose bark was worse than his bite', took a particular interest in sport, notably rugby and squash, while Gerard ('Dub') Wathen taught French, English and Literature. Former pupils recalled the impact of Wathen's 'revolutionary ideas', including the so-called 'Dalton plan', which allowed free periods on afternoons deemed too wet for games, and a general broadening of the school curriculum. Wathen was quick to defend the school's principles – 'We are always fighting against anything that tends to make education narrow' – and was admired by at least one public school head for offering a 'liberal and refreshing' approach and being in the 'vanguard of educational reform'.[12]

Klugmann thrived in this environment, was an outstanding pupil and took full advantage of the opportunities it afforded for pursuing creative interests. School records show him consistently at the top of his class and as a pupil who willingly took part in a range of school activities. This extended beyond the confines of Belsize Park. On Tuesdays and Fridays, the boys could go to the swimming baths on Finchley Road, a busy London thoroughfare also popular for visits to the toy shop or Stewarts for buns and cakes. For school recreation, there were exciting journeys on the Metropolitan Line underground from Finchley Road station to Selfridge's Sports Ground at Preston Road, near the new Wembley Stadium.[13]

It was at The Hall School that Klugmann developed what would be a lifelong interest in chess, influenced by the eccentric but inspiring Maths tutor, W.H. Copinger. Of conservative political opinions, but with an enlightened attitude to learning, Copinger was passionate about chess and would encourage the boys to take part in lunchtime matches, often moving between tables to participate in simultaneous games himself. According to *The Hall Magazine*, Klugmann, representing the Purple House, was: 'A silent type of player who greedily snatches his opponents' pieces. His adversaries find his little sighs (in more senses than one) not a little disconcerting.'[14]

Klugmann undoubtedly benefited from the liberal philosophy and tolerant atmosphere of the school. His outstanding academic performance was helped by the expansion of the school library, which stocked a rich variety of subjects and over 1,000 books on art, adventure, school tales, biography, classics, fairy tales and poetry. It was here that he first developed his love of books. As his literary interests flourished, it is likely his family would have enjoyed his minor role as Salerio in a school production of *The Merchant of Venice* – notwithstanding its depiction of anti-Semitism and the Catholic church venue – which played to a packed audience at nearby St Peter's Church in Belsize Square in 1925.

He also took an interest in poetry, the first route into politics for many of his generation. His poem 'On the Lower Fourth Debating Society' reveals the observations of a 14-year-old on the precocity of his classmates and their naivety in setting out early political opinions on the issues of the day, including the General Strike of that pivotal year, 1926.

> A very small boy
> With a very large head,
> Proceeds to deliver
> On what he has read;
> A speech very long
> He quotes very often
> From Byron and Tennyson,
> Milton and Emerson,
> But sad to relate
> His quotations are wrong.
> A diminutive child
> Then steps out to speak
> On the strike. And he talks
> Of the T.U.C's cheek
> In calling a strike –
> Mr. Baldwin he says,
> Is the only Prime Minister.
> He is not sinister.
> But Ramsay Macdonald
> He never would like.
> A minute baby infant
> Advances and squeaks,
> That in Mars, he believes
> Live some leopards with beaks,
> And he furthermore states,
> With an air of great knowledge,
> That they only eat Keatings,

> And have Mothers' Meetings,
> And much to their hatred
> Have lessons at college.
> My dear little babies,
> Before you spout forth
> On aeroplanes, ostriches,
> Stamps and the North,
> If you take my advice,
> You will thoroughly learn
> Both your measures and weights
> And all history dates.
> And then I am sure
> Some marks you will earn.[15]

The General Strike dominated Klugmann's last term at The Hall, which was also Kitty's last term at Kingsley. Kitty was now engrossed in her studies and drawn to radical politics. She would remain a significant political influence on her brother, and as they made the short walk to school during that summer the strike would have been a topic of conversation. Ramsay MacDonald, who had lived in nearby Howitt Road until the previous year, would become a contentious figure for both over the next few years, while the strike itself would be the subject of one of Klugmann's later history books It is likely that their discussion of the strike, together with Kitty's growing political awareness, were the first causes of family disagreements, which would intensify over the next few years.

The strike itself caused some disruption to the day-to-day running of The Hall, though with most staff and pupils living nearby, it had less impact than it did elsewhere. The lack of coal, however, did have an effect, 'for the baths were not warmed until the last week or so of term, with the consequence that bathing was sadly limited and the annual swimming display could not be held'.[16] Perhaps more disappointingly, from the boys' point of view, was that they were deprived of Mrs Mildred's ices for the entire summer term.

Despite these constraints, Klugmann enjoyed an immensely happy final term at The Hall. With his cousin Charles Rosenheim he founded and edited a small school newspaper, *The Upper Sixth Former*, whose motto was 'Justus Omnibus'. It was the first tentative introduction to journalism for the future editor of *World News and Views* and *Marxism Today*, and he and Charles showed some awareness of the wider political world in a section on 'International Upheavals', though this was often limited to schoolboy jokes. The first editorial declared that 'we propose to issue this paper weekly, gratis [...] All contributions must be handed in to the editor by Thursday 6.0pm.' As well as editor, Klugmann was the main writer, contributing poems on the 'greedy tale' of 'Percival Archibald Edgar Snell' and on his experiences on the cricket field:

> The languid longstop spends his hours
> In taking sleeps and picking flowers.[17]

Klugmann and Charles also contributed entertaining instalments of the escapades of the detective duo Hammond Eggs and Roland Buter, inserted cricket reports, spoof ads and a not altogether sympathetic comment on the departed French master Major Drake-Brockman. The paper was widely admired by the teachers and reveals its editor to have been a popular, witty and engaging fellow among his peers, well on the way to a successful academic career. Wathen's son Mark was a school contemporary who knew Klugmann well and 'always rather admired him for his cleverness'.[18]

During that last term Klugmann excelled in his academic studies, confirmed by his final report in 1926, which was exceptional, in length and praise, while providing some insight into his character and attitude.

> Klugman is by nature the most modest of boys and would be wretched to hear his praises too loudly sung, but we cannot refrain from saying he is one of the cleverest boys we have ever had at The Hall, that his scholarship was not at all a surprise to those who knew his capabilities and that he is sure to distinguish himself in later life. His contributions to the Upper Sixth weekly were delicious, and showed that like so many quiet folk, very little escaped him. We wish him happiness and recognition in his school life.[19]

Klugmann's performance won him a scholarship to Gresham's School in Holt, Norfolk (Rosenheim won a scholarship to Shrewsbury). He did not forget his prep school, nor in the years after did it forget him, though the staff and pupils might have been surprised by the manner in which he would 'distinguish himself in later life'. In 1928 he attended an Old Boys' dinner at the fashionable Café Monico in the West End, presided over by Mr Wathen, who recalled his 'literary contribution' to *The Upper Sixth Former*.[20]

2

Outsider at Gresham's

Gresham's School in Holt, Norfolk, which James Klugmann entered in 1926, was at that time run by a progressive headmaster, J.R. Eccles, a critic of the competitive public school tradition who wanted to instil a sense of trust, loyalty and a civic public service ethic among his pupils. Gresham's had gained a liberal reputation under the previous headmaster, George Howson, for being tolerant, committed to an 'honours' system based on trust and promises rather than the more punitive regime typical of many other public schools. Eccles continued this tradition, which influenced the decisions of many liberal-minded parents to send their children to Gresham's. Indeed, Klugmann's classmates included Roger Simon and Donald Maclean, sons of liberal politicians who had prospered in the post-1906 era of Edwardian Liberalism, while a couple of years below were Roger's younger brother Brian, and Bernard Floud, a future friend and comrade of Klugmann's, and the son of the diplomat and civil servant Sir Francis Floud. His older brother Peter was also a Gresham's pupil.

The role of Liberal Party families in supporting Gresham's cannot be underestimated. Donald Maclean's father, Sir Donald Maclean, was first elected as a Liberal MP in Bath 1906, then Peebles and South Midlothian from 1910 to 1922 (which also saw him briefly as leader of the opposition) and North Cornwall from 1929 until his death in 1932. He was a well-respected committee man and administrator, a reformist liberal and Asquith supporter. The presence of the son of a leading Liberal Party politician in the school ranks was regarded with pride by Eccles and gave wider purpose to his mission at the school. He ensured that Maclean junior, along with the children of other liberal figures, (including the sons of C.P. Scott, editor of the *Manchester Guardian*, and Walter Layton of *The Economist*) were all members of his own house, Woodlands.

The background of Klugmann's classmate Roger Simon was arguably an even more significant reflection of the school's liberal ethos. Roger and his younger brother Brian were the sons of Ernest Simon, Baron Simon of Wythenshawe, a Liberal MP for two years while the boys were at the school, and the close links between their father and the headmaster were always evident. Eccles was a strong supporter of Lloyd George's politics and adhered to his belief that unemployment in the Great Depression could be overcome, and Ernest Simon helped to strengthen links between Liberal Party politics and the school, while regularly updating his sons with news of the government's economic policy. A school motion supporting the Liberal Party won a close vote of 80 votes to 76 after the intervention of Eccles and was achieved, according to the school magazine, 'amidst scenes of unprecedented enthusiasm'. Brian Simon later recalled his 'four impressionable years' in the headmaster's house and the role of Eccles as a 'substitute father'.[1] However, he added that 'it would be giving a wrong impression that Eccles' political liberalism dominated the school'.[2]

Ernest and Shena Simon were both prominent liberal thinkers and social reformers who were close to Sidney and Beatrice Webb, Fabian intellectuals and fellow social refomers with whom they were often compared for their commitment to public service and the belief in the importance of producing an educated elite. The Simons shared Eccles's belief that pupils should be instilled with the civic and social values which would later enable them to play a leading role in public life.[3] Correspondence between Ernest Simon and his sons, as well as the former's own diaries, confirm that he was clearly impressed that Gresham's shared his ideals.

The school encouraged the airing of public issues through debating societies [... which] enabled Ernest and Shena to dovetail their interests with the schooling of their children. For example in 1932 Ernest led debates on the 'slum problem' and on the 'stupidity of public opinion', while Shena delivered a lecture on the licensing commission.[4]

As Robert Cecil, Donald Maclean's biographer, remarked: 'Eccles was delighted to have at Woodlands these sons of distinguished fathers, certain that they would help to form a real aristocracy of merit and give a lead to the whole school.'[5] Klugmann, despite his achievements at The Hall, was put in Kenwynne House, regarded as less academically gifted and mainly consisting of day boarders. It is likely he was placed there because his two older cousins, Frank Norman (at Gresham's 1918–22) and John Donald Klugmann (at Gresham's 1920–5), the sons of Felix, had been recent Kenwynne pupils. They had achieved reasonable academic success: Frank winning a prize for French and John excelling in Maths, and both were good rugby and hockey players; after Gresham's they both went up to Cambridge. Klugmann's parents, despite their successful business interests, did not have the same public status as the Simons or Macleans, and this may have been another reason he was put in Kenwynne.

The liberal ethos of the school marked it out from the more austere environments of other public schools, and there were no beatings by masters and less bullying from older pupils. Many have testified that it was a happy place, enhanced by its location overlooking the marshes at Salthouse village and within walking distance of Hempstead watermill, in an area of outstanding countryside. W.H. Auden, who left Gresham's the year before Klugmann arrived, remembers 'plentiful hot water', 'adequate cooking' and 'dormitories with cubicles', which meant pupils were not 'unduly herded together'.[6]

Gresham's liberalism was also shaped by the legacy of World War I, during which around 100 former pupils had been killed in action. This cast a long shadow over the next generation and brought a new urgency to avoiding further war. The death of the headmaster, Howson, in 1919 was said to have been accelerated by his grief at the scale of the loss. The fear of war was reflected in the support for the League of Nations, and Gresham's became the first public school to be a member of the League of Nations Union. It also had a marked effect on the political outlook of Benjamin Britten, another of Klugmann's contemporaries, whose music was influenced by the pacifism nurtured by his experiences at Gresham's. Britten refused to join the Officer Training Corps (he would later become a conscientious objector), and, as alternatives to the OTC drills, he spent more time on the cricket field and in the music room. He shared some common experiences with Klugmann, who also avoided the OTC, and arrived at his political radicalism partly through a critique of militarism. It is not difficult to speculate on some of the conversations the pupils might have had with their friends, including the Floud brothers, on the changing international situation. Britten was initially attracted to the left, interested in Marxism, and later collaborated with the communist Montagu Slater and worked within the social realist genre popular among left-wing writers and artists. Klugmann would follow Britten's career over subsequent years and was profoundly moved by his *War Requiem* in 1962.[7]

Klugmann had begun to feel he was an outsider – an oddity', as he put it later – in what was a very different setting from the comfort of The Hall. Partly estranged from the more confident sons of MPs in Woodlands, and with his natural modesty and the fact that he lacked any notable sporting or musical talent, he put all his energies into studying. The Hall had aroused his intellectual curiosity in history, literature, poetry and world affairs, and at Gresham's he found the perfect mentor in Frank McEachran. McEachran had arrived at the school in 1924 in his early twenties and had taught W.H. Auden in the latter's last year at the school in 1925. Auden acknowledged McEachran's crucial formative influence on his early poetry and philosophy and, according to the Auden scholar John Bridgen, he arrived at the 'basic literary and philosophical framework of his lifetime's enquiry while he was still at Gresham's'.[8]

McEachran, 'a remarkable man and a teacher of genius', according to Bridgen, saw Auden's intellectual abilities and gave him special attention, while Auden, on his part, 'looked up to him, at least in the early stages of their friendship, as a father figure'.[9] McEachran's influence on Klugmann would be arguably even more extensive. McEachran was officially teaching French, but it was the sheer scope and depth of his intellectual interests, ranging from classics, philosophy, poetry, literature and history, which marked him out as an inspirational figure. In the four years McEachran taught Klugmann, he introduced him to the world of history and philosophy, nurtured his radicalism, while imbuing him with a set of values to live by, including the importance of holding a 'worldview', or an 'outlook', to use one of Klugmann's later favoured expressions. McEachran's highly original teaching methods, which became epitomised as the model for Hector in Alan Bennett's *The History Boys*, as well as influencing the *Private Eye* set at Shrewsbury School in the 1950s, had a major impression on Klugmann. At the heart of his teaching method were 'spells': extracts of classic prose and poetry recited aloud in class.

Perhaps McEachran's most significant influence, as Europe entered its darkest hour, was stressing the importance of European culture and civilisation. This was reflected in his classes on the origins of European civilisation, particularly on the French Enlightenment and the history of the liberal tradition, which he traced back to the Middle Ages and the work of Dante. McEachran championed a form of liberal humanism, and his belief in the capacity of European culture to unify nations and peoples was optimistic, indeed utopian. Yet, he went beyond defending the liberal tradition – then in crisis – and warned of the dangers of nationalism and romanticism which threatened to divide Europe. These concerns were later set out in his books, *The Civilised Man*, *The Destiny of Europe* and especially *The Unity of Europe*, where he warned against what he saw as the 'religion of nationalism' sweeping across Europe:

> The fever of nationalism which now rages round the world has not only shattered into fragments what little common feeling it once possessed but has also nearly destroyed the unity of Europe, the focus in modern times of human civilisation.[10]

These interests in the history of ideas, French literature and the Enlightenment helped shape Klugmann's perspectives on life, his desire to become a history teacher and his interest in the French Revolution. McEachran nourished Klugmann's heretical views and, crucially, introduced him to the ideas of Karl Marx, though he himself was not a Marxist, having been drawn to Marx through his interest in Henry George. As a contemporary of Marx, George shared some similarities, in particular an empathy for the condition of the worker, a condemnation of economic inequality and a belief in progress, though for George this was to be along an evolutionary rather than revolutionary road. Later, Klugmann would reject the 'reformism' of thinkers such as George (whose views also influenced the Fabians, George Bernard Shaw and David Lloyd George), but at the time McEachran's enlightened liberalism influenced Klugmann, whose early political journey was driven by the humanism of the early Marx and the philosophy of emancipation derived from it.

According to Klugmann, McEachran's 'teaching methods opened our eyes to new horizons of ideas, new excitements, to rouse imagination in books and theories and liberalism and languages'.[11] He was clearly indebted to McEachran, whom he must have considered a father figure – as Auden had – as well as his first intellectual guru. In fact McEachran, like Klugmann later, was clearly an excellent 'talent spotter', given his ability to pick out and encourage those with particular aptitudes. There were some similarities in character too: McEachran, brilliant in the classroom, was modest, if no less passionate about his wider ideals; likewise, Klugmann was later regarded as a 'born teacher' with a genuine interest in the ideas and welfare of his mentees.

Klugmann owed McEachran a further debt. This brilliant and highly original schoolmaster was unimpressed with some of the restrictions of the school honours system, which did not appeal to his 'anarchic' side. Klugmann, too, had resisted impositions such as the OTC and the excessive moral constraints which made him feel an outsider. Nourished by McEachran's own gentle liberal anarchism, he started to call himself 'The Communist' as an early sign of this rebellion without fully understanding its meaning at the time:

When I was at Gresham's, I felt so much out of things as the clever oddity who got most of the prizes, but not even the humblest office, that I cast around for a title to bestow on myself. I hit on an ingenious one in my last year, and I surmised at once that the authorities wouldn't like it. They certainly didn't. For I called myself 'The Communist', advertising myself as the only specimen for miles around. I hadn't any clear idea, to begin with, what a good Communist really stood for; but having a very inquisitive mind, I soon remedied that. The books I read opened my eyes a little. Being also one of nature's rebels, I became a distant sympathizer.[12]

Ironically, it was the honours system itself, the innovation that had so appealed to liberal parents, that made him feel most uncomfortable. Auden had also found the system ultimately oppressive. The commitment not to swear, smoke or do anything 'indecent' was to be implemented by the individual responsibility to 'self-police' one's own behaviour, and to report any transgressions, either of one's own doing or that of fellow pupils, to the headmaster and housemaster. Auden accepted that by and large the system succeeded; he 'almost never saw anyone smoking or heard swearing or smut'.[13] However, in his view, demanding loyalty and honour from 14-year-olds was fraught with danger, helping to either suppress emotions or encourage inner conflicts of loyalties that would have consequences for their future lives:

> It meant that the whole of our moral life was based on fear, or fear of the community, not to mention the temptation it offered to the natural informer, and fear is not a healthy basis. It makes one furtive and dishonest and unadventurous. The best reason I have for opposing Fascism is that at school I lived in a fascist state.[14]

Some of these fears would have been felt by James Klugmann, who would suffer from conflicts of loyalties for much of his life. A suspicion of informers and spies was a continuing preoccupation for him in later years, together with a distrust of the state and its representatives, while the unappealing responsibility to inform on friends could only have increased his sense of isolation from authority. At the same time, given what we know about the sexuality of some of his friends and contemporaries – Maclean, for example, was bisexual, Britten and Auden were gay – the repressive atmosphere had another dimension. Auden, Britten and others suggested there was no sex and painted a picture of pupils going around with their trouser pockets sewn up. This could only have increased the sense to Klugmann – himself a repressed homosexual – that he was an outsider, while at the same time leading him to 'bottle up' his emotions and keep his feelings to himself, as he would do in the future. Expressing his opposition to the 'school system' surely helped to drive his early political identity.

Clearly, many found it inhibiting and restrictive. Brian Simon himself later commented in a letter to his future wife Joan Peel in 1940 that at Gresham's 'most of the really creative instincts and emotions had been driven out of me or deep underground'.[15] Benjamin Britten was another who found the atmosphere repressive at times. It had nurtured his pacifism and introduced him to politics but he endured a lonely existence in Farfield (Auden's old house), and in his diary he noted that the honours system was a 'positive failure in Farfield. It is no good trying the Honours System on boys who have no honour. Boys, small and rather weak are turned into sour & bitter boys, & ruined for life.'[16]

Despite already calling himself a communist, Klugmann had at that time little contact with the working class. While the school's Sociological Society did bring him and others in touch with the Norwich factory workers, this was at a fairly superficial level. However, he gave expression to his growing political radicalism in the pages of *The Grasshopper* magazine, founded by McEachran in 1930, and the school Debating Society, which became the two main forums for political discussion. In these circles, outside the confines of the house system, 'Kluggers', as he was known to friends – he had also by now substituted 'Norman' with 'James' – was admired for his political understanding and lucid analysis. The honours system did at least encourage the kind of small reflective discussion circles in which Klugmann, always impressively well read, thrived. Encouraged by McEachran to read Marx, he imbibed the core ideas on the state, class struggle and historical materialism, and he disseminated their meanings to a growing circle.

He had a good audience, including both the Floud and Simon brothers, who would be friends and comrades of his for many years afterwards, while his chief ally and closest friend was Donald Maclean. His friendship with Maclean would grow in his last two years at Gresham's and then continue at Cambridge, when they would become leading activists in the Socialist Society and Communist student group. Maclean, like Klugmann, prospered under McEachran, and records show them regularly at the top of the class. Both boys were outsiders in the sense that they preferred their own or each other's company and were not very clubbable, though Maclean did take a full part in sporting activities, doing well at cricket and rugby. Of the two, Klugmann was the stronger and more independent character, whose political principles were beginning to mature earlier, and he was more adept and convincing in political arguments.

Maclean and Klugmann had different experiences at Gresham's. Maclean, sporty, tall and handsome, was more conventional in attitudes and behaviour, joining the OTC (where he rose to the rank of lance corporal). He was more formal and even more accepting of the school authorities, with his 'natural capacity to exercise authority'.[17] His chosen future career as a diplomat would not have surprised any of his contemporaries at that time. Politically, under the growing influence of his friend and the intellectual stimulation of the environment, Maclean became increasingly critical of the policy of the Liberal Party, though he was very wary of making his opposition to his father's politics public. When Sir Donald Maclean addressed the school in November 1930 on the value of the League of Nations, Donald junior was a proud son. Yet over the following months, as the political crisis unfolded – it would later bring his father to a belated ministerial role as president of the Board of Education – his own radicalism took him in another direction.

By contrast, Klugmann, chubby, bespectacled, hopeless at games, suspicious of power and orthodoxies, and looking to rebel, hated the OTC and never became a prefect. If less confident in public speaking at this point, he was more idealistic, less burdened by convention and more inspired by McEachran's teachings on the European radical tradition. Despite his antipathy towards the school authorities, his own academic performance was outstanding and he won a series of prizes, including English (1928) and French (1930). His academic merit was achieved without being distracted by the allure of school office; his principles of intellectual rigour and political commitment were taking shape.

Both Klugmann and Maclean spent a lot of time in the library (serving on its committee) and in their last year at school were both active participants in the Debating Society. In one of these debates – hinting, perhaps, at the different emphases and personal mentalities which later drove their beliefs – they spoke on different sides of the motion: 'In the opinion of this House modern progress is a departure from civilisation.' Klugmann argued in October 1930, in a contribution which clearly owed something to McEachran's influence, that 'modern man' 'had lost his sense of values and was treating soap and machinery as ends in themselves, instead of as means to a fuller and more satisfying experience', while Maclean suggested that 'man was at last beginning to "know himself", through the science of psychology, and to realise that true liberty was to be found in social service'.[18] In a later debate, Maclean, speaking against the motion 'This House condemns socialism both in theory and practice', 'deplored the distinction between private and public morality. Socialism would carry into a wider sphere the domestic virtues of service, liberty and justice.' Despite his and Klugmann's interventions, that motion was lost.

The Gresham's School Debating Society helps illuminate some of the communist affiliations of students in the 1930s as its leading participants, Klugmann, Maclean, Peter and Bernard Floud, Roger and Brian Simon, would all become prominent communists or communist supporters over the next decade, with Klugmann providing the intellectual force and linking thread across their different paths at Cambridge, Oxford and the London School of Economics. Bernard Floud was a frequent contributor to debates, speaking in favour of the League of Nations, while the Simon brothers argued in favour of a motion to extend democracy.

Klugmann and Maclean both contributed regularly to McEachran's *The Grasshopper*. Klugmann, on a similar theme to his contributions in the Debating Society, wrote two significant pieces on the threat to the civilised values of man. In one of these, 'The Quest of the Eternal Glob', the philosopher, in search of the human enlightenment offered to him in a vision, ends up losing his soul to the corruptions of modern life. The young Klugmann's way of illuminating his dilemma is expressed through the temptations of the tuck shop, where 'all evil is a sticky bun, the doughnut of death was the eternal glob and the soul of man is the jam of human existence'.[19]

Maclean's account of 'The Sandwichmen' in the third edition of the magazine may have been influenced by the visits of the Sociological Society to poorer parts of London. His story depicted the lives of those who until now Gresham's pupils had barely encountered, but would know better following the arrival of the hunger marchers in Cambridge. The Sandwichmen were a 'bedraggled lot, with their ramshackle bowlers, muddy trousers [...] Their boots that oozed mud as they slumped along in the gutter. Their faces were studies in abject misery; dirty hair hung over their coat collars.' Both Maclean and Klugmann were already intent on bringing the realities of class inequality, and the decaying capitalist system which had produced it, to the attention of their privileged cohort.[20]

The two boys were friends outside school too and would meet regularly in the holidays. In his biography of Maclean, Robert Cecil asserted that 'Kluggers' 'was a frequent visitor at the Macleans' house in London'.[21] Yet, Klugmann told Andrew Boyle that, while they became close friends, their meetings were usually away from the family home because Maclean was worried that his father would not approve of their friendship; Klugmann, older by a year and more mature in his convictions, was openly expressing his new political creed by the end of his time at Gresham's. Maclean was uncertain at this time of the implications of his developing political views, was still living in the shadow of his father and was gradually losing his Presbyterian faith. Klugmann, on the other hand, had a sister who was already a communist with whom he could discuss his politics. She and her boyfriend, a philosophy student called Maurice Cornforth, were already active in Cambridge student politics and were waiting for him to join them in the autumn of 1931. After excelling in his studies, he won a Modern Languages exhibition to Trinity College, Cambridge, while his friend Donald Maclean had also succeeded in winning a scholarship to nearby Trinity Hall.

3

A Cambridge Communist

Cambridge University at the beginning of the 1930s showed few signs of radicalism. The previous decade had been dominated by what T.E.B. Howarth called a 'conservative outlook', reflected not only in its more arcane practices, and what many perceived to be a decaying, decadent class culture amongst the students, but also in their politics. 'Their main political enthusiasms were hostility to Bolshevism, suspicion of the motives of trade union and Labour politicians and a belief in the continuing utility and virtues of the British empire.'[1] Cambridge students had played a major role in breaking the General Strike, with over half of all undergraduates taking up volunteer positions with the emergency services on trams, trains and buses.[2] The Conservative Party dominated what existed of student politics, and while the occasional Labour MP – Arthur Greenwood and Jennie Lee, for example – spoke at meetings, left-wing students were thin on the ground. The only communist of any influence was the economics don Maurice Dobb, the leading figure in a small unofficial communist university group. Moreover, the bohemianism of the aesthetes and experimentalists of the 1920s generation, under the influence of Bloomsbury, did not translate into lasting political commitments on the ground in the years prior to mass unemployment, the rise of fascism and political crisis.

James Klugmann knew something of Cambridge's conservative culture from his sister Kitty, who had gone up to Girton College (one of only two women's colleges) in 1926 to study Moral Sciences. Her introduction to philosophy and history at school, through the teaching of Hilda Gavin, Susan Stebbing and Kay Beauchamp, had given her a greater political maturity than many of her Cambridge contemporaries.

When she arrived in the autumn of 1926, she encountered a university that showed little sign of any political radicalism. Indeed, the college had recently commended the public service spirit of the many students who had volunteered to drive buses, work in the docks or act as messengers in the General Strike a few months before. This was some way from the enlightened and critical thinking of Susan Stebbing.

Kitty and her contemporaries were confronted by many repressive obstacles for young women at university at this time, which put restraints on political activities, meetings and social and cultural life. As one of her Girton contemporaries recalled:

In our first term most of us did not visit men in Cambridge colleges because we did not know any. Only students who had former school mates or relations in the university had contacts. Later we rather benefited from the rule that students visiting or entertaining men must have 'chaperones'; no girl could visit or entertain alone.[3]

Another of Kitty Klugmann's peers was Kathleen Raine, later the distinguished poet and writer, whose Ilford family background was modest in comparison to many of her fellow students. It was the custom at Girton to put students into small mutually supportive 'families' of four or five which would remain together throughout their time at college. Kitty Klugmann was in the same family as Kathleen Raine and became an important political influence on her friend. Raine recalled:

The most interesting member of my 'family' was the senior scholar of my year, a Jewish moral scientist, the first Marxist I had met. She, as a member of a persecuted race, I an 'outsider' by reason of class were thrown together. She introduced me to the avant-gardism of the time, to the books of Aldous Huxley, Virginia Woolf, E.M. Forster, Lytton Strachey and the rest of the Bloomsbury school; and to Roger Fry's and Clive Bell's books on painting.[4]

According to Raine, it was Kitty who first recommended the poetry magazine *Experiment* edited by William Empson, in which Raine published her first poems, and, through her friendship with Empson, Raine joined a circle of left-wing writers and poets, including the surrealist Hugh Sykes Davies (who became her first husband), Anthony Blunt and Julian Bell. Raine would go on to marry Charles Madge, another communist poet, founder of Mass Observation and a Cambridge contemporary of James Klugmann.

Kitty Klugmann and Raine were both active in the Girton and Newnham Joint Debating Society, with Kitty acting as president and Raine secretary during the academic year 1928–9. Despite the restrictive impositions of the time, Girton aspired to be a progressive and intellectually exciting place for young women who were regarded as the early heirs of the suffragettes. The college had distinctive feminist origins, and this continued into the 1930s with the likes of Virginia Woolf and Edith Sitwell among visiting speakers.

Kitty and Raine were also members of the Girton College Labour Club, which held Sunday teas and study circles, invited outside speakers and cultivated local links with Girton village. During the time that Kitty was its president (1929–30), Girton Labour Club's own meetings became less frequent and it was decided to amalgamate with the larger Cambridge University Labour Club. This may be partly explained by Kitty's disillusion with the Labour Party and the attraction of working within broader political organisations like the Cambridge Socialist Society.[5]

Alongside her political interests, her academic studies progressed very well; she became an outstanding student of philosophy. Her enthusiasm for the subject had brought her into contact with Ludwig Wittgenstein and Bertrand Russell and others through the Moral Sciences Club. It was in these circles that she began to see a lot of Maurice Cornforth, a young postgraduate who, after taking his philosophy degree at University College London, had arrived in Cambridge in autumn 1929 to study Analytic Philosophy under G.E. Moore and Wittgenstein. Cornforth was regarded as a brilliant student by Moore, and well suited for an academic career.

Kitty achieved a first class in Moral Sciences but did less well in Economics. The decision to study Economics was popular among left-wing students at the time and her decision may have been influenced by Maurice Dobb, the leading communist don at Cambridge, known for cultivating bright left-wing students, while the chance of attending Keynes's lectures would also have appealed. At the time of the Great Depression, there was a feeling that economics was the discipline which could provide the key to understanding the way society was organised and how it needed to change.

Yet it was philosophy which continued to drive her imagination, and on the back of her success in this subject, Kitty won a Rose Sidgwick Studentship to Columbia University for a year between 1930 and 1931, where she studied under Professor William Pepperell Montague, the author of *Ways of Knowing*, and one of the advocates of the new realist manifesto. She found her work interesting and living in New York 'exciting', though, as she told Girton's mistress, Miss Major, in April 1931,

I have finally decided that I don't like it. It is the quintessence of city-ness and there is nothing in it corresponding to the Bloomsbury Squares, and the Inns of Court. The sky scrapers are some of them beautiful I think, but their beauty is the same as that of a very fine machine.

She told Miss Major that she was looking forward to returning to Cambridge and wanted 'to go on working at philosophy next year. I must look for a post or a scholarship. I would much rather be in Cambridge than anywhere else.'[6]

Back at Cambridge, it was her relationship with Cornforth and the circles they moved in that would be instrumental in getting the communist student movement off the ground. Crucially, it would provide the organisational nucleus for the emergence of a strong communist presence amongst the student body, which her brother would eventually lead. Cornforth was one of Wittgenstein's brightest students; he studied under him at the time when the former had just returned to Trinity College on a fellowship to begin work on what would become his *Philosophical Remarks*. According to Cornforth,

Wittgenstein immediately caused an upheaval in the circles of students (and lecturers) who were studying philosophy. He proceeded to tear all our preconceived ideas to pieces. He taught that no proposition had meaning unless one could demonstrate what experiences would verify it; and everything which could not be verified (that is, most propositions which philosophers believed) he attacked as meaningless metaphysics, or as he expressed it, 'nonsense'.[7]

Cornforth's closest friend among the philosophy students was David Haden Guest, son of a Labour politician, who had started as an undergraduate at Trinity at the same time as Cornforth arrived as a postgraduate. They were both early disciples of the Austrian philosopher. Cornforth remembered, 'We used to sit at Wittgenstein's feet, drinking in his new ideas, and at the same time we argued furiously, both with him and with one another.'[8] Wittgenstein had opened their minds and made clear to them the importance of grounding their ideas in experience, in what was a rapidly changing international political situation.

Indeed Wittgenstein had a substantial following among left-wing students during this period. He was often in the company of Maurice Dobb and took Russian lessons from Fania Pascal, wife of Roy Pascal, another communist and German tutor. He was also a close friend of another economist, Piero Sraffa, who was an influential confidant of the Italian communist Antonio Gramsci, then writing his notebooks from a Mussolini prison. Wittgenstein himself rejected Marxist theory, but had great sympathy with the cause of the working class and began to adopt a very positive and hopeful attitude towards the Soviet Union. He would later tell Rowland Hutt: 'I am a Communist at heart.'[9]

Guest was to become the first notable leader of the Cambridge communist students and with Cornforth and Klugmann would establish the first organised cell. The formative moment in making him a communist was the year spent at the University of Gottingen during 1930–1 studying Mathematical Philosophy under the formalist David Hilbert. Whilst at Gottingen, he was struck by the sense of decay and collapse around him and the strength of Nazi support among the student body. At an anti-Nazi youth demonstration in Braunschweig on Easter Sunday 1931 he was arrested and imprisoned for two weeks, kept in solitary confinement and accused of spreading alien communist propaganda. After a short spell on hunger strike, Guest was finally granted access to a lawyer and released; he had been shaken after seeing Nazism in action and his political consciousness had been aroused.[10]

These experiences meant that Guest returned to Cambridge a committed communist. At a meeting of the Cambridge Moral Sciences Club he produced Lenin's *Materialism and Empirio-Criticism*, and his espousal of its arguments variously shocked and inspired those present. It made a 'big impression' on Cornforth:

> I went straight home and read the book, and thereupon decided to join the Communist Party. To this extent it was David's influence that made me join the Party. I was thinking about doing it, but his directions and enthusiasm made me quite decided.[11]

In the event, Cornforth and Guest both joined the Communist Party in the summer of 1931. On the back of Guest's revolutionary fervour and a visit by Clemens Palme Dutt, who then had responsibility for the Party's work among students and wanted to test the water, it was decided to establish a more formal communist presence at the university. Initially, there were only four or five other students who joined them, including ex-miner Jim Lees and Bugsy Woolfe, along with Dobb, 'who had done most to prepare the ground',[12] and Roy Pascal. Guest was therefore the first leader of the communist student group at the university, and his energy was crucial in establishing a collective student voice beyond Dobb's drawing-room discussions. Initially, the main focus of the cell was targeted at the Cambridge working class, with street-corner sales of the Party weekly, the *Daily Worker*, support for rent campaigns and canvassing amongst the building and railway workers of Romsey Town, a densely populated stretch of terrace streets which had strong labour traditions. Cornforth was put in charge of the town branch and, following his marriage to Kitty at Hampstead Register Office in the autumn of 1931, they moved into a flat over a pawnbroker's in the centre of the town, which would be the base for regular communist gatherings.

Therefore, when James Klugmann arrived in Cambridge in October 1931 to take up his place at Trinity College, he already had good connections to the embryonic Cambridge communist group which had come together over the previous months. 'Verily James Klugman [sic], you are the universal provider', his friend Donald Maclean quipped on hearing the news of Kitty's new husband.[13] Klugmann remained Maclean's political mentor, a constant source of advice for his friend, until the latter's recruitment by the Soviet security and intelligence agency (NKVD) after graduation. The Gresham's cohort would be increased the following year with the arrival of Brian Simon, who would go on to become president of the National Union of Students, and Klugmann kept in touch with the Floud brothers, Bernard and Peter, at Oxford and the London School of Economics (LSE). Unsurprisingly perhaps, the Greshamites appeared more politically mature and serious than some of their more hedonistic public school contemporaries who 'came to play and grow up'.[14] For some, this gave the impression that they were arrogant and self-assured. Klugmann, of course, already had the added advantage of the political circles opened up to him by his sister and brother-in-law, and he was less politically naive than many of his contemporaries.

Trinity College, along with King's, was one of the largest Cambridge colleges, and a symbol of great wealth and privilege. It was large enough, however, to absorb its fair share of outsiders and eccentrics. Klugmann was allocated K2 on the second staircase in Whewell's Court, the Gothic stone building partly designed by William Whewell, master of Trinity in the mid-nineteenth century. The entrance to Whewell's Court was directly opposite the main entrance to the college on Trinity Street. Klugmann was to remain here throughout his time at Trinity. Later, from the autumn of 1933, when he took over the leadership of the communist organisation, his part of Whewell's Court increasingly became a central meeting point for communist students, and political discussions would be held there until curfew. However, during his three years in these rooms he also made a serious commitment to his academic studies and won the respect of his tutors as a likeable and brilliant student who would often drop in for early evening discussions on international affairs.

Above him in the top of Whewell's Court tower was the poet and classical scholar A.E. Housman, by then in his mid-seventies and in the last three years of his life. Housman was a reclusive figure, a repressed homosexual with a reputation for being generally dismissive towards students. Below Klugmann on the ground floor was Cornforth's mentor Ludwig Wittgenstein, a more fruitful source of political conversation. It is fitting perhaps that these two remarkable and in their own way eccentric intellectuals, both gay and inhabiting rather austere existences – with Wittgenstein's barely furnished rooms and Housman's reclusiveness – were among Klugmann's neighbours. (Housman famously refused to share washing facilities with Wittgenstein or his other neighbours.)

Klugmann's sense of being an 'outsider' started to diminish at Cambridge, and though he shared the general rebellious tone and dress – limited in his case to wearing his hair longer than normal and opting for Oxford 'bags', the loose-fitting trousers worn by some undergraduates – he retained a measure of social conservatism, reflected in a clear preference for books and serious study over sherry parties. He enjoyed cinema and theatre and even joined Donald Maclean on an occasional bet on the horses at Newmarket. He must have felt free from some of his earlier moral constraints, and his sexuality would not have faced the same imposed inhibitions he might have felt at school.

He was good company. Pictures of him punting on the Cam offer a lighter side and he was generally regarded as an affable and witty companion, while his impressive knowledge of world events gave him an advantage in his favoured small political discussion circles. Here and in his convivial chats with his tutors, his lucidity and confidence in argument impressed his different audiences. It was an advantage to have his sister and brother-in-law close by and they would have recommended him to their own circles. Shortly after arriving, he found a note pushed under his door: 'We understand you are an "intelligent" – please join us at our regular gatherings.' It was signed Q.D. Leavis and was an invitation to the English Society's regular discussions which she hosted with her husband, F.R. Leavis.[15] The Leavises were then both at the peak of their intellectual influence, and the following year his *New Bearings in English Poetry* and her *Fiction and the Reading Public* would be published, as well as *Scrutiny*, the journal much influenced by their ideas.

Nor was Klugmann afraid of tackling tutors for their conservative views. 'Tell me James, why is it that so many of my brightest students seem to be on the left?' Trinity's Classics don Andrew Gow asked him. 'Well sir,' Klugmann replied, 'you have to think of the common factor. And that's you, sir.'[16] Nevertheless, he respected their status and deferred to them on normal academic procedure; after all, he remained part of a generation that was still wary of upsetting parents and peers.

In any case, the Cambridge he encountered imposed its own social restrictions, as Victor Kiernan, another Whewell's Court neighbour, friend and an early Klugmann recruit to the Communist Party, discovered. Kiernan, who went up to Cambridge at the same time to study History, described Cambridge as 'oppressively genteel and ritualistic. [...] There was in general a stifling atmosphere of closed windows, drawn blinds, expiring candles, sleep-walking.' His own room, on the ground floor of Whewell's Court, below Klugmann,

> was not an ideal residence. When a gust of wind blew, the small fire, over which toast could be made with the help of a long fork and much patience, threw out billowing clouds of smoke, enough sometimes to drive me out into the court gasping for breath.[17]

Michael Straight, who moved into Whewell's Court in 1935, also remarked on the stark surroundings:

> in order to take a bath in Whewell's Court you had to march across the cobbled stones of the courtyard in a dressing gown and slippers, carrying a towel and a bar of soap. You went down a flight of stairs into some dark catacombs. You felt your way around until you slipped on the greasy floor of the showers. Then you turned on a tap and jumped up and down under a cold stream of water.[18]

Klugmann's austere Cambridge social environment was nevertheless a privileged one and has to be set alongside the bigger picture of economic crisis. Britain at this time was a society of widening class division, economic hardship and political inertia. After the relative stability of the late 1920s, when 'Fordism' was widely thought to be the road to lasting prosperity, the biggest world slump, following the Wall Street crash, left Britain's economy rocking, with rapidly rising unemployment (which would reach 3 million in 1933) and escalating class divisions, leaving 'poverty in the midst of plenty', as those on the left characterised it. Britain had also entered a serious political crisis, with Ramsay MacDonald's Labour government falling and the subsequent National

Government – regarded as an act of betrayal by the left – lacking popular support. Looking back over 40 years later, Klugmann himself described the state of Britain at the time he arrived in Cambridge in October 1931:

> Life seemed to demonstrate in an early way the total bankruptcy of the capitalist system and shouted aloud for some sort of quick, rational, simple, alternative. There was in this period a very strong feeling of doom, doom that was not very far off.[19]

This sense of 'impending doom' had a profound impression on the political outlook of Klugmann's student generation, manifested in growing disillusion at the betrayal of the Labour government, a strong opposition to war and fascism and a new class awareness, where privileged undergraduates were confronted for the first time with the conditions and struggles of the working class. The Soviet Union was then in the midst of big construction projects; its Five Year Plans appealed as the embodiment of progress in contrast to the decay and backwardness of capitalist Britain. These factors culminated in a shift to the left and the catalyst for a distinctive student cohort: the first student 'movement' of modern times, in which Klugmann would play a leading role.

Disillusion with Ramsay MacDonald and lack of enthusiasm for the Labour Party in general had led to the dissolution of the Cambridge University Labour Club and its replacement by the Cambridge University Socialist Society, (CUSS), an alliance of left-wing social democrats, Marxists and Independent Labour Party (ILP) supporters. Initially under the leadership of its secretary, Harry Dawes, a mature student and former coalminer who had been through the General Strike, the CUSS was the focal point of left-wing radicalism from the autumn of 1931. Klugmann and Maclean quickly became members of its committee, which often met at Trinity College, with Maclean put in charge of publicity. Kim Philby, another Trinity College student, then studying economics under Maurice Dobb, and much influenced by Dawes, became treasurer in 1932. Philby would owe his early political education, in which he moved from left-wing social democrat to Marxist, to his time in CUSS. Other leading members included Labour socialists A.L. Symonds (later the Cambridge MP); Anthony Blake, who succeeded Dawes as secretary, R.W.B. Clarke and John Midgeley. Jim Lees, like Dawes another ex-miner, was also a key figure and by now a member of the ILP. However, it was the core group of communists, under the direction of the student cell, which would shape the CUSS and its activities. Meeting in St Michael's Café and other central Cambridge venues, the CUSS was to become the organising vehicle for the range of anti-fascist and peace movements over the next few years.[20]

The rise of the student left at Cambridge was part of a wider shift among the student generation. At University College London (UCL), the Gower Socialist Society was formed in autumn 1931. A Marxist society was set up at the LSE, which would later involve Peter Floud, Michael Straight and briefly John Cornford, before the latter two went up to Trinity College. In Oxford, at the end of 1931, Frank Strauss Meyer, a wealthy American postgraduate, and Dick Freeman set up the October Club, inspired by the Soviet revolution and without any official help from the Communist Party of Great Britain (CPGB). The October Club for a while matched the activities of the Cambridge communists. Its founding objective was: 'the study of communism in its world, social, economic and cultural aspects'.[21]

Meyer had previously been an active member of the Oxford Labour Club and had set up a 'Marxist study group' after becoming 'impatient with the Labour Party and the left'. Freeman was a friend of the left Labour intellectual John Strachey and had 'worked on a collective farm in Russia the summer before, coming back full of enthusiasm'. Meyer explained that he and Freeman (and others they nominated) would have 'complete control over its policies and activities'. Through their contact with the CPGB leaders they initially used the Party as a vehicle for organising speakers and Meyer claimed that Emile Burns, the Party's head of propaganda, 'was taken aback by the whole thing and didn't know quite what to do about it'.[22]

The major breakthrough in bringing together the different communist student organisations took place at Klugmann's house in Hampstead during the Easter vacation in 1932, when his parents were away. The meeting followed a circular from Harry Pollitt, the Communist Party's general secretary, which – almost certainly acting on Comintern instructions – encouraged the formation of student cells. Klugmann, Kitty and Maurice Cornforth set up the meeting in discussion with the Party leadership at King Street. Present at this meeting were representatives from the communist cells and societies of Cambridge, UCL, the LSE and the October Club, as well as Clemens Palme Dutt from the Party leadership, and Dave Springhall, who had recently been at the International Lenin School in Moscow and had just been elected to the Party's Central Committee.[23] Springhall, a tough-talking organiser, would later be convicted for espionage and expelled from the Party. At this time he was a rising influence in the leadership, with a special interest in cultivating Comintern links and along with Clemens Palme Dutt would be one of Klugmann's main contacts at King Street while he was at Cambridge. The meeting established a National Student Bureau – with Meyer its first secretary – and identified the need for a stronger communist strategy in the universities in order to win leading positions, bring in outside speakers and dominate existing left and labour associations. This strategy quickly paid off, with more cells, members and a growing communist presence beyond the three largest centres (Cambridge, Oxford and the LSE) to include 12 more universities in Britain. They also set up their own newspaper, the *Student Vanguard*, which replaced the *Outpost* (a Cambridge communist paper), and was edited by Meyer, Guest and Cornforth.

This strategy strengthened communist presence in the colleges as a rival to Labour student associations, culminating in the disaffiliation of the CUSS and other bodies from the University Labour Federation (ULF) and the creation of the Federation of Student Societies the following year. For all present at the Lancaster Road meeting, the message was clear: they were joining an international political organisation with roots in the October Revolution which drew its inspiration from the Soviet Union. No one present at the meeting would have been in any doubt that the Party had close underground links with Moscow, though these were regarded as official and authorised by the Party.[24]

Despite his now firm communist convictions, Klugmann was not yet an open communist. In fact he did not officially join the Party until the following year. Like Donald Maclean, his decision not to join earlier was partly the result of familial pressure; to varying degrees, they both lived in the shadow of their fathers. Maclean had endured growing tensions with his father, who had served as a minister in what his son saw as Ramsay MacDonald's 'traitorous' National Government. Despite this, Maclean felt unable to join the Communist Party until his father's death in June 1932. Klugmann's father was not a government minister but a respected businessman and free trader. Klugmann had experienced many arguments at home about his and his sister's political views. Only after his father's death on Easter Saturday, 26 March 1932, did he feel sufficiently liberated to make the full commitment that his politics were now demanding.

4

Organising the Movement

James Klugmann was on the way to becoming an open communist, as he would remain for the rest of his life. It was not unusual to take part in communist activity prior to officially joining the Party. Much of the work of the Student Bureau, like that of the Party as a whole, operated in clandestine ways; according to Frank Strauss Meyer, it communicated on a 'strictly conspiratorial basis', involving 'mail drops, coded references to individuals' and secretly maintaining its HQ in a private apartment, with records held in code.[1] This is not surprising. Communists had until recently regularly been imprisoned for perceived subversive activities in the General Strike or agitation among servicemen. The Hampstead meeting had an immediate effect in Oxford just weeks later when a group of ten leading communist students joined the CPGB, and attendances at October Club meetings grew rapidly, resulting in an estimated rise from around 150 to 300 by the end of 1932. Oxford communists would soon be strengthened by the arrival of Bernard Floud and Philip Toynbee, who would go on to be leading officers. According to Meyer, by the end of its first year the October Club had around 25 actual Communist Party members and links to various other left-wing associations. Meyer went down from Oxford in June 1932 to take up a research position with the social anthropologist Bronisław Malinowski at the LSE, where he continued his communist activities, leaving Freeman in charge of the October Club.[2]

Meyer found that the LSE suited his political activities, and his role as secretary of the CPGB's Student Bureau enabled him to coordinate political activities, leading the LSE communist 'unit' into – in his words – 'a powerful organisation which eventually controlled most of the student activities of the School and was able to achieve my election as President'.[3] The expansion of communist influence in university colleges and the work of the Student Bureau led to more united work, supported by the growth of radical student literature. The *Student Vanguard* newspaper offered a forum for discussion of communist activities across the country, with the tone of the new journal reflecting the rapidly changing political atmosphere. It proclaimed, 'The Student Vanguard makes no pretence at impartiality. It is written by students who are convinced that conditions in every section of social existence are more and more forcing a radical alteration in society.'[4]

Much urgency was given to opposing war, following the League of Nations' inability to prevent Japan's invasion of the Chinese region of Manchuria and the rise of fascism and militarism during 1933. At the Oxford Union in February, the motion 'This House will in no circumstances fight for king and country' was passed with a large majority, an unprecedented development described by Winston Churchill a few days later as 'shameless and squalid', and the subject of virulent attacks on communists and pacifists by the conservative press. In fact, the procrastination of the League of Nations had weakened the pacifist case for many on the left, a growing number of whom were now looking towards the Soviet Union for an alternative. Maurice Dobb's visits there had informed his politics. At the Cambridge Union in May 1932, in a debate which revived the union from its 'smug contentment' and 'air of aggressive Victorian prosperity',[5] Dobb spoke in favour of the motion 'That this House sees more hope in Moscow than Detroit.' He spoke enthusiastically of the increase in literacy, the Five Year Plan and the yearly increase in production, contrasting it with the millions of unemployed in America, gangsterism and the consequences of capitalist crisis. According to the reviewers, it was 'an outstanding speech, [...] the most interesting and competent speech that the house has heard for a long time'.[6] The motion was passed by 62 votes to 36 and contributed to growing confidence amongst students on the left. One of the speakers against was George Kitson Clark, Klugmann's personal tutor. Despite the difference in their political views, Kitson Clark was to remain an important friend to Klugmann, offering support and advice on his academic career and future plans, and they would spend early evenings together discussing world affairs. Kitson Clark argued, no doubt with some difficulty given the depression and rising unemployment, that the worker was 'better protected' in England than in Russia.[7]

Like many of his contemporaries, Klugmann had been excited about the events taking place in the Soviet Union. This sense of enthusiasm and optimism was not confined to the economy but included the wider society, revolutionary ideals and the notion of progress they embodied:

> Literature, art, the whole culture of the Soviet Union, was dominated by construction, great buildings, great dams, great schemes. The novels were full of it, the hero was the hero of construction, the villain, the saboteur. And this

contrasted with 'poverty in the midst of plenty', the destruction of wealth that was taking place under capitalism in its crisis.[8]

What Klugmann saw as the Soviet Union's 'cultural achievements' included the silent films of the era – he had already seen some of the early socialist and avant-garde cinema with Donald Maclean in London in school holidays at the end of the 1920s. Now he devoured the silent films of the Soviet director Sergei Eisenstein, notably *Battleship Potemkin* and *October,* and Vsevolod Pudovkin's 'revolutionary trilogy': *Mother, The End of St Petersburg* and *Storm Over Asia.*

If the Soviet Union was the country which had made the first communist revolution, then Klugmann turned his thoughts to Germany for the next. In addition to studying German at university, he had taken vacation language classes in Munich and Berlin as well as occasional family holidays to Wiesenbronn and was impressed by the way in which Marxism had influenced German left-wing culture. He was an 'addict' of German expressionist theatre and had become well acquainted with the works of Bertolt Brecht, Georg Kaiser and Ernst Toller, and would see their plays at the Festival Theatre in Cambridge, or when he was back in London, at the Gate Theatre in Villiers Street, Charing Cross. In the plays of Brecht and Toller Klugmann found a deep revolutionary culture.[9]

It was therefore a terrible shock – a 'bombshell' – to hear of Hitler's advance in January 1933 and the dismantling of the progressive advances made by the German left. This was probably the event which finally triggered Klugmann into joining the Party a month later. The Reichstag fire and the rise of Nazism in the German elections had crystallised the threat of fascism and war. His Marxist beliefs, shared and nurtured in regular discussions with Kitty, Maurice Cornforth, David Guest, Kiernan, Maclean and others, now had a much wider audience and he was proving himself an able theoretician and organiser. There were other reasons for him to join the Party at this time. He had just turned 21, the age of majority, and was finally free of some of the family and personal inhibitions, given his father's death and his mother's apolitical nature. However, in other ways it was easy to join an organisation on whose behalf he had already been agitating for a considerable time. The international crisis, combined with lack of political solutions at home, demanded more active commitment. He would have been buoyed too by the foundation of the Federation of Student Societies (FSS) at its Easter Congress. Free of the Labour-controlled ULF, communist students now had the chance to build a more resilient anti-fascist strategy. This reaffirmed the feeling that the student movement was moving into its most militant stage.

Shortly after joining, Klugmann was sent by the Party to get firsthand experience of the working class in the South Wales valleys at the time of the Rhondda East by-election, where the communist candidate, Arthur Horner, was standing. It was standard practice to send new middle-class recruits to spend a week with working-class comrades and it was a formative experience in Klugmann's development as a communist. At the heart of the depression, this was a period when the condition of the workers' lives on the margins were being documented in the writings of George Orwell (*The Road to Wigan Pier*), J.B. Priestley (*English Journey*) and Walter Greenwood (*Love on the Dole*) or through the realist films and documentaries of the era, including *Night Mail*, made with the help of W.H. Auden's poetry and Benjamin Britten's music. The voices of working-class people themselves were being heard, perhaps for the first time, by a mass audience. Klugmann later wrote:

> When I was first sent, after a few weeks membership of the Communist Party in 1933, to a South Wales mining town, I met people (I was then twenty one) older than me who had never worked at all, didn't know what work was. I saw empty houses furnished with bits of wood and orange boxes, children without shoes, rickets everywhere; small shopkeepers ruined because their customers couldn't buy; illness, tuberculosis, (TB in those days was a dread word rather like cancer is now – it often signified that you were waiting for the end); emigration, either to countries or anyway out of South Wales.[10]

His visit to South Wales and experience of poverty had also acquainted him with deep respect for working-class culture which would take on an almost deferential disposition in later exchanges with industrial leaders. It made him aware of the degree to which his Party was a working-class organisation, one that shared the ethos and culture of struggle and solidarity with its deep roots in the National Unemployed Workers' Movement (NUWM) and the National Union of Mineworkers. He would have concurred with Orwell in *The Road to Wigan Pier*:

> [The miners] treated me with a kindness and courtesy that were even embarrassing; for if there is one type of man for whom I do feel myself inferior, it is a coal-miner. Certainly no one showed any sign of despising me from coming from a different part of the country.[11]

This experience would stay with Klugmann, influencing his own perception of himself as an intellectual in a working-class party.

On his return from South Wales he assumed a leading role in the communist cell at Trinity. His partner was David Guest, and their styles and personalities complemented their leadership, with Klugmann learning from his older friend some of the tactics and organisational nous that were to mark him out over the next few years as the most prominent student figure of the British Communist Party. He and Guest put in many hours during the final term of 1933 – the end of his second year of academic study, and the last for Guest, who would graduate with a first-class degree in Mathematics. As one of their comrades put it later:

It was a period of frenzied action, rendered vital by the thrill of intellectual discovery, a period of searching study and tireless tactical discussions, often in all-night sessions. However unshaven and dishevelled our appearance [...] however ridiculous we might make ourselves in our 'sectarian' fanaticism, [...] we succeeded once and for all in putting communism on the map in the universities.[12]

The primary objective was to recruit heavily among those thought to be in the slightest way like-minded or sympathetic to the anti-fascist cause. Not everything went smoothly at first, however. A Trinity contemporary, Kenneth Sinclair-Loutit, remembered Klugmann's first attempts to recruit him to the CUSS in 1933, when Klugmann turned up at Sinclair-Loutit's rooms accompanied by his more confident partner.

My first meeting with James Klugman [sic] had been when he and Haden Guest had been doing a recruiting drive [...] Klugman had tripped up coming into my room and twist[ed] his ankle. He had had to sit down, and I noticed that he was wearing heavy leather shoes while his companion, Haden Guest, was wearing rubber-soled gym shoes. As a chronic non-joiner, we failed to find common ground. The footwear is relevant, because, in a rather touching way, it served as a paradigm. Haden Guest had tried to smooth over the minor contretemps of their clumsy entrance by remarking 'the bother with James is that he will wear those great heavy things; it's much better like this', showing his own gym shoes. I had asked why he preferred them, as they had no heels they could not have been comfortable for walking. 'That's the whole point', said Haden Guest. 'I don't want to walk, I run. I reckon I win one hour per day for something useful by running. I run everywhere. I cover twice the ground in half the time. While old James is plodding along I can be reading.'[13]

The growing threat of Nazism in Germany and the prospect of war were the major preoccupations for Cambridge communists during 1933. Guest set out his view on the rise of Nazis to power in Germany in an article for the Trinity College magazine. He argued that the 'reactionary press' had welcomed Hitler's accession to power as a way of curbing Bolshevik influence and as a 'new prop of the capitalist order in Europe'.[14] In Britain there were also signs of fascist advance 'in the wave of attacks by reactionary students on progressive societies which has swept through the British universities in the last year'. Seeing 'everywhere' 'decline', 'decay' and 'death', he argued that 'we must work to overthrow the power of capital before ever a fascist movement is able to develop and in so doing avoid the terrible period of suffering which might otherwise be passed through'.[15]

Guest left Cambridge in 1933 to work for the Young Communist League (YCL) in Battersea, South London, later going to Moscow and subsequently to Spain, where he would be killed defending the Spanish Republican government. As Cornforth before him and Klugmann later, he was among the first of that generation to sacrifice a promising academic career in deference to his high ideals.

John Cornford's arrival at Cambridge in the autumn of 1933 on a History scholarship gave a new direction to the student movement. He took over from Guest after Charles Madge, originally chosen for that role, had to withdraw to look after his girlfriend Kathleen Raine (Kitty's college friend), who was pregnant with their child. The Klugmann–Cornford partnership transformed the student movement in Cambridge and would make a major contribution to the wider cause of the intellectual left in the movement against fascism and war.

As a precocious 16-year-old, John Cornford had taken a two-term course at the LSE prior to going up to Cambridge. The son of distinguished Cambridge academic parents and a descendant of Charles Darwin, Cornford had become politicised at an early age at his public school, Stowe. Like Klugmann at Gresham's, he resented the Officer Training Corps, became anti-militarist and atheist in outlook, and had taken an anti-authoritarian stance in opposition to the school authorities, debating, amongst other things, religion with the school chaplain. He read voraciously and, according to his brother, had become a socialist at 14. Taking after his mother Frances, he was also a talented poet from an early age, though he rejected the romantic poetry of Shelley, Keats and Rupert Brooke, who had been a friend of his mother and after whom he was named (Rupert John), in preference for Auden and Eliot. In letters home to his mother he debated politics and art and his impatience with the school. However, he enjoyed debates on Marxism with his closest schoolfriend, Tristan Jones. He and Jones, who had visited Russia in 1932, read *Capital*, *Wage Labour and Capital* and the *Communist Manifesto* together and they both considered joining the Communist Party. History, however, was his abiding passion and helped to drive his Marxist ideas.

He eventually joined the Communist Party at the LSE, where he immediately became involved in a whole range of political activities. He was one of Frank Strauss Meyer's younger comrades during the spring and summer terms – Meyer referred to him as his 'protégé'. He took over the editorship of *Student Vanguard*, became secretary of the Labour Research Department Group (LRD), sub-edited *Young Worker*, was a member of the LSE Anti-Fascist and Anti-War Committees and joined the Marxist Society. Very soon, he became secretary of the FSS.

However, his priority was to get involved in working-class action and he spent considerable time organising demonstrations, including supporting a strike in tram depots. His role in the LRD meant that he had to address groups of workers in explaining the Transport Act, a daunting task for a teenager. Meyer's activities as president of the LSE student union would lead to his extradition in 1934 for disciplinary reasons, but his friendship with the young Cornford was important in channelling the latter's political energy, cemented further when they and their girlfriends holidayed together in the summer of 1933 on the Norfolk coast.

The leadership duo of Klugmann and Cornford was the catalyst in the transformation of the student movement in Cambridge. Together, they ran the Cambridge student communists, not only building a strong base at Trinity, but taking communist politics to the wider student body. Their impact on a notable generation of students would become more profound even than this, exercising political leadership over the CUSS and the wider Cambridge left, impressing the Party leadership and the national student body with their imagination and commitment. Cornford would take this commitment to Spain; Klugmann, to Paris as an international student leader working for the Comintern, on the recommendation of the Party leadership. Despite their academic prowess, both had decided early on in the conversion to communism that their political commitment was for the long term.

As individual personalities they were very different. Cornford had Guest's energy and impetuosity and, like Guest, he was determined to erase any sign of 'dilettantism' or 'careerism' and immersed himself in working-class struggles.

Tall, handsome but often shabbily dressed and confrontational, he was a natural contrast to the slightly chubby, bespectacled and softly spoken Klugmann. They were both brilliant students and despite the fact that the precocious Cornford was still in his first year as an undergraduate and Klugmann entering his final year, they shared a political intensity. Although neither at this time was a particularly brilliant orator, they were extremely effective in delivering the political message.

Victor Kiernan recalled Cornford's first speech to members of the CUSS at a Sunday tea gathering. It was an uncompromising speech delivered very fast and impatient with student politics in the wake of the changes taking place in the wider world. As Kiernan recalled, 'he did in fact *enjoy* finding himself in an epoch of storm and stress, oppression and revolt, tyranny and heroism'.[16] From the start, and no doubt drawing on his experience in London, he urged the CUSS to take a more radical direction to confront the international political crisis at a time when the Labour Party and social democratic 'reformist' solutions were clearly failing. The combination of the worsening international crisis and the impotency of domestic politics added strength to his arguments and communists started to win key positions in the CUSS.

During the autumn of 1933, Cornford and Klugmann were influential voices in setting out a new strategy. This plan had two main objectives: first, to build a strong anti-fascist student movement and, second, to create a large revolutionary body. This required a great deal of propaganda work and countless hours in engaging students in political discussions, organising meetings, winning political arguments and forming broad political alliances.

It was the international crisis which provided the momentum for the first part of this strategy. The Cambridge Anti-War Council, whose secretary was Maurice Dobb, was 'an independent non-party body representing some 23 organisations in the town and the university',[17] including pacifists and church leaders. Its meeting at the beginning of November in the Guildhall was addressed by Ellen Wilkinson MP, J.D. Bernal and F.M. Cornford (John's father) and included a collection in support of the victims of German Nazism. This was part of a more concerted effort to raise the consciousness of local people about the fascist threat and was followed by an anti-war exhibition at St Andrew's Hall.

On the back of these developments, Klugmann and Cornford took the anti-war movement to the student body. Their first major public demonstration was against the showing of *Our Fighting Navy*, a naval training information film which was seen by the left as little more than militaristic propaganda. Two months before, at a showing of the same film in Swindon, six people (including two Oxford students) had been arrested after staging a protest inside the cinema, which involved shouting three slogans – 'Take it off', 'We won't fight for king and country' and 'Workers unite to fight war'. After walking out of the cinema, without being stopped and without any disturbance, the protestors had been arrested on the grounds that a 'breach of the peace' could occur if the protest was continued. They were convicted, kept in Gloucester Prison overnight and subsequently agreed to be 'bound over' for six months (the alternative would have been a month in prison).[18]

Klugmann and Cornford organised a similar protest outside the Tivoli Cinema at the beginning of November. Since Gresham's, Klugmann had been moved by the horrors of war, something which had made a further impression on him through the Nie Wieder Krieg! (No More War!) movement, which published graphic images of the worst atrocities. For Klugmann and Cornford, it also made sense strategically for student communists to mobilise around the rapidly growing peace movement, with its broad Christian and pacifist influences. Students were being drawn to anti-war protests which would escalate over the next two years through initiatives such as the Peace Pledge Union and the Peace Ballot.[19]

However, the demonstration was met with a large counter-demonstration by right-wing students and ex-servicemen, who arrived with a brass band singing wartime songs, waving Union Jacks and promising to 'rag the cads'. This precipitated a fierce fight outside the cinema, with the anti-war demonstrators largely on the receiving end. The consequences of this fracas went on for weeks afterwards and marked a shift towards more militant student action.

The protest against *Our Fighting Navy* marked the beginning of intense anti-war activity during Armistice Week. On Armistice Day itself, a demonstration jointly organised by the CUSS, the Student Christian movement and assorted pacifists marched through the centre of Cambridge to the War Memorial. Many opposed the 'jingoism' and 'anti-intellectualism' of previous days. The threat of further attack and disruption by right-wing students was almost certainly another factor contributing to the large numbers on the march. For Klugmann, Cornford and other communists in the CUSS it was important to avoid the occasion being reduced to that of a 'student rag for poppy day'. They inserted on a large wreath the inscription: 'To the victims of the Great War, from those who are determined to prevent similar crimes of imperialism.'[20] The insistence on using the word 'imperialism' prevented the participation of the League of

Nations, which objected to the term, and police later removed the inscription on the grounds that it could lead to a breach of the peace.

The march had been preceded by a meeting on Parker's Piece which had to be cut short after attempts by right-wing students to disrupt proceedings. The demonstration itself attracted larger numbers than organisers had expected and was able to continue despite heckling, sporadic fights and attempts to overhaul the CUSS banner as the march began. There were enough people from the town as well as many students in support to see it off. As some of the participants recalled:

> There was a certain amount of throwing things and cat-calling, but it was not so bad; you could walk along with some dignity, pretending not to hear [...]
>
> It was as the demonstration reached the narrowing of the road by Peterhouse that it ran into the big fight. An organised attempt was made to bar the road with cars and to cut the demonstration in half. There was a terrific mob, and the police drew their batons. Most of the demonstrators, of course, couldn't see what was happening up at the front, where the banner pole was broken and several nasty knocks given. Then, from somewhere, as the column pushed and fought its way round by the Art School, came a cloud of flour and white feathers. We knew that was what they gave to anti-war militants during the Great War; it made it seem like the real thing. Some of the students proudly stuck the feathers in their coats as trophies. We got through somehow or other, and marched to the war memorial, pursued by relays of toughs who went into shops for eggs and tomatoes [...] Triumphantly we formed a ring round the Memorial, and the wreath was laid there.
>
> The event itself had been exciting enough to those who took part in it: it had made them feel that there was a need for protest and action on behalf of peace in a way that no orderly meeting would have convinced them. A large number of the demonstrators became from that time very active in the anti-war movement.[21]

The Armistice Day demonstrations were a pivotal moment in the development of a large militant student movement in Cambridge, as well as being formative in the experiences for many.[22] The two events also took up several pages of debate and discussion in the press, with fears about the consequences of the growing student agitations. As a *Cambridge Review* editorial warned:

It might be argued that it was perhaps unfortunate to introduce politics into a day which is essentially one of personal remembrance. But surely freedom both of speech and action are menaced, if an orderly procession of people is not to be permitted to lay a wreath upon the war memorial, whatever may be your point of view. As it was a crowd of intolerant hooligans was so far lacking in any sense of decency or chivalry as to attack the procession, which included many women and to assault it in a most brutal fashion. We must condemn unreservedly this resort to violence, reminiscent more of lynch law than of the actions of educated people, as entirely unworthy of Cambridge.[23]

Among those who took part was Guy Burgess, who in the heat of the hostility during the Armistice march had navigated while Julian Bell drove a car buttressed with mattresses to keep the counter-demonstrators at bay. Burgess, who was an exceptional history student, had initially been drawn to left-wing politics under the influence of Jim Lees, the former Nottinghamshire miner and ILP member and had got to know Klugmann, Guest and others at Trinity and in the CUSS. Now, he found that his anti-war position had put him at odds with the League of Nations and pacifism and was protesting against the system which produced war. 'If you think like that, your place is in the Party', Klugmann told him.[24]

The demonstrations and clashes in 1933 may have been deemed 'unworthy' by the university authorities but for Klugmann and his comrades they were indicative of a fast-moving international political situation. It had been a long and eventful year, which had seen the rise of fascism, struggles against unemployment and militarism and his first real experience of a working-class community. He had played a leading part in the growing student movement at Cambridge and, while he continued to excel in his studies, was coming to the view that politics was going to be a big part of his life.

5

Mentor and Talent Spotter

According to James Klugmann's friend and tutor, Anthony Blunt, the end of 1933 was the moment at which 'Marxism hit Cambridge'.[1] Klugmann himself believed that the situation in Britain, combined with the fast-developing international events, confirmed his new Party's prognosis: 'We simply knew, all of us that the revolution was at hand. If anyone had suggested that it wouldn't happen in Britain, say for thirty years, I'd have laughed myself sick.'[2]

Communists at Cambridge University now occupied a leading strategic position in the Cambridge University Socialist Society. The CUSS grew rapidly from the end of 1933 with a membership of around 200 members, to peak at 600 by 1936, with approximately 25 per cent of them communists. The big expansion took place under Klugmann's and Cornford's leadership, a result not only of the more intense political agitation and organisation on their part, but also of their ability to present communism as the only reasonable political solution on offer. Margot Heinemann, one of those who joined the Party under their influence at this time, informed her family that she was 'being converted to communism by some very efficient members of the Party. They charge round leaving pamphlets & leaflets and conversational missions everywhere and very well they do it.'[3]

Their recruitment drives were adapted according to whether their intended candidate was considered ready for the CUSS or the communist cell and involved different categories of membership. Some would join the communist cell openly; others would keep their membership secret, while a third group might have shared the broad politics of the CUSS but were not prepared to take the final step to identify themselves openly with the Party. Within the CUSS, the communists were the best organised, theoretically informed and strategically adept. They helped put Trinity at the centre of this organisation and indeed it became 'the focal point of student communism in Cambridge and the whole of Britain'.[4] Its leading student members, Klugmann, Cornford, Burgess, Brian Simon and Victor Kiernan, were influential in some of the university societies (including the Trinity Historical Society and economic and science discussion groups) and received encouragement from Maurice Dobb, the communist don who had connections with the Party leadership and the Comintern. The Trinity College cell met weekly in student rooms to discuss the political situation and to decide on 'immediate tasks' such as organising demonstrations, winning political battles in the broad movements and raising funds for campaigns. Other strong bases grew in King's College and Pembroke College, while members in colleges with fewer members were grouped together. Margot Heinemann at Newnham, for example, was in a group which also included Gonville and Caius College and St Catherine's College. Klugmann's and Cornford's intensity of work and attention to detail meant that there was a system in place to integrate those drawn to communist ideas and build on their political interests:

> The steady undramatic work of Marxist study groups in the colleges, of anti-war study groups, of arranging weekly lectures, above all, of private conversation, was the sure basis on which the successes were built up. Elaborate lists were kept of sympathisers, near-sympathisers, and in general of everyone a Socialist student knew; and systematic collecting and recruiting and converting were his main occupations.[5]

More breakthroughs in numbers and influence were achieved at a time when communism in Britain began to enjoy wider intellectual hegemony over the culture and ideology of left-wing politics. Organisationally, the Party was now benefiting from stronger student cells and associations, which would lead to the first full-time student organiser, Jack Cohen, who would later go on to be one of Klugmann's closest friends in the Party's education department. Beyond the colleges, intellectuals, writers, poets and scientists were drawn to the Party in the mid-1930s, while their growing political influence within the struggles of the unemployed and anti-fascist movements challenged mainstream labour politics.

One of the attractions for many of the students was the closer links formed with working-class struggles which, combined with firsthand experiences of fighting fascism and brushes with the law, went well beyond the rebellious strains of youth. These commitments also distinguished the student communists from the earlier generation of radical aesthetes who had expressed their opposition to the status quo in radical and avant-garde ways but had not forged deep political alliances or connections with 'mass' organisations. These commitments carried costs: working in a clandestine way remained a reality for many who joined, though the Cambridge University authorities seemed less censorious in their responses in comparison to the LSE or Oxford University, which had banned the October Club in autumn 1933 after it issued publicity attacking OTC recruitment. A follow-up meeting protesting against the 'violation of free speech' was attended by university proctors who took down names and subsequently confined students to their rooms after 9 p.m.[6]

Following the anti-war protests in late 1933, the second defining moment for many who went on to join the Communist Party[7] was the Hunger March of February 1934. This was the second national hunger march organised by the NUWM, which was communist led, and was given heightened significance by the growing disillusion with the National Government and the escalation of fascism. The Labour Party and Trades Union Congress (TUC) remained hostile to the NUWM, though the ILP had supported the Party's call for united action. For many Cambridge students who were coming into contact with workers for the first time, this experience left a marked impression, while unprecedented solidarity with workers helped to remove mutual barriers of suspicion. The wider political crisis certainly helped to amplify the ferment of activity and worked to the communists' advantage as they were instrumental in making links between opposition to fascism and war and the political situation at home. Every town visited by the hunger marchers had a 'Public Assistance Committee' which took responsibility for feeding them, and in Cambridge the CUSS worked with communist and other supporters to organise support and raise money for food and clothing. This took place in an atmosphere of some tension, given the opposition of the government and the threat of police charges.

Nevertheless, as the marchers arrived in Cambridge they must have been surprised by the warmth of their reception. Some Cambridge students, among them Guy Burgess, joined the marchers at Huntingdon, but it was the reception in the town that was striking. Women students from Girton College were the first to meet them on the outskirts of the town, handing out refreshments and then joining with them to march together into the centre of Cambridge.

At first, some of the students were a bit shy and self-conscious, wondering whether they had a right to be there, wondering whether it would be cheek to buy packets of cigarettes for the men. Gradually they began to enjoy it, singing Pie in the Sky and Solidarity for Ever and the rest of the marchers' songs. Going through the town, shouting 'Down with the Means Test!' you would see some student you knew slightly, standing on the pavement, staring, a little frightened, at the broken boots and the old mackintoshes. The phrases about the power of the workers and the right to a better life suddenly meant something quite concrete and real.[8]

The 100 or so marchers were put up in the Corn Exchange and, with the help of the Public Assistance Committee, provided with food and blankets. The police arrived early next morning to ensure they left, and despite 'some rough handling no blows were struck'.[9]

Later that day, a packed meeting heard a passionate speech by Wilf Jobling which elicited an enthusiastic reception from students, some of whom accompanied the marchers on the next stage to Saffron Walden. Margot Heinemann was one of the students who met the marchers. She recalled Jobling – who later died in Spain – making a stirring speech in the evening, while the whole experience reaffirmed her earlier decision to join the Party after the anti-war protests. It was the 'first time it ever occurred to me that the working class could have a central role'.[10]

For Klugmann himself, the experience of the hunger marchers was another important rite of passage in his development as a communist. The previous year in the Rhondda Valley he had observed the unemployment and poverty of a mining community facing the ignominy of the means test. Those sparsely furnished little houses with crooked roofs dug into steep slopes were inhabited by some people who had never worked, their children without shoes and with TB endemic. This had come as a shock to Klugmann, whose life since he left the secluded environs at Belsize Park had remained a privileged one, his active politics notwithstanding. He also knew that his empathy had its limits; he was not of the working class and could never know their poverty.

Yet he also met people there who had participated in the General Strike, and their humanity and dignity made a lasting impression on him. Now, in Cambridge, he witnessed the fight back, as the unemployed brought their struggle to the citadels of power. For Oxbridge students like Klugmann, the 'fraternization of students with the hunger marchers and, be it said, of hunger marchers with the students, which wasn't so easy going into these centres of the rich [...] were quite traumatic elements in the birth and growth of the student movement'.[11]

He admitted that he and his generation had been intellectually 'arrogant'; 'We were still "lost" at the beginning of the thirties; often with immense knowledge but no philosophy, immense mental effort and activity but no purpose.' However, he and his comrades in the CUSS and the communist cell were committed and in search of a cause, when 'they came across this new species, the British working man, in action and in struggle, not the British working man in inverted commas, but the working man and woman in reality'.[12] For Klugmann, support for the hunger marchers was something more than an act of philanthropy. It meant that the students were losing their arrogance and no longer remaining adrift from working-class struggles and could share common ideals with workers.

David Guest had earlier failed in his attempt to set up a branch of the NUWM at the university, but now under the leadership of Cornford and Klugmann, meeting regularly in Klugmann's rooms in Whewell's Court, Kitty and Maurice Cornforth's flat in the centre of Cambridge, or McLaurin's bookshop in All Saints' Passage, the students took a more public role in support of working-class struggles. It helped that Kitty was secretary of the town branch, and she and Maurice had established a presence in working-class communities, canvassing on housing estates, and organising a rent strike. The bus strike in Cambridge in the autumn of 1934 involved early morning pickets of the bus garages and included several students. This was the first occasion Margot Heinemann met John Cornford. It was in a transport café at 6.30 a.m., and despite his 'slightly scruffy' appearance in a grey polo-neck sweater she was impressed by his leadership and ability to convey to students the importance of supporting working-class struggles.

The communist attitude to the relationship between students and the working class was not straightforward, however. The 'Class Against Class' strategy adopted by the Comintern during its Third Period (1927–32) was rigidly tied to a sectarian analysis which characterised social democrats as 'social fascists' and dismissed the 'pretensions' of 'intellectuals'. This had left its mark. Rajani Palme Dutt, editor of *Labour Monthly* and at that time the Party's most prominent in-house thinker, issued a warning in *Communist Review* to young writers and technicians: 'First and foremost he should *forget* that he is an intellectual (except in moments of necessary self-criticism) and remember only that he is a communist.'[13] As late as October 1933 – that is, just prior to the big peace demonstrations and clashes which sparked the communist student movement in Cambridge – he was still denouncing 'petty-bourgeois' students.[14]

There had been some indications of scepticism towards left intellectuals in the early period of the Cornford–Klugmann leadership as they asserted their newfound Party identity; their long hours of commitment organising meetings, taking stands and preparing briefings left little time for what they saw as the frivolous posturing of some of the poets. In what he later called 'a lonely personal demonstration', Klugmann recalled how he and Cornford made their point in a resolve to 'Keep culture out of Cambridge', a slogan taken from one of Cornford's own poems. It was written during his first term at Trinity, and was symptomatic of the harsh and unforgiving politics of young activists who were seeking an uncompromising 'pure' revolutionary ideal, in the early days of party membership:

> Wind from the dead land, hollow men,
> Webster's skull and Eliot's pen,
> The important words that come between
> The unhappy eye and the difficult scene.
> All the obscene important names
> For silly griefs and silly shames,
> All the tricks we once thought smart,
> Kestrel joy and the change of heart,
> The dark mysterious urge of the blood,
> The donkeys shitting on Dali's food,
> There's none of these fashions have come to stay,
> And there's nobody here got time to play.
> All we've brought are our party cards,
> Which are no bloody good for your bloody charades.[15]

Cornford stopped writing poetry in his second term because of his frenetic political activities and both men gave much of their time, when not studying, to politics – around 14 hours a day in Cornford's case, according to his comrades. Though they had broad cultural interests, they had less time for university societies, although the Cambridge Film Society regularly showed political films and a 'workers' newsreel'. Through the film agency KINO they had been able to see several Soviet films, and experimental theatre was another way in which culture and politics were joined at this point; they were often the subject of intense debate among critics and participants.

Maintaining such a sectarian position would, then, have been uncomfortable for Klugmann, who by nature and schooling had come to Marxism via the humanist traditions of the Enlightenment. However, any dilemmas he may have had were lifted following a visit to Cambridge by Willie Gallacher in 1934. Gallacher, a working-class Scot, Clydeside trade unionist and foundation member of the Communist Party who had earlier been imprisoned for his politics, was seen as a working-class hero by middle-class Cambridge students. The following year he would be elected as a Communist MP. The visit had a significant effect on Klugmann's future career. Gallacher was initially offenced at the attitudes and appearance of some of the Cambridge communists who wanted to join the workers in the factories or become full-time revolutionaries. Gallacher told them that they should stay and study hard and make their contribution to the struggle in other ways. This led to the slogan 'Every communist student a good student'. He told the students that only 'one or two of you' might become full-time revolutionaries but the Party also needed good scientists and teachers.

Gallacher's advice presented an attractive solution to Klugmann's immediate career prospects, which he was now forced to consider at the end of his degree in the summer of 1934. His tutors encouraged him to do research and to opt for an academic career. At the same time, the Party also had plans for him. In June he graduated with a double first in French and German, and his intellectual prowess had left a deep impression with his tutors. Kitson Clark, who was very fond of him and maintained a paternal interest in his welfare for some years afterwards, sent a warm message on hearing his results: 'A thousand congratulations – I was most extraordinarily glad when I heard the news and now all that you have to do is go from strength to strength.'[16] As an outstanding student with aspirations to be a history teacher, Klugmann saw a way ahead whereby it would be possible for him to be both an intellectual and a communist. He was offered a research scholarship in the history of French Literature under the supervision of Henry Ashton, with permission to visit Paris the following year to study under the French intellectual historian Daniel Mornet at the Sorbonne. More widely, the Gallacher mantra – 'Every communist student a good student' – had instant results, with many of his contemporaries also graduating with firsts; he later calculated the percentage of communist students gaining firsts at Cambridge rapidly went from under 5 per cent to 60 per cent.

The warm regard in which he was held by his tutors partly reflected the fact that his radical politics was not accompanied by the more direct confrontational approaches of Burgess, Cornford and Guest, and he was rarely seen to lose his temper or raise his voice. His geniality was very useful in the division of responsibilities he enjoyed with Cornford as they found renewed vigour for their organisational work in the autumn of 1934. Cornford continued to believe that his priority was to organise amongst the working class in the town (he was now living with his girlfriend Rachel 'Ray' Peters, a working-class woman from South Wales, with whom he would have a son, James, named after Klugmann, in January 1935), and that he needed to convince students to renounce their lifestyles and privileges. A more romantic and impetuous leader, he was impatient with the restrictions of the college environment. The older Klugmann, however, was the one who had been most taken with Gallacher's argument and it was he who took the lead in recruiting new college arrivals. Some of these had been recommended to him by comrades at other colleges, whereas on other occasions it was a case of following up the sympathetic 'doubters' of previous encounters. This suited him, as outwardly he was more conventional in manner and appearance, and at his strongest in winning intellectual arguments with his student contemporaries through charm and tact. This difference of emphasis between the two in fact amounted to a brilliantly successful and complementary recruitment strategy.

Margot Heinemann, now a regular participant in many of the meetings, recalled that they 'read everything as it came out' and were 'tremendously briefed' on the latest developments in the Communist International. Klugmann and Cornford saw their key political tasks as convincing undergraduates of the communist cause, recruiting them to their ranks, and ensuring that the Party policy and strategy was disseminated. They spent hours visiting possible recruits and talking with their fellow students. Cornford, despite being four years younger than his co-leader, was, in Heinemann's view, 'very mature. Very determined not to be an amateur in politics.' He was not a particularly good orator and, as a fast talker and quick thinker, would often have to check himself and slow down, but he was a 'clear logical speaker', 'burned up with enthusiasm', who 'would hit the table with his fists' when making his points. Like Guest, he was always on the move, and 'never had any spare time'.[17]

Klugmann, Cornford's 'closest friend', according to Margot Heinemann, adopted the role of the patient persuader, explaining the significance of the historical moment and the Party's analysis of the situation. He showed a genuine enough interest in the backgrounds and opinions of his potential recruits to spend an evening talking with them, where his growing command of Marxism and the international situation put him ahead of others. Given the Labour Party's capitulation in 1931, he presented the Communist Party as the only alternative, and besides, it was now in the forefront of left politics at Cambridge, occupying a key role in the leadership of the CUSS, with the Trinity communist cell the linchpin of the movement. His continued success as a student leader would be built on his perception that the real potential of communism at that moment was its capacity to explain the multiple crises.

Some of his recruits had seen the rise of Nazism in Germany or witnessed, as he had, the big Mosley fascist demonstrations of the previous summer. In the Olympia exhibition hall in London in June, counter-demonstrators – many communists among them – were roughly treated by fascist stewards, with several needing hospital treatment. In a subsequent demonstration in Hyde Park in September, a large police force of 7,000 was seen to defend a fascist demonstration of an estimated 2,000 people. In these and other anti-fascist and peace movements, the communists were seen to have played an important role in an escalating crisis, and Klugmann's strength was his ability to articulate his Party's policy – at the time when Labour was at its lowest ebb – as the only credible alternative on offer.

The long evenings talking and debating were for him stimulating social events. Neither he nor Cornford shared Guy Burgess's taste for extravagant sherry parties and, though there was punting on the river and the occasional society dinner, Klugmann's social life became increasingly dominated by Party commitments. At times it must have been a lonely existence; his shyness and inhibited sexuality preventing – as far as anyone could tell – close personal relationships outside politics, though he remained popular with fellow students and tutors and acquired acquaintances easily. His reading remained expansive, however – if now tailored more to his revolutionary ends. Overall, the combination of his personality and lifestyle, his hunger for ideas, intense political engagement and the need to spread the message must have resembled the religious commitment of a missionary.

One who saw him in this way was Charles Rycroft, then studying Economics and History at Trinity College. Rycroft, who had experienced the rise of Nazism at firsthand in 1933 before going up to Cambridge later that year, was surprised to discover that 'it was only the extreme left wing undergraduate organizations that were aware of what was going on in Germany'.[18] He found many of them,

> unlike anything I had known before. They had accents and scholarships, wore polo sweaters and Mackintoshs and were obviously contemptuous of anyone who appeared to take superficial matters seriously or serious matters lightly. From them I learnt that intensity, which I had previously thought a vice, was really a virtue, and also that I, poor thing, was decadent, a dilettante, a member of a dying class, precluded by the dialectic of history from ever having any understanding of the modern world.[19]

Nevertheless, it was clear to Rycroft that he was seen as a potential recruit. This was largely down to Klugmann, whom Rycroft refers to as 'Mark', the 'intellectual Jesuit', as distinct from Cornford's Matthew, 'a romantic puritan' who believed 'individual bourgeois [...] should renounce their private incomes, or give their capital to the Party [...] change their accents and their clothes'. Klugmann's rooms were near Rycroft's and, after a 'marathon series of indoctrination sessions lasting far into the night', he finally succeeded in recruiting him, impressing Rycroft with his knowledge and empathy.

> He was by far the best-read person I had hitherto met and he took more trouble over me than any tutor or teacher had ever done. He also had a very ecumenical approach towards communism, which enabled him to convert people to it without requiring them to change their opinion on any important matter [...] Mark believed that communism was the heir to all that was best in liberalism, socialism, conservatism, rationalism, Catholicism and Anglicanism. It was 'Forward from Everything' and he encouraged his recruits to live exactly as they had before their conversion [...] He held that culture was a weapon in the class struggle and that even research in aesthetics was a legitimate form of revolutionary activity. Prolonged meditation at the foot of a Chippendale Chair would, I once heard him say, bring a Marxist to a closer understanding of the class structure of eighteenth century England.[20]

Rycroft felt that Klugmann's 'view of communism' 'suited me down to the ground', enabling him to carry on attending sherry parties on St Augustine's principle of 'I love God and do what you will'.[21]

According to Rycroft, Klugmann's leadership style and organisational acumen were crucial factors in accommodating the less reliable, but intellectually expansive groupings; the 'crème de la crème of the liberal intelligentsia', as he put it. It was Klugmann and not Cornford who had the 'ear of King Street' and this enabled him to include those who may have had 'doubts about the validity of Marxist ideas' and were less constrained by party discipline – distinct from Cornford's target group of grammar school cadres.

> it was understood that their contribution to the class war would be made not at the barricades but on the cultural front. Their historic tasks were to infiltrate senior common rooms, the corridors of power, Bloomsbury and Mayfair, and to

hold themselves in readiness to re-establish cultural life after the chaos of the revolutionary period.[22]

Rycroft was one of the more loosely affiliated communists, whose interest in Marxism rarely extended to commitment beyond the university. While they were less reliable than the dedicated cadres in the so-called 'category A' of Party recruits, they remained invaluable to Klugmann because of their potential intellectual influence in wider political circles. Winning them over helped bring communism in from the cold, taking it from the margins to the mainstream of politics. Moreover Rycroft was not alone in being attracted by 'Mark's' all-embracing interpretation of the revolution. Kenneth Sinclair-Loutit, the medical student who had rebutted Guest and Klugmann the year before, had since been inspired by the hunger marches and had witnessed the rise of Nazism in Germany. He could not resist in his next encounter:

> My second meeting with James Klugman [sic] must have been after my return from Germany. He was accompanied by John Cornford. As contemporaries we all knew each other by sight, and Klugman remembered his previous recruiting visit. They said, very reasonably, that it was only by working together that people sharing the same goals could hope to achieve them, so I really could not do other than join the university Socialist Society. I had already told James the year before that I was not a joiner. His manner had a hint of recognition that at last virtue was starting to prevail, that I was beginning to see the light.[23]

Sinclair-Loutit never joined the Communist Party but was typical of many who were drawn to the left through anti-fascist movements, describing himself at this time as a 'non-Party radical intellectual, frightened and disgusted by the inhumanity of the depression'. He later went to Spain to head a medical unit and subsequently joined Stafford Cripps and Aneurin Bevan on the left of the Labour Party in opposing appeasement. His and Klugmann's paths would cross again towards the end of World War II.

6

The Making of a Communist Intellectual

Willie Gallacher's visit to Cambridge in the summer of 1934 had been a timely revelation for James Klugmann, a 'dramatic moment' which justified his long evenings of intellectual discussion with his comrades. From Gallacher's talk Klugmann derived two main incentives for his own future. First, he started to see himself as a communist intellectual. Not an aloof, decadent thinker removed from the practicalities of the real world, but one organically linked to the working-class movement with sufficient knowledge and expertise to teach and educate at the service of the Party. He was already regarded by his peers as an expert exponent of Marxism and the one who could make the case for the Party and its policy in lucid and imaginative ways through his application of Marxist theory and knowledge of European history. Now he assumed a stronger meaning and purpose to his endeavours. Eventually he would become one of the Party's leading theoreticians and one of the few intellectuals to rise in the hierarchy.

More widely, as a communist intellectual, Klugmann now sought to apply Marxism as an explanatory framework for understanding a range of economic, historical, scientific, cultural and artistic questions. He argued that the middle class and professional sections would become politicised in response to the pressures capitalism was imposing on many vocations, from doctors to scientists to teachers. What, for example, was scientific research to be used for, or – in the pre-welfare state days – what would be the constraints placed on doctors serving working-class communities? The university curriculum was still detached from the pressing concerns of social change and world affairs. Klugmann's own subjects, French and German Literature, were still disconnected, he felt, from society. He found the syllabus more restrictive than the one he had encountered as a schoolboy; there was little of McEachran's idiosyncratic but stimulating reading of the anti-war writers such as Barbusse (*Under Fire*) or Remarque (*All Quiet on the Western Front*), but instead a diet of romanticism, classicism and Goethe.

Was there anything on Goethe that hadn't been written? [...] And then, suddenly, there was nothing done, there was hardly a book about Goethe that was worth reading. Suddenly you realised that everything still had to be done. From feeling stilted, cynical, fed up, you saw that the whole of intellectual life had to be restudied [...] Marxism made everything rich. Although it didn't do the work, it opened you to do more work than you'd have done with a bourgeois philosophy.[1]

The interests of middle-class students, professionals and intellectuals were not antithetical to workers but were bound up with the same struggle. For Klugmann, it was Marxism which offered a unique insight into the world and provided a holistic way of interpreting and changing that world. This was something that remained with him throughout his life and continued to be reflected in his education work in Paris, Cairo, Party schools and in the 1970s at the Communist University of London.

The second incentive he took from Gallacher's talk was the view that only a few would have the qualities and opportunities to become full-time revolutionaries. It was an important and privileged role. Eric Hobsbawm felt that it was the 'only really desirable career' for communist students in the 1930s, but he himself ruled it out on the grounds that he did not have the organisational skills needed.[2] This did not apply in Klugmann's case, as he had already demonstrated to his peers and leaders at King Street that he had what it took. It was becoming clear to him that he was one who could take that path. He had made the transition from 'rebel' to 'revolutionary', and that distinction was one he now prioritised in his recruitment drive, trying to move the slightest critical or rebellious student to a position where they would see communism as the only alternative. He later described the approach he adopted in Cambridge to a group of young communists in London in the 1970s: 'When freshmen came I would go out and look at them.' He would search for signs of rebellion in clothes, dress or lifestyle. If he saw long hair, velveteen trousers, or Oxford 'bags', he would take it as a sign of rebellion and something to cultivate. These signs of rebellion were

very welcome. To be cherished by us [...] If I took this as a starting point, I could take this further and win them to the Party [...] The rebel, man or woman, boy or girl, when they dislike some aspect of capitalism, but they have not yet – this is the point – reached the stage when they know what they are for, this is the important thing.

On the other hand, 'the revolutionary is *for* something. For socialism.' There was, he said, 'no future in just being a rebel'.[3] His success in recruitment would enhance his reputation as the Party's leading talent spotter at Cambridge, bring swift promotion in the Party and a new vocation.

In the autumn of 1934, Klugmann first met John Cairncross, who had recently arrived at Trinity following earlier studies at Glasgow and the Sorbonne in Paris. It was to be a fateful meeting for both parties. They shared an interest in French and German literature, with Cairncross finding his older friend's ideas on those subjects 'stimulating'. Cairncross's tutor, Professor Henry Ashton, an expert on Molière, was now Klugmann's postgraduate supervisor, and the three would have long discussions late into the evening. It was through common intellectual interests that Klugmann won Cairncross to the 'communist circle', by convincing him that the communists were the only ones in Britain committed to opposing Nazism. It was Cairncross's 'first contact with organised Communism and I felt compelled to look into it'.[4]

Another of Klugmann's tutors was Anthony Blunt, who held a fellowship at Trinity. The two got to know each other well from the end of 1934, on Blunt's return from a sabbatical year in Italy and Germany. Returning briefly in January 1934, Blunt had noticed that 'most of my friends [...] had either joined the Communist Party or at least were very close to it politically'. When he returned permanently to Cambridge at the end of his sabbatical in September, he 'soon found that the grip of communism on Cambridge had got even stronger'.[5] Blunt had had little contact with communism at this point, being, in his own words, an 'art for art's sake' Bloomsbury aesthete. The politicisation of Guy Burgess over the previous year was one of the important factors in his conversion, with Blunt impressed by his friend's command of the Marxist dialectic of history. The other factor was his friendship with Klugmann.

Blunt, as a young Trinity don, was close to many of his students and took a keen interest in their welfare. He sought to cultivate the intellectual development of his brightest students, and Klugmann was a regular visitor to his rooms in Neville Court. Klugmann benefited from Blunt's knowledge of French culture, and it was almost certainly Blunt who stimulated his later interest in drawings, prints and engravings. Their discussions on European history and culture would have reaffirmed Klugmann's belief that communism was the heir to the progressive traditions of the Enlightenment. For his part, Klugmann was able to impart his knowledge of Marxist theory and explain how art needed to be understood in its social and class contexts and that political struggle needed to be waged on the cultural front. Blunt regarded Klugmann as a 'brilliant student of mine and also a friend'. He was impressed by Klugmann's political knowledge, understanding of Marxism and ability to translate theory into political practice. Klugmann, as Blunt commented later:

> was the pure intellectual of the Party. He was a very good scholar and also an extremely good political theorist. He was the person who worked out the theoretical problems and put them across. He ran the administration of the Party with great skill and energy and it was he who decided what organisations in Cambridge were worth penetrating and what were not.[6]

If Blunt was his mentor on art, Klugmann reciprocated on communist politics and Marxist theory. They were both in the process of becoming talent spotters and mentors. Though he had been his tutor, Blunt was in fact a typical Klugmann target for recruitment.

Another of Klugmann's recruits who would later be embroiled in espionage controversy was Michael Straight. From a wealthy American family who had taken over the ownership of Dartington Hall in Devon, Straight had become politicised after spending a year at the LSE working under Harold Laski (whilst living with a valet in P.G. Wodehouse's Mayfair flat). Arriving at the LSE at the same time that Cornford departed for Cambridge, Straight had joined the Marxist Society, where he too came under the influence of Frank Strauss Meyer, at the same time forming a close friendship with Peter Floud, a former Gresham's contemporary of Klugmann and Maclean, whose younger brother Bernard would accompany Klugmann on the World Student Association's China delegation in 1938.

Straight went up to Trinity College in October 1934 to study Economics, initially under Maurice Dobb. However, unlike some of his communist contemporaries, he was not initially won over by Dobb, whom he described as 'a shy man, but a persuasive one when he turned to politics; as an economist he had little influence'.[7] In contrast, Straight was immediately impressed by John Maynard Keynes, whose lectures on the general principles of his economic theory Straight compared to 'listening to Charles Darwin or Isaac Newton'.[8] Enthused by Keynes's work and that of his protégés Joan Robinson and Denis Robertson, he 'left Dobb as soon as I could', though he was to work with him later on his anti-fascist exhibition.[9]

Nevertheless, Straight was won over to communism by the two visitors dressed in black gowns who arrived at his lodgings, initially some distance from the college, one November evening.

> One had a birdlike head and manner, his name was James Klugmann. The other had black, curly hair, high cheek bones, and dark, deep-set eyes. His entire body was taut, his whole being seemed to be concentrated upon his immediate purpose. His name was John Cornford [...]
>
> James and John wandered around the room, looking at the paintings, then James slumped into my easy chair. He sat there, smiling. John stood by my fireplace. When he grinned, it was as if the grin had been wrenched out of him. [...] James explained why they had come to see me [...] My name had been passed along to them by some comrades at the London School. They asked if I would join the (Cambridge Socialist) society. I said that I would. [...]
>
> I went to the Society from then on and spent many hours with James and John, arguing about political priorities. They were patient but persistent [...] In the course of that winter I learned that at Cambridge, as at the London School of Economics, the Socialist Society was dominated by a Marxist core. It was at heart, the point of entry into the student communist movement. That movement, which took its direction from the head office of the British Communist Party in King Street, was led by James and John.[10]

Straight recalls that there were around 'a dozen' members of the Trinity College cell when he joined in early 1935, and he did not see it as a 'major step to move from

> the outer fringes of the Socialist Society to the inner core of a communist cell [...] We wanted to believe. We carried our little green cards in our pockets; we took no Party assignments with us when we left Cambridge at the end of each term.[11]

Straight's commitment to the Party extended to passing regular funds through Klugmann to the leadership in King Street. Raising funds for the Party, another Klugmann duty, was more easily achievable from wealthy supporters like Straight, but they also appealed on humanitarian grounds to others who felt sympathy for hunger marchers and anti-fascist causes.

Klugmann's part in developing the group of loosely attached sympathisers was crucial in gaining wider credibility for the Party. This task, of course, was helped by the wider international situation. In fact, the internationalism of students in Britain was reflected not only in their opposition to fascism and appeasement, but also through a rejection of British colonialism. Communists had good links with the Cambridge Majlis, a long-standing political debating forum for 'colonial students', and included in their milieu notable activists like the scientist Ram Nahum and Mohan Kumaramangalam, president of the Cambridge Union. Victor Kiernan and later Eric Hobsbawm both participated in the Colonial Group's activities and Nahum and Pieter Keunemann, a Ceylonese activist, would later be part of Klugmann's international student movement.

The internationalist outlook of the students was reinforced by being part of the wider Communist International, and at the end of 1934 Klugmann travelled to Brussels to attend the first Congrès Mondial des Étudiants Contre la Guerre et la Fascisme (World Student Congress Against War and Fascism), which had emerged on the back of the World Committee Against War and Fascism, a broad anti-fascist front set up by Willi Münzenberg on behalf of the Comintern.

The Comintern, or the Communist International, had been founded in 1919 as the association of national communist parties and ultimately sought to create an international Soviet republic. It held seven World Congresses, with the last one in 1935, and was abolished by Stalin in 1943. One of the purposes of the Comintern was therefore to cultivate a presence through various broad organisations. One such organisation was the World Student Congress, which would launch the Rassemblement Mondial des Étudiants (RME – World Student Association). The theme of its first Congress was opposition to the militarisation of young people and promotion of the role students could play in the anti-fascist movement. Leading the Cambridge delegation, Klugmann was one of 55 who travelled from Britain out of a total of 375 delegates from 31 countries. The political composition of delegates was mixed, with 74 communists, 67 socialists and 117 members of non-aligned anti-fascist organisations; 70 of the delegates were women. Among academic subjects humanities and social science students were the best represented. The Congress had the support of an impressive list of left-wing professors and intellectuals, among them Henri Barbusse, writer, pacifist, communist and inspirational founder of the movement.[12]

Klugmann and the other British delegates reported on developments at their universities, anti-fascist activities and strengths and weaknesses of the movement. They referred to the 'new armaments race', the growing militarisation that was aided by Baden-Powell's appreciation of Mussolini and the promotion of the OTC in schools and colleges. They also pointed out differential treatment of fascists and anti-fascists by police, with the recent experiences of Olympia and Hyde Park fresh in their minds. In sharing their experience of student anti-fascist activities, they pointed to the anti-war exhibitions, films, photographs and journals and argued that, with more cooperation, effective anti-fascist action could be achieved:

> Up till now students have been grouped in many organisations with similar aims but different in methods of work and it is one of the main tasks of our delegation to learn from other delegations how best they may be welded into a unity.[13]

The real urgency of the anti-fascist struggle, however, was brought home by the speech of a German delegate who described the impact of Nazism on student life, and the growing discrimination against Jewish students:

> [the] crazy theory of blood and soil [which] urges a return to the land and back to primitivism. [...] says that the Jews are inferior and that the Jew was poisoning the German universities, that Jewish students and professors whom we consider valuable and scientifically very capable men should be chased from the universities.

The German delegate ended with an emotional appeal to the Congress:

> We know that our struggle will and must end with the defeat of Hitler, and in this struggle we are assured of your support [...] We [are] also certain that you will stay in permanent contact with us and support us in every respect. This for us will be one of the great accomplishments of this congress. In this spirit we grasp hands. Down with war! Death to Fascism! Long live the unified battle of students of all countries, the united front against fascism, on both sides of the frontiers.[14]

Klugmann warmly endorsed – and was possibly a contributor to – the manifesto issued at the end of that first RME Congress. Addressed 'To the student youth of the world, to the mental workers of the new generation', it declared:

> We men and women students who met in the last days of December in Brussels, and in comradely discussion, and solemn decisions, created a strong tie for the

coming times, call upon the millions who share the same fate as ourselves, to engage in a common fight for a new future [...]

Now our prospects, the prospects of the student youth, of the new generation, are the future battlefields, trenches and artillery.

Of what use is it for us to learn and study for an intellectual profession [...] We cannot make use of our degrees and diplomas [...] Thus we are experiencing the efforts of a society which is based on the exploitation of man by man, a society which has entered a period of utter decay, a regime preparing the way for fascism and war.

Fascism is the instrument of capitalism. Its natural element is war. War is the last way out for the ruling class.

In the Soviet Union we see a tremendous factor for peace, a fighter for complete disarmament, for fraternisation of the people over all frontiers.[15]

Klugmann had experienced international solidarity and the excitement of sharing a worldview that was now capturing the imagination of a generation. The Congress made clear the potential that now existed for broad alliances between liberals, Christians and socialists. The Comintern and the CPGB had long supported the idea of the 'United Front', which had been proposed as an alliance of workers from different sectors brought together in opposition to capitalism. This would be led by the revolutionary component of the working class, transforming the political outlooks of other workers in the realities of struggle. This strategy, of course, had been abandoned in the 'Class Against Class' period. Now, as the anti-fascist struggle was fought at an international level, it was to be succeeded by the 'Popular Front' of all those opposed to fascism. This was officially adopted by the Comintern at its seventh (and last) Congress in July–August 1935, at which Georgi Dimitrov, the Bulgarian communist leader, argued that the 'Popular Front' would not limit the alliance to the working class, but would incorporate all those groups opposed to fascism, though officially it would still be led by a united working class.

In practice, evidence of this strategy was already taking place, notably in France, where the left's Rassemblement Populaire was making gains and communists had been building alliances on demonstrations, exhibitions and in meetings. The official endorsement by the Comintern – with Stalin's blessing – gave wider credibility to this strategy and would have an immediate implication the following year after the election of Léon Blum's 'Popular Front' government in France and in the defence of the Spanish Republic. Both those developments would be very important in the next stage of the life and career of James

Klugmann, and the politics of the Popular Front was a perfect match for his own philosophy. Indeed, Dimitrov's critical proviso that communists must address the people 'as they are, and not as we should like to have them'[16] had long been adopted by Klugmann in his own recruitment strategy. Although one of the objectives of the Popular Front was to unite all those opposed to fascism and to defend rights and freedoms under threat, it was more than a defensive strategy. It sought to dislodge fascism's 'mass' base, bring in wider sections and develop in embryo an alternative to capitalism, of which fascism was regarded as the 'dying embers'. In this way liberal democratic opposition to fascism was regarded as perfectly compatible with the communist position in its first stage. This was precisely the approach adopted by Klugmann when he explained to potential recruits that 'communism was forward from everything'. However, it had gone way beyond Cambridge, and in Britain, as elsewhere in Europe, communists were now forming alliances with socialists and liberals.

The first year of Klugmann's research on the French Revolution had been funded by a Peter Leigh Exhibition and a grant from Cambridge University's Scholarship Fund. His personal tutor George Kitson Clark supported his application and held out the hope that he would apply for a Trinity Fellowship the following year. At the end of Klugmann's first year, Kitson Clark was able to tell him that he had been offered a Jeston Exhibition with the hope that it would be sufficient to finance vacation trips to Paris.[17] In fact, Klugmann was no longer certain he would follow an academic career and the first RME Congress had shown him new horizons. The RME was a Comintern front organisation, with new offices in Paris set up by the Comintern agents Willi Münzenberg and Otto Katz. Klugmann's rise as a communist student leader was now recognised at King Street, and the prospect of combining his study in France with playing a leading role in the student movement would have appealed to both sides. Maurice Dobb was used to finding roles for his underlings – he had sent Philby to Paris on Comintern work the previous year. The chance to work for the Comintern was an ideal opportunity for Klugmann to take his commitment further and to assume the role of professional revolutionary that Gallacher had dangled before him.

The role of a revolutionary, however, and in particular that of a communist intellectual, also demanded loyalty and sacrifice to the Party. For those in leadership positions in King Street it also involved upholding Communist Party discipline and taking necessary measures to curtail dissident elements.

On the back of his early success in getting the student movement off the ground at Cambridge, Klugmann had his first taste of this on being put in charge of its public school section. Here, with his own political dissent at Gresham's still a recent memory, he was confronted by an unprecedented revolt by communist rebels at some of the leading public schools. The leader of this revolt was Esmond Romilly, nephew of Winston Churchill and a pupil at Wellington School. Romilly, in his precocious radicalism, had moved swiftly from Tory Jacobite to communist sympathiser and by the 1933 Easter vacation was already calling himself a communist and reading the *Daily Worker*. Like Klugmann, Romilly was opposed to the OTC and practised his propagandising in the school cloisters. At the end of his summer term he visited the Parton Street bookshop, off Theobald's Road in central London, which was run by David Archer, a recent Cambridge graduate (and counted Klugmann among its regular customers). As well as a bookshop and lending library offering Marx and Engels classics, Soviet literature and a plethora of pamphlets, the shop had become a regular rendezvous for left-wing poets and intellectuals.

By autumn 1933, Romilly was promoting communist literature at Wellington, writing a letter to the *Student Vanguard*, redirecting communist propaganda to one of his masters and supporting the anti-war movement on Armistice Day – which in his case amounted to inserting anti-war statements into the school hymn books. For these activities, which had provoked Scotland Yard to make contact with Wellington's headmaster, he was given a final warning as to his future behaviour.

His activities and contacts had also come to the attention of Klugmann and fellow leaders of the FSS, which, in light of the leftward shift amongst students, had started to look towards the public schools as a fertile ground for recruitment. A circular distributed to Romilly and other communist sympathisers in schools called for a 'coordinated opposition' to the public school system which 'must also be linked with the work of progressive students in the universities, and with the organized working class, who are the most effective, indeed the only allies in the fight for a live advancing culture'.[18]

Romilly and his comrades were invited to a special meeting of the FSS in Bloomsbury in January 1934, where future campaigns would be agreed. In the event, Romilly's reluctance to conform to the line dominated the meeting. According to one of the participants, Romilly's speech, which argued for a magazine first and organisation later, 'threw the meeting into confusion'. As the student leader with the task of securing acquiescence amongst the rebellious schoolboys, Klugmann was given a difficult time and had to call for 'revolutionary discipline' before gaining their agreement. Nevertheless Romilly went ahead regardless and issued a manifesto in advance of the production of his own student paper *Out of Bounds*, which set out its opposition to the role of the public schools in generating support for militarism. It generated considerable press attention, with the *Daily Telegraph*, *Daily Express* and *Daily Mail* carrying the story, and the latter warning of the 'Red Menace in Public Schools'. The paper claimed – wrongly – that Romilly and his comrades were financed from Moscow. In the aftermath of the notoriety created by the press attention, Romilly ran away from school and started to work full-time at the Parton Street bookshop, where he also produced the magazine. This prompted other left-wing schoolboys, including Philip Toynbee – who would go on to be the first communist president of the Oxford Union – to do likewise. It resulted in more discomfort for Klugmann, who was given the job of urging Romilly to return to school where he would be more use agitating among his fellow pupils. Klugmann would later dismiss this in a light-hearted way:

> For my sins, I was put in charge of the Communist public school movement in the middle thirties, a new phenomenon in the Communist International. I was in Cambridge at the time and small boys from all over the country used to run away from the public schools. [...] My job was to say that the line of the Communist Party was that they should go back to school, and I lost a whole number of willing recruits in the process of carrying out the party line![19]

It is not surprising, perhaps, that teenage schoolboys were unlikely to conform to strict party discipline, given that they were attempting to escape the disciplinarian environment of the British public school. However, carrying out his leadership duties was Klugmann's mild introduction to the contested loyalties that would come to dominate much of his life. In his book *Communism and British Intellectuals*, Neal Wood writes of the 'mental adjustments' and transformations in the mind and outlook of an intellectual who becomes a loyal member of the Party.[20] Intellectuals, he argued, faced particular difficulties because they subscribed to a different value system, normally uncompromising in the pursuit of truth or the common good, which would inevitably be tested by the demands of Communist Party loyalty and discipline. For those, like Klugmann, who would devote his working life to the Party, the demands and compromises were increased several times over. Moreover, as he began his next phase as a professional revolutionary, he had a new master to contend with.

1 James Klugmann's father, Samuel Klugmann

2 Norman (as James was then known) and Kitty in 1917

3 James Klugmann's mother Cissie and his grandmother Martha

4 Kitty Klugmann

5 Punting on the River
Cam while a student at
Cambridge

7

Working for the Comintern

By the end of 1935, James Klugmann had a promising academic career ahead of him, if he chose that path. His first year of research had gone well and he was preparing to spend the next two terms in Paris. His intellectual prowess complemented his political acumen. According to Eric Hobsbawm, five years behind him, Klugmann was 'a person of enormous prestige, even a sort of guru'.[1] Victor Kiernan, his friend and Cambridge contemporary, and another distinguished historian, thought Klugmann 'the equal of any Marxist scholar Britain has produced'.[2]

They were in awe of him; he carried authority, confirmed by his double first, and was held in high regard by his tutors, who had great expectations of him. He had told Kitson Clark he intended to apply for a fellowship. He had developed a strong interest in French history, notably the historical significance of the French Revolution, a journey he had first started under Frank McEachran at Gresham's and subsequently encouraged by Ashton, Blunt and Kitson Clark himself. Ashton was his Cambridge supervisor, and in Paris Klugmann was to work under Daniel Mornet. In 1933 Mornet had published *Les Origines Intellectuelles de la Revolution Francaise 1715–1787*, a seminal text which would shape scholarship on that subject for the next 50 years. Mornet argued that to understand the ideas which influenced the Revolution, it was necessary to assess the institutions, salons and public spaces where the ideas were produced and disseminated, and within that the role of intellectuals.[3]

The opportunity to study under Mornet presented Klugmann with an ideal research topic and outstanding supervisor. It also provided the perfect solution of how to combine his academic career with his political commitments. His research topic – intellectuals and the French Revolution – suited his own political circumstances, given that he believed revolution was almost inevitable and communist intellectuals had an important role to play. Like others, he sought a role which would enable him to use his intellectual and political gifts for the service of the Party. Others, including his friend from Gresham's,

Donald Maclean, would make a very different choice to serve communism. For Klugmann, who had always avoided military training and by instinct was a public proselytiser for the communist cause, another opening now beckoned for him in the international Communist movement. Following the 1934 Congress in Brussels he had become a member of the RME Secretariat. He would lead it from 1936 and the role would take him to China, India, Yugoslavia and the Balkans, the Middle East and the United States. It was to increase his status in the Comintern, enhance his career in the British Communist Party and put an end to any academic ambitions.

Kitson Clark had initially questioned whether Klugmann needed to spend entire terms in Paris, believing vacation visits would suffice for his research. By early December, however, Klugmann had received official confirmation from the Board of Research Students that he had been 'given permission to spend the Lent and Easter Terms 1936 working in Paris under the supervision of M. Daniel Mornet, while keeping in touch with Dr Ashton by correspondence subject to the approval of the Degree Committee'.[4] To augment his scholarship funds, he had the added supplement to his income of £130 from his grandmother's dividend from Phoenix Telephone shares, organised for him through the offices of Rosenheim, Ross and Rosenheim in London.[5]

Paris in the mid-1930s could not have been a more appealing venue for Klugmann's research and the next stage of his political career. It had become the 'mecca for political exiles', a city of émigrés, where left intellectuals, workers' movements and anti-fascist activists converged at a time when the French left (including both the French Communist Party and the Socialist Party) were gaining support. The Comintern's adoption of the Popular Front strategy meant Paris was the base for a plethora of broad anti-fascist Comintern-sponsored groups, which included Klugmann's RME. Willi Münzenberg, the Comintern agent who was the key figure in the formation and rapid rise of these groups, had escaped from Germany in February 1933 on a false passport after warrants were issued for his arrest in the immediate aftermath of the Reichstag fire. He was smuggled into France in March 1933 and quickly shifted his operations as the instigator, fundraiser and organiser of Comintern-backed political alliances to Paris. According to his biographer, 'he enveloped Paris in a multi-tiered network of fellow travelling fronts that could be disassembled and reassembled at a moment's notice'.[6]

The first of these was the 'World Committee for the Relief of the Victims of German Fascism', into which Münzenberg had channelled an estimated $3,000 of Moscow money by the autumn of 1933. This committee, which Münzenberg founded with the help of his lieutenant, the Czechoslovak Comintern agent Otto Katz, had won support and influence in Britain, where Katz, on Münzenberg's instructions, had raised funds through Lord Marley, its honorary chairman. Münzenberg enjoyed significant influence among French intellectuals, and one of his closest collaborators in Paris was the novelist Henri Barbusse, a thinker and activist who – along with his fellow novelist Romain Rolland – was long admired by Klugmann and the Cambridge communists for their opposition to war and fascism. In 1932, Barbusse and Rolland had published an appeal for an international Congress of 'War Against War', following the Japanese attack on Manchuria. According to Barbusse, this attack was part of the 'preparation for war of the great imperialist powers against the USSR, and that all men, all women, whatever their political affiliations, and all working class organizations – cultural, social and syndical – all forces and all organizations, en masse' should come together in a Congress to 'confront the masters which threaten them'.[7] After the first Congress in Amsterdam in 1932, a second was organised by Münzenberg shortly after he arrived in Paris in June 1933 at the Salle Pleyel, at which the 'European Committee for the Struggle Against Fascism' was born. Münzenberg and Barbusse merged the two Congresses into a 'World Committee for the Struggle Against War and Fascism', often referred to as the Comite Amsterdam-Pleyel.[8] At the same time the emphasis on imperialism was gradually replaced by broader anti-fascism to reflect Comintern policy.

This movement helped the campaign for a Popular Front government in France and had much significance for James Klugmann as it spawned the RME. Münzenberg's money provided the offices and staff for these organisations, while Katz, on Münzenberg's instructions, did much of the groundwork. Münzenberg had organised a counter-trial of the Reichstag fire inquest in London, with the help of lawyers and politicians, including D.N. Pritt and Stafford Cripps, in which the blame for the fire was laid at the door of the Nazis. This produced *The Brown Book of the Reichstag Fire and Nazi Terror*, which Katz helped publicise during his visits to Britain, cultivating support among significant British left figures such as Ellen Wilkinson, Ivor Montagu and members of the CPGB leadership. Katz's regular visits between 1933 and 1936 were closely observed by MI5, and were only authorised on the recommendation of Lord Marley and Ellen Wilkinson on the understanding that he was raising funds for the Relief Committee.

It is likely that Katz, whose lifestyle has been variously depicted as 'seedy' or 'glamorous' (and, according to his biographer, was the model for Victor Lazlow in the film *Casablanca*[9]), had made contact with Klugmann on one of his visits to London, probably through the Communist Party leadership, who were well aware of his work, while Carmel Haden Guest, mother of David, was one of Katz's regular contacts. Katz was regularly in touch with Isabel Brown, secretary of the British Section of the Workers' International and a leading communist, and Dorothy Woodman, of the German Relief Committee. Klugmann's language expertise, together with his work in the Cambridge student movement, his growing commitment to the politics of the Popular Front and to the Communist Party, made him the ideal British representative of the international student movement.

On arriving in Paris, Klugmann initially found lodgings in a furnished apartment at 71 Rue du Cherche Midi, a busy street in the 6th arrondissement. He would have cherished the discovery that Laura Marx (daughter of Karl) and her husband Paul Larfargue had resided a few doors down in the 1860s, while the same street had earlier been the home of Pierre Augustin Hulin, a French revolutionary agitator who had taken part in the storming of the Bastille and was later one of Napoleon's generals. Another near neighbour, until his death in 1936, was Eugene Dabit, a key figure in the 'proletarian literature' group and author of the short-story collection *Hotel du Nord*.

From there Klugmann was within a 15-minute walk of the bookshops and bars of the Left Bank, the Sorbonne and university buildings. His journey to the RME offices was a more complicated one. The RME then shared an office with Münzenberg's other organisations at 1 Cité Paradis, a five-storey building built in 1910, which had also been identified by British Security Services as one of Otto Katz's private addresses. Eric Hobsbawm, who visited Klugmann there, recalled it as 'one of those small dusty Balzacian backstairs offices so characteristic of unofficial pre-war politics' in a 'gloomy dead end in the 10th arrondissement'.[10] It meant a metro or bus ride and some acquaintance with more remote parts of Paris.

At the RME offices, Klugmann was one of a three-member secretariat, and part of a larger political bureau made up unofficially of representatives from left-wing student organisations. Though in theory he was subject to the constraints of Comintern policy, and dependent on Katz and Münzenberg (whose own relationships with the Comintern were to become increasingly tense in the following years), he was given a reasonable amount of autonomy and the chance to introduce his own ideas.

Indeed, his first major contribution went some way to imposing his own political strategy and outlook on the organisation. Together with the Belgian and Czechoslovak members, he proposed a change of name at the enlarged RME Secretariat of 22–3 November 1935. In place of 'Against War and Fascism' the RME should now be called Rassemblement Mondial pour la Paix, la Liberté et la Culture (World Student Assembly for Peace, Freedom and Culture).[11] Significantly, the new name reflected a proactive political strategy which fitted into the Comintern's revised position. Perhaps more importantly for Klugmann, it reflected his own political priority of not merely opposing but setting out an alternative vision.

It did not alter the need to mobilise for peace. The secretariat heard reports on resistance to war and rearmament from student associations around the world. The National Committee for Student Mobilisation for Peace in the US issued a statement calling for 'neutrality' to prevent the entanglement of the United States in war'. The National Student Federation of America, the YMCA/YWCA, Youth Congress and the American League Against War and Fascism issued 'An Eleventh Hour Demonstration Against War' on Armistice Day. In Paris on 11 November there had been a student 'demonstration for peace', while Klugmann was able to report on large demonstrations and meetings in Oxford (including the Oxford Peace Ballot), Cambridge, Sheffield, Manchester and Aberystwyth.[12]

Significantly, the same RME Secretariat heard reports from leading intellectuals and university professors involved in anti-fascist activity, including Professor Paul Langevin, founder of the Comité de Vigilance des Intellectuels Antifascists; the German novelist Heinrich Mann; Helene Stessova on the development of culture in the USSR; André Malraux, French novelist and art critic – and later minister for culture under de Gaulle – and Louis Laloy, musicologist at the Sorbonne, writer and secretary general of the Paris Opera House, on China. The RME Secretariat passed a motion establishing a 'Presidium of Honour' to recognise the contributions of anti-fascist intellectuals in their work.

Klugmann also gave his first report on China, a subject which was to preoccupy him for much of the next few years and would culminate in his 1938 visit and meeting with Mao. He wrote a series of articles on the worsening situation in China in *La Voix des Étudiants*, RME's monthly bulletin, warning (in the January and February 1936 editions) of the threat and consequences of Japanese occupation. He had a sound grasp of the international situation and was regularly in touch with Chinese student associations on the ground and through their representative in Paris, Wang Hai King. Klugmann argued that there was a 'vital need to organise for peace on a global scale' and that the Chinese people's struggle 'would be decisive in the preservation of world peace'.[13]

He recognised the role of Chinese students, who were in the vanguard of popular resistance to Japanese aggression, and referred to large student demonstrations in Shanghai and Peking. He called for 'concrete' measures of support from the international student movement, citing as an example the collaboration between the Chinese Student Association and the Friends of China organisation he attended in London. Complimenting Lord Marley on a speech he had made in the House of Lords, Klugmann announced new initiatives in London and Paris involving Chinese, British and French student associations and leading intellectuals. To his fellow student comrades he argued: 'The World Student Association proposes that all students take part in a campaign of solidarity with the struggle of Chinese students for safeguarding their territory and their country.'[14]

As he settled in Paris during the early months of 1936, dividing his time between studying in the Bibliothèque Nationale and working at Cité Paradis, the French left was making big gains in the face of the economic crisis and resistance to fascism. It had been gaining ground since early 1934, when the Croix de Feu, the French fascist league, had been responsible for an attack on the Palais Bourbon in February, leaving 20 dead and leading to the resignation of the Daladier administration and the formation of a temporary government of national unity with a new opening for the left. The French Communist Party (PCF) had committed itself to a 'United Front' strategy at its Congress in June 1934. Maurice Thorez, the Moscow-trained PCF leader, was well aware of the potential of the new strategy and in October founded the Popular Front for Work, Peace and Freedom, a movement typical of Comintern influence which resonated with the wider anti-fascist politics to which Klugmann was now well accustomed.

During 1934–5 there had been a big shift to the left, with the PCF winning councils and substantially increasing its vote. Large demonstrations (notably on Bastille Day, 14 July 1935) increased the tempo for change, particularly after Thorez had persuaded the hitherto reluctant Socialists to join what was now widely referred to as the Popular Front; the latter's support, together with that of the Radicals, was necessary to form a future government. The Comité National de Rassemblement Populaire called for the defence of civil liberties, the disbanding of fascist leagues, the nationalisation of the arms industry and a series of economic measures, including the reduction of working hours. The

Communist trade union federation, the CGT, demanded a 'new social policy', and by the time of the general election in May 1936 there existed a 'feverish atmosphere' for change amidst prevailing political tensions.[15] In the event the Popular Front government was elected with a majority of 100, with the Socialists the largest party with 146 seats and the PCF 72, with big losses for the Radicals. 'It was a triumph for the socialists and communists whose united action had beaten back fascism, and who now seemed to represent the best hope for all who really wanted to fight for bread, peace and freedom.'[16]

The election victory was followed by spontaneous celebrations and strikes, with workers extracting major pay concessions from their employers. The strikes continued in the aftermath of the election as a statement of intent and show of strength, which at its peak involved 2 million workers in engineering, mining, catering and construction industries. The official position of the PCF, which had played the key strategic role in the electoral victory, was to remain loyal to the government (headed by the Socialist Léon Blum) but to avoid taking up ministerial posts. At the same time it maintained unwavering support for the strikers, which raised the question of whether more revolutionary action could be taken, a position favoured by Trotsky (who was then exiled in Paris) and his supporters. Despite many factories being under workers' control by 11 June and the need for mediation, the position of the PCF was to avoid putting at risk the existing alliance between the working class and the wider Popular Front. Instead it should seek to widen its base and reach.

This made a lot of sense to James Klugmann, whose own political endeavours on behalf of the RME had already turned in that direction. In his view, the policy was right for two reasons. First it put democracy and liberty at the centre of the political struggle, thereby opening up the prospect of aligning with the broadest anti-fascist and peace movements. Second, it sought to reconcile internationalism and patriotism, which enabled the communists to be at the forefront of defending the nation against fascism. This was particularly true in France, and Klugmann was profoundly influenced by the way in which the French left sought a positive identification with its own history: 'They retook possession of the French Revolution, they repossessed the tricolour, the colours of France. They put the red flag side by side with the tricolour, and at the end of their meetings sung the Marseillaise and the International.'[17]

He was enthused by the wider feeling for change and liberation embodied in the Popular Front, which had 'transformed a defensive movement of anti-fascism into an authentic movement of liberation'.[18] This summed up his political identity as a communist, which he sought to impose in the fluctuating episodes of his life, from the political strategy he adopted while working for the Special Operations Executive during World War II, to his lectures at Party education schools.

Klugmann's own life in Paris was becoming absorbed in his political activities and brought new international contacts, friendships and allies. These included Blahoslav Hruby, a fellow member of the RME Secretariat from the Christian student movement, who had fled Czechoslovakia and had been working underground defending the rights of Jewish people under the Nazi regime. Klugmann's relationship with Hruby, who would go on to be a Protestant minister monitoring religious persecution in the communist regimes of Eastern Europe, was one indication of the breadth of his allegiances. Another figure closely involved with RME was Raymond Gurot, the leader of the French Young Communists and secretary-general of the Young Communist International (ICJ) who had twice been imprisoned in the early 1930s for agitating amongst the military. In 1935 Guyot became a member of the Comintern executive and was likely a key figure in enhancing Klugmann's political connections. It was in the RME too that Klugmann first met Ivan 'Lolo' Ribar, the future Yugoslav communist and Partisan leader who, as a militant student communist, had got to know Klugmann at Congresses in Brussels and Geneva and hosted his visits to Belgrade. By the time Hobsbawm was working for Klugmann, Ribar was a 'familiar figure at RME'.[19] This friendship was crucial in Klugmann's later contacts with the Yugoslav Partisan leadership while working for the Special Operations Executive, as it was through Ribar that he was able to maintain links with Tito.

Together with Hruby and the French communist André Victor, his fellow members of the secretariat, Klugmann was responsible for running the RME Congresses, galvanising support for students fighting fascism, and organising meetings with prominent anti-fascist intellectuals. Much time was spent in the office writing reports and circulars of international student activities and acting as a liaison point between different political groups and associations. He excelled at this work and was able to impose some of his own ideas on the future political strategy of the RME.

He remained in contact with his British friends and comrades, many of whom, including Margot Heinemann, Bernard Floud, Eric Hobsbawm and others, visited him in Paris and worked for him on the RME Congresses, printing and packing letters and packages and distributing solidarity messages. Denis Healey, the future Labour politician, was then an Oxford student communist and recalled taking Klugmann a message during the Aid for Spain campaign.[20] Klugmann was a tireless worker, with socialising confined to games of chess and table football in the basement bars near Cité Paradis, combined with his book-collecting and occasional dining in the Left Bank.

Klugmann would have felt that politics at home, though lacking the political temper of Paris, was showing signs of moving in his favoured direction. The left was extending its influence among an intellectual culture that developed rapidly through 1936, signified by 'the omnipresent orange of the limp, cloth-bound volumes published by the Left Book Club'.[21] The Left Book Club had been formed by John Strachey, Stafford Cripps and the publisher Victor Gollancz and was a very timely response to the new openings. The club's founding aims were:

> to help in the struggle for world peace and a better social and economic order and against fascism by [...] increasing the knowledge of those who already see the importance of the struggle and [...] adding to their number the very many who [...] hold aloof from the fight by reason of ignorance or apathy.[22]

Its popularity went way beyond the hopes of the founders, with 6,000 members after its first month, 40,000 members after the first year and 57,000 members by April 1939, with an estimated readership of 250,000.[23] The membership was heavily concentrated amongst white-collar workers and intellectuals, though it did recruit and hold 'vocational discussion groups' among busmen, taxi-drivers, teachers and commercial travellers.[24] It had more than 1,000 discussion groups, and held film shows, rallies, 'knit-ins', established a children's section, scientific groups, amateur theatre groups, and organised dances, football matches and tours to the Soviet Union and was a leading protagonist in Britain for the Republican side in Spain. All this activity amounted to an impressive intellectual and cultural force. Politically, the Left Book Club was close to the Communist Party and was arguably the most significant beneficiary in Britain of the Popular Front politics. The Party influence was of some concern to Gollancz as membership of the Left Book Club and holding a Communist Party card in this period were often regarded as virtually synonymous.[25]

Despite this surge of left-wing consciousness and the optimism it brought, the next two years had profound moments of sadness for Klugmann as his two fellow student leaders and close friends, John Cornford and David Guest, were killed while fighting in support of the Spanish Republican government. Like France,

Spain had elected a Popular Front government involving the left and centre parties (though not the anarchists). Cornford had been offered a studentship from Trinity to study the Elizabethans, but he decided to go to Spain to help defend the Republic, expecting the fighting to be over in a short time. He and his girlfriend Margot Heinemann had originally planned to go on holiday to the south of France; now they changed plans and he left early for Spain, intending to join her later, while she stopped over in Paris to see Klugmann along the way, at the end of August. 'James knows heaps of people and so one has a very good time', she wrote home.

In a brief summer respite from his work, Klugmann took her to a Cézanne exhibition, a tour of the 'Grands Boulevards' and the Elysées – 'all floodlit with the lighted fountain in the concord' – Notre Dame, and the bars and restaurants of the Latin Quarter, which by this time, he knew well. 'I eat too much and everyone seems to drink coffee without stopping', Margot reported. They could not stay out of politics for long, though, and Margot reported a 'terrific feeling' in the Paris streets: 'Everyone is awake + alive to things.'[26] Cornford, meanwhile, aided by a letter of introduction from the *News Chronicle*, spent two and a half days in Barcelona, where he initially joined the Workers' Party of Marxist Unification (POUM), the 'left-sectarian semi-Trotskyist' militia,[27] because he did not have relevant papers or his Party card necessary for the Unified Socialist Party of Catalonia (PSUC) group of socialists and communists. Writing to Margot from Barcelona, Cornford described the crowded streets and squares, where 'the mass of the people [...] simply are enjoying their freedom'. This brought him an understanding of 'what the dictatorship of the proletariat means'.[28] It was clear to him that he was at the heart of a revolution.

John Sommerfield captured that moment of hope and sense of historic opportunity in his novel *May Day*, written in the first few months of 1936 and one of the few optimistic novels of the decade: 'Communists had tremendous tasks [...] tremendous responsibilities; they were men of the future, the men destined by history to change the world.'[29] By the later part of that year Sommerfield was in Spain fighting alongside John Cornford, whose death he would later commemorate in public meetings.

While some of his closest Cambridge contemporaries were fighting in Spain, Klugmann devoted much of 1936 to organising support for Chinese students. China was then almost as significant as Spain for the British left, with many campaigns organised in support of its resistance to Japanese aggression. At Cité Paradis, Klugmann was receiving regular telegrams from Chinese students and activists, which informed his long monthly articles on the changing situation there for *Voix des Étudiants*. He warned of the dangers of war in the Far East and detailed the struggles of the Chinese students in 'defending culture and national independence'. He called for solidarity between international student associations, and cultivated closer links with the 'Friends of China' and Chinese student federations in Paris, London and Amsterdam, and the offices of Lord Marley in London. Klugmann warmly complimented Marley's speeches in the House of Lords and with his support had organised a conference at Bedford College in London where he urged European students to give practical support to their Chinese comrades. Addressing the broad group of supporting organisations, which included the Student Movement for Peace, Freedom and Cultural Progress, the Central Union of Chinese Students of Great Britain and Northern Ireland, the London Chinese Association, representatives of the National Union of Students and the League of Nations, Klugmann promised that he would send an international student delegation to China, something he would fulfil two years later.[30]

Beyond China, Klugmann continued agitating on behalf of the Indian students' struggle for independence, keeping in contact with Cambridge comrades who organised the Colonial Group there, notably Victor Kiernan and S.M. (Mohan) Kumaramangalam, general secretary of the Federation of Indian Student Societies in Great Britain and Ireland, as well as P.N. Haksar, then at the LSE, who would later go on to be principal secretary to Indira Gandhi.

However, by the end of 1936, it was Spain that was gripping the attention of the RME. At its bureau of 12 November, it had called for solidarity with Spanish students and pledged support for those fighting on the Republican side. For Klugmann, the struggle in defence of the Spanish Republic embraced the highest values of democracy and anti-fascism. Many volunteers on their way to Spain stopped over in the RME offices to pick up papers or resources or to bide their time as they waited to be assessed in recruitment centres.

Spain became a symbol of the entire anti-fascist movement, illustrated in poetry, art and voluminous Left Book Club editions. Though the communist and ILP influence was particularly strong in enlisting volunteers, the cause had appealed to many liberals and democrats. Klugmann was not part of the international student delegation which spent ten days in Spain at the end of the year, but it included people well known to him of broad political persuasions: Gerald Croasdell of the British Universities' League of Nations Society, Hugh Gosschalk, of the University of London Liberal Association, Philip Toynbee of the University Labour Federation and Rajni Patel of the Indian university students' group.

After his first trip to Spain, which had lasted longer than the short break he originally envisaged (you 'can't play at revolution', he wrote in a letter to Margot Heinemann), illness had meant John Cornford's early return in mid-September. Back in England, he spent time with Margot in Birmingham and Michael Straight in Devon, before returning to Spain with his own group of volunteers in early October, having confirmed to Trinity that he would not be seeking a fellowship. By this time, the Comintern had formed the International Brigades, the vehicle through which Communist Party members could be recruited to fight. Paris was the crucial meeting point for volunteers passing through to pick up papers and instructions, and among those helping in the recruitment was one Josip Broz, who was organising his 'secret railway' for Eastern European volunteers from a Left Bank hotel. It was almost certainly here that Klugmann first got to know Broz, the future Marshal Tito, whom he would support through his work in SOE and the United Nations Relief and Rehabilitation Administration (UNRRA) and in whose future communist leadership he would invest much hope until the fateful split in 1948.

After seeing Klugmann in Paris for what would turn out to be the last time, Cornford returned to Spain with his group of volunteers, which had by now been incorporated into the International Brigades, via Marseille to Alicante and then to Albacete, where they received training. From there they reached Madrid and supported a successful attack on Nationalist-held Casa de Campo, though their own losses included Griff McLaurin, the Party bookseller in Cambridge. Cornford was by now leading a battalion, had spent some time in hospital from a freak head wound suffered from his own side and had killed his first fascist. Over Christmas his battalion received orders to go to the Cordoba front. Taking position just outside the village of Lopera, they were engaged in protracted battles without sufficient ammunition or promised backup, and in these battles Cornford, together with many of his comrades, was killed on or around his twenty-first birthday, 27–8 December 1936.

News of Cornford's death was sent through Comintern channels to the Party's headquarters in mid-January 1937. It is possible that Klugmann may have heard of it through his own Comintern base in Paris, but the first news reached Cornford's family and Margot from Michael Straight, who travelled to Birmingham to break the news. One of Cornford's last poems from Spain was dedicated to Margot:

'Heart of the Heartless World'
Dear heart, the thought of you
Is the pain at my side,
The shadow that chills my view.

The wind rises in the evening,
Reminds that autumn is near.
I am afraid to lose you,
I am afraid of my fear.
On the last mile to Huesca,
The last fence for our pride,
Think so kindly, dear, that I
Sense you at my side.

And if bad luck should lay my strength
Into the shallow grave,
Remember all the good you can;
Don't forget my love.

In his last letter to her, Cornford told her,

> I love you with all my strength and all my will and my whole body [...] The party was my only other love. Until I see you again, bless you my love, my strength. Be happy. I worked for the party with all my strength, and loved you as much as I was capable of. If I am killed, my life won't be wasted.[31]

Shortly after telling Straight, 'I am absolutely all right and very proud',[32] Margot left for Paris to see Klugmann, who had been organising a conference for Hindu students. They would remain close friends for the rest of their lives. The death of Cornford brought them closer together, while their commitment to the Party, Cornford's 'other love' (and Klugmann's primary one), they would endure together through some turbulent times. In remembering John, the romantic and principled revolutionary whose impatience with the pace of the struggle always took him to the front line, they took solace in his political legacy.

Cornford's ultimate sacrifice would be followed by that of Julian Bell and David Guest, among over 500 British volunteers to die in Spain. The escalation of the international crisis, with civil war in Spain and the battle against rising

Nazism in Germany, took Klugmann's work in Paris to new levels of urgency. Though his studies would continue to inform his politics, his ambitions to become an academic now seemed a peripheral concern and his priorities inevitably shifted to his political work.

8

The Professional Revolutionary

In 1937, the RME faced its biggest organisational challenge to date, with its Congress due to be held during the Paris International Exhibition. The polarised world of contrasting futures represented by Nazi Germany and Soviet Russia would be reflected in the arts and culture as polemics continued on the wider political stage. The Congress, held in August at the majestic Maison de la Chimie, just off the Boulevard St Germain (and not far from the National Assembly), brought together 120 delegates from 35 countries. Klugmann and his helpers found them accommodation and planned an agenda of political meetings and visits to the exhibition – for which they were offered a 'Carte de Legitimation' with student discounts at restaurants, museums, hotels, theatres and French railways. The exhibition brochure promised delegates

[the] wonders and discoveries of science. The greatest artists, painters, sculptors, architects and decorators will exhibit the best of their talent. For the first time in the history of exhibitions 43 nations will be gathered together in this apotheosis of work, invention and thought and each of them will present in its own national pavilion its most up-to-date achievements.[1]

The international exhibitions of the past had often been regarded as exaggerated bourgeois spectacles. This one, held at such a defining moment, was an exception. Paris had been

the city of the peace treaties that had sealed the end of the First World War and created the new European order. And Paris in 1937 was also the place where the front lines of the coming conflicts and catastrophes came into view. The spectacle that was to display the state of our civilization two decades after the Great War led straight into the coming war.[2]

Indeed, the exhibition reflected the fact that Paris, the temporary home of anti-fascists, Gestapo spies and Comintern agents in the midst of a strong workers' movement, had 'become a contested terrain'.[3] Pablo Piccasso's painting *Guernica* dramatically illustrated the suffering of the Spanish Civil War, while the German and Soviet pavilions, representing their contrasting perspectives of the past and future, stood opposite each other, with the Eiffel Tower in the immediate background.

In fact, the USSR pavilion provided the biggest spectacle. For Klugmann, and many of the RME delegates, this was the showpiece of the whole event: 'an emblem of the Soviet Union's entrance into the world stage'.[4] The Paris exhibition was regarded as an occasion of great importance in the Soviet Union, dominating the Soviet press, and leading Soviet 'artists, actors and prominent Soviet visitors of every kind assembled at Belorusski station for the Paris express'.[5]

The message was that since the October Revolution the Soviet Union had been the epitome of progress. It was the driver of technological change, industry and culture, with Vera Mukina's 24.5-metre stainless steel sculpture *Worker and Kolkhoz Woman* symbolising the epoch of Soviet communism. The rooms of the Soviet Pavilion were divided into science and planning, architecture, education, libraries and museums and sculpture, painting and art, and cinema and radio and music, while the centrepiece of the Great Hall was Sergei Murkurov's 35-metre statue of Stalin.

> The Soviet leadership wished to demonstrate above all how much the country had changed in recent years. In its pavilion the USSR celebrated the twentieth anniversary of the October Revolution. Visitors were invited to take a journey through the map of the USSR. The pavilion contained a map of the country that was 19.5 metres square finished in minerals and semi-precious stones. All the Union's achievements – the conquest of the north, the development of air travel and construction, were to be put on display, with the aid of models of recently completed buildings, such as the Kuznetsk Iron and Steel works, the Moscow–Volga canal and a section of a Moscow metro carriage.[6]

This view of the Soviet Union retained a vivid political vision for Klugmann and many of the RME delegates. His Congress programme reflected the compatibility he saw between the exhibition themes and the RME perspectives of hope, progress and peace. Following the opening discussion on the 'Right to Culture', delegates spent the first evening, of 25 August, at the Pavilion de la Paix in Place du Trocadéro. A regular tourist spot in the heart of Paris, with its view of the Eiffel Tower, it now became an even more international meeting point for exhibition visitors and students. After the second day's report and discussion on 'Students and the Nation', delegates spent the evening at the exhibition and then, after the final morning, they took an excursion to Versailles. In between, the Congress held discussions on the material situation of students, the role of intellectuals and academic freedom in the university, and heard appeals by Professor José Gaos, a prominent Spanish philosopher and rector of Madrid University, and Professor Yang, who spoke on behalf of Chinese intellectuals in light of the Second Sino-Japanese War which had finally broken out the previous month. Klugmann once again used his political acumen and growing list of contacts to draw messages of support from leading anti-fascist intellectuals, including A.D. Lindsay, master of Balliol (who would fight the Oxford by-election on a Popular Front platform the following year); Gilbert Murray, Regius Professor of Greek at Oxford and liberal humanist; P.M. Blackett, a future Nobel Prize physicist; the painter Henri Royer and Marcel Prenant, a zoologist, then preparing a book on biology and Marxism. Prenant would later be captured twice by the Germans for his anti-fascist and resistance activities. British delegates included close comrades of Klugmann, Ram Nahum and Kutty Hookham, who would go on to be secretary of the World Federation of Democratic Youth, the successor to the World Youth Congress, like its predecessor, a Comintern-backed front. Eric Hobsbawm, an undergraduate at King's College Cambridge, was there too, working for Klugmann as a translator. There were several delegates from the University Labour Federation, testament to closer links between communists and Labour students.

Klugmann remained optimistic that the best of European democratic culture could be reconciled with the overwhelming sense of hope in the emerging Soviet society. He would have heard the first rumours of conspiracy against the Soviet leadership and the show trials of alleged traitors, but his loyalty to the Comintern – his employer – meant he would keep faith, and indeed would refuse to countenance any truth in the worst allegations for years to come, while publicly justifying some of the later trials of the 1950s. However, he must have known that Willi Münzenberg was already in trouble with Moscow, even if the extent of the purge among Comintern agents and leaders was not yet evident.

Münzenberg, the prime mover behind the broad Comintern anti-fascist fronts, had grown disillusioned with Stalin's leadership and had refused to help purge the German Communist Party (KPD) on Stalin's orders. Victims of these purges included Heinz Neumann and other KPD comrades of Münzenberg who had not provided 'self-criticism' and were detained or executed. By 1937 Münzenberg too was under suspicion, with his fellow KPD leader Walter Ulbricht observing his behaviour and reporting back to Moscow. Münzenberg left the KPD, continued his anti-fascist work but avoided returning to Moscow, knowing he would be arrested. Eventually, Münzenberg left Paris in 1940; he was briefly interned by the Daladier government and then murdered – presumably by Comintern agents – in the south of France in October of that year.

The suspicion mounting against Münzenberg may have been one of the reasons the RME moved offices at the beginning of 1938 to the more central Boulevard d'Arago, nearer to the bookshops and cafés of the Left Bank. Here, it was easier to merge into the broader intellectual milieu, but after the efforts of organising the RME Congress, there was little let-up in Klugmann's hectic daily schedule. His earlier commitment to send an international student delegation to China was realised in the spring of 1938 and now had heightened significance in light of the Second Sino-Japanese War. He led the delegation, which also visited India, Ceylon, Singapore and Hong Kong, and was accompanied by his friend Bernard Floud, whom he had known since Gresham's days. Floud had been active in the October Club in Oxford (though his Party membership had been kept secret) and was one of the RME volunteers working for Klugmann, though on the delegation he officially represented the British Youth Peace Assembly. They were joined on the China part of the trip by Molly Yard and Grant Lathe of the United States and Canadian student associations.

This trip was the first time that British Security Services monitored Klugmann's political activities. He had first come to their notice in October 1934 in Cambridge, when his name was linked to a CUSS event, though they had little knowledge of the extent of his political activities there. They had noted his presence at the founding RME Congress in Brussels in December of that year, his arrival at Cité Paradis and some of his activities in support of Chinese and Indian students.[7] The Security Services also drew on their contacts in several of the scheduled stops and were able to obtain detailed accounts of Klugmann's activities on the trip through intercepting the regular reports he sent to Penelope Brierley, who had just taken up a role in the RME offices as a member of its secretariat. It is probable that Bernard Floud had recommended Brierley to RME. She was a former student of St Hilda's College, Oxford, who divided her time in Paris between working as a translator for an American travel agency and the RME offices. She would become a good friend of Klugmann and Margot Heinemann, though there would be much concern over her period of internment during the war. At the RME she was also romantically linked to Otto Katz; it was almost certainly Brierley whom

Donald Maclean's biographer Robert Cecil described as the 'personable young woman from one of the Oxford women's colleges [who] was a good deal closer to Katz than his wife, Ilse, would have wished'.[8]

The trip was a whirlwind tour which saw them address big student rallies and participate in meetings with prominent leaders, culminating in an interview with the Chinese communist leader Mao Tse-tung. The intelligence files tell us that Klugmann and Floud boarded the SS *Strathallen* at Port Said for Bombay on 30 March 1938 to begin their trip, and would then travel on to Ceylon, Singapore, Hong Kong and China.[9] They arrived in Bombay on 8 April and headed to Allahabad for a meeting with Indian student leaders and an interview with J.L. Nehru. On 19 April they arrived at Lucknow, where Klugmann gave a talk on the history of the student movement and urged Indian student activists to campaign broadly in the fight against colonialism, a position which closely followed his general Popular Front strategy. While in Lucknow they visited a student strike and Klugmann promised to organise support, disseminate literature and 'preside' over an all-India student conference. After arriving in Patna on 20 April, Klugmann gave an interview to the Associated Press on the situation facing Indian students in which he described them as 'strong and well-organised'.[10]

From Patna Klugmann and Floud went on to Calcutta, where Klugmann addressed an audience estimated at 500 at the Albert Hall. For someone who just a few years earlier was nervous of speaking in public he now gave a wide-ranging speech on the potential of the rising student movement, called for the removal of the colour bar in the US, the extension of education in Yugoslavia, the boycott of Japanese goods in support of China that was taking place in England and for support of the anti-fascist movement in Spain. He urged Indian students to carry on their struggle against colonialism and complimented the strong organisation behind their student associations. Prior to this rally, Klugmann and Floud had held a secret meeting with the representatives of different Indian student groups, where they proposed the 'line of action' of the international student movement. First, Klugmann argued, they had to 'defend liberties and promote peace and culture'. Secondly, they must mobilise broad opposition to fascism in defence of civil liberty. Thirdly, he called on them to organise for peace against the prospect of war and finally to 'expose imperialism'. 'But', he added, 'only then can the question of national freedom be taken up.' This 'line of action' gives a clear indication of Klugmann's ability to interpret and apply Comintern political strategy to the student movement in a very lucid and rational style – a skill which had already won him many admirers.[11]

The day after the Calcutta rally, the pair went to Cuttack, where Klugmann spoke to another student gathering, MI5 noted, 'upon whom he urged the necessity of unity in order to assert their rights'.[12] The duo had more private discussions with student representatives in Madras before sailing the following day to Colombo, Ceylon, where they shared a room at the Bristol Hotel. 'Nothing is known about their movements in Ceylon', MI5 reported, but in any case, they were only there for two nights before sailing third class to Hong Kong on the *President Doumer*, passing through Singapore on 4 May. In Hong Kong they met members of the National Government Propaganda Ministry and leaders of the Hong Kong Students' Relief Association. While in Hong Kong they also met H.D. (Derek) Bryan, one of the vice-consuls, who had been a couple of years ahead of Klugmann at Gresham's School and subsequently a fellow Modern Languages student at Cambridge; he was also a friend of Julian Bell and a committed Christian. At Cambridge, although he had turned down Klugmann's offer to become a member of the Communist Party, Bryan had expressed sympathy for their struggle. In response to MI5's request, Bryan said that Klugmann 'may be a communist [but] he did not think either he or Floud are likely to be engaged in activities damaging to the British Empire'.[13]

It was the visit to China that was the centrepiece of the tour. As Tom Buchanan has made clear, it is important to recognise the significance China held for the British left at the time. Although not rivalling Spain in attracting volunteers to fight, China nevertheless elicited much sympathy in the cause against Japanese imperialism. Sympathy for the Chinese struggle went beyond the student movement and was an important part of the internationalist, anti-colonialist and anti-fascist arguments that were growing on the British left at the time.[14]

From the first moment of their arrival, it was clear that the delegation had entered a place of revolutionary agitation. Their every movement throughout the liberated areas was feted by their Chinese hosts, the Chinese Communist Party and left-wing student and youth associations who, while grateful for the recognition the delegation brought for their struggle, also sought to maximise it for propaganda reasons. Their reception exceeded anything they had encountered in India. The journey was not without alarm, however. MI5 were informed by their people in the Far East that Klugmann and Floud had approached the British Consulate-General to ask if their British ship would be intercepted if it passed through Japan. The trip itself coincided with the Japanese bombing of Canton in June, and many of their meetings were held in an intense atmosphere of hope and resistance.

On their arrival in Hankou on 21 May, the two were guests of honour at a reception lunch given by Dr Chu Chia-Hua, president of the Chinese League of Nations Union, where there was an early opportunity to exchange views on the League's activities. The following day they were joined by Yard and Lathe, and a further reception committee was held in the auditorium of Hankou YMCA. The *China Forum* reported that there were:

> brilliant and inspiring speeches giving vivid accounts of the sympathy of their peoples towards China as well as the practical work they have undertaken to aid the Chinese people. They were given long and cheering applauses during and after the speeches.[15]

Chinese political leaders used the efforts of the international student movement to highlight their plight and to negotiate practical aid to students, through fundraising for dormitories, book distribution, scholarships for Chinese students abroad and visits to China by leading professors. Wang Ming, a senior Chinese Communist Party (CCP) leader who had just returned from Moscow, in a speech in Hankou on 26 May attended by an estimated 15,000 Chinese students,[16] thanked the 'honourable delegates' for visiting China

> at a time when our nation is in distress and when our war of resistance is in full swing in its second stage. These Delegates of repute and prestige have come at the right moment to inspire our students and youth, to encourage our soldiers and people to protest against our enemies' atrocities and inhumanities and to support our struggle for self-preservation.

The struggle, he said, was against 'Japanese fascist militarists'. He called for increased resistance to Japanese aggression, a boycott of Japanese goods, embargo on arms and financial loans to Japan, protests against Japanese air raids and the blockade of Chinese coasts, as well as for more war supplies, volunteers and relief for refugees. He ended a rousing speech with a call to the youth of the world which must have inspired Klugmann and reinforced his faith in the wider struggle: 'We who believe in communism, in peace, in world brotherhood have immense love for youth. Unite students and youth in the world! For a new China! For a peaceful world!'[17]

The delegation was still in Hankou in June when Canton came under an unrelenting bombing campaign by Japanese forces. They were at a roundtable conference with Hun Lih-Wu of the Chinese League of Nations Union and took part in spontaneous demonstrations, carrying photos of Chinese communist leaders. They were taken to liberated areas or 'revolutionary bases', as they were often known, to see the informal schools that had been dug into caves away from the firing line. Students of all ages were regularly mobilised by the slogan: 'Let the air raid siren be the sound of the classroom bell.'[18]

The meeting with Mao Tse-tung, held in his cave hideaway on 12 July, was the pinnacle of the trip and an opportunity for Klugmann and his comrades to assess the United Front strategy on the ground. The Chinese Communist Party's membership had increased five-fold between 1937 and 1938, and it was the communist-backed United Front's control of the Border Region that was of particular interest for the delegation, which spent several hours with the Chinese Communist leader. Mao started by talking about the effects of the extension of the franchise to illiterate peasants and the democratic election of public servants, which distinguished the Border Region from the rest of China and was crucial in the coordination of the Sino-Japanese War. 'I am inclined to think', Mao told his four young interviewers,

that the whole country should adopt the same duel policy; the prosecution of the war by the practice of democracy; the external victory over Japan by the internal triumph of democracy. If all the people have sufficient freedom of speech, freedom of publicity, freedom of assembly, and freedom of association, if all the military officers and soldiers live on the best of terms, if people and soldiers help each other, if education promotes democracy, if economic construction propels the power of resistance of the people and ameliorates their livelihood, and if administrative organs of all grades are constructed on the basis of universal suffrage and co-ordinated with representative assemblies, China will surely win a final victory over Japan.

In response to the next question, on the current role of the Chinese Communist Party, Mao told them it was pursuing a three-sided strategy: a 'war of resistance', the United Front and a 'long war'. This would have made a lot of sense to Klugmann, for whom the opposition to fascism evoked some similar objectives. When asked about the 'principal task of the Chinese Communist Party after the final victory of the war of resistance', Mao outlined the commitment of the CCP to a process of national and democratic reconstruction involving a representative parliament, land and tax reform and the removal of illiteracy, but couched in Marxist-Leninist terminology:

> Such a state cannot yet be called a socialist state. Such a government cannot yet be called a Soviet government. But such a state and such a government will put into full play democratic principles and systems and will not persecute private property [...] With such a government China will emerge from her present condition of a semi-colony and a semi-feudalist country.

The final question to Mao concerned the 'mission' of the world student and youth movement and what it could do to support China. His response must have warmed the hearts of the young revolutionaries and went some way to vindicate their own efforts:

> Students are messengers of peace. Through them, the peoples of the world will come to understand what students and youths [sic] understand through you, namely, the necessity of opposing Japan and the benefit of supporting China. You can discharge this honourable mission by means of propaganda and publicity. You will persuade your governments and peoples to give China ample material support, to boycott Japanese goods, to lay an embargo on goods and materials to Japan, to organize international volunteers, and to send them to China when the call comes. Representing great numbers of students and youths [sic], you have come to China, bringing with you an important mission and the sympathetic voice of the world. The Chinese people thank you. On behalf of the Chinese Communist Party, I pay you highest respects. [...] We shall be permanently united with you. You and we shall fight together for China's freedom and equality and for universal peace and happiness.[19]

Meeting Mao was a memorable event for Klugmann, one which capped an extraordinary trip. He knew that few would have experienced the feeling of revolutionary struggle and it strengthened his communism. From China, the delegation went on to the Second World Youth Congress at Vassar College in New York State, at the end of August, where they shared their experiences with delegates, and launched their appeal for aid and an embargo on war materials to Japan. They were joined by a large RME delegation which, in addition to André Victor and Penelope Brierley from the secretariat, included Ahmed Abbas of the All India Student Federation, Ricardo Suay of the National Union of

Spanish Students, L.S. Peng from China and Michael Young of the University Labour Federation. The Congress produced the 'Vassar Peace Pact' signed by all delegates as a commitment to upholding international law and to support the growing number of war victims.

The trip to the Far East did much to cement James Klugmann's faith in the Party and Communist International. He had witnessed Chinese students play a leading role in guerrilla units, the desperate plight of thousands of refugees escaping from war zones and the impact of sustained Japanese bombing in Canton and elsewhere.

He had now spent the best part of six months travelling and speaking and had met student leaders from many parts of the world. It had given him insight into the broad politics of anti-fascism at an international level and must have strengthened his sense of purpose as a rising figure within a world revolutionary movement. The trip had raised his profile and status within the World Student Association. On his return to Paris he was much in demand as a speaker, reporting back on his experiences at meetings in Brussels and Amsterdam. At the same time, Bernard Floud embarked on a speaking tour of British universities, calling for more solidarity and a boycott of Japanese goods, while Yard and Lathe were invited to similar meetings in the US and Canada.[20]

Klugmann gave a full report of the visit to the RME's Executive Bureau in October, where he sought to explain the Chinese struggle within the broader Popular Front strategy. He talked emotionally and optimistically of the 'international spirit' of Chinese youth who had welcomed them and given them such warm hospitality in the face of suffering. This experience influenced him deeply and throughout his life he retained respect for those he saw in 'struggle' – workers and peasants.

Klugmann's optimism resulting from his China visit was tempered, however, by the new international realities which now confronted the RME. The Munich Agreement, in which Italy, France and Great Britain agreed to Germany's annexation of Czechoslovakia, had recently been signed and its implications for the spread of Nazism were brought home to the 27 members present by the report of Blahoslav Hruby, Klugmann's Czech colleague on the RME Secretariat. Hruby recounted the 'heavy defeats' of recent years, 'the fall of Austrian democracy, German rearmament, the Italian invasion of Abyssinia, the foreign invasion of Spain, the Japanese aggression against China, the annexing of Austria by Germany, the Polish threat against Lithuania, and, finally, the mutilation of Czechoslovakia'. His own country, Czechoslovakia, he said, was abandoned by the very nations which should have come to her help. The consequences of the Munich 'peace' agreement are extremely serious; the aggressors have been encouraged, and their regimes [...] have been strengthened [...] The Munich Peace is a dangerous threat to Spain and to China, defending their independence against aggression.

Hruby concluded his talk by quoting from the theologian Karl Barth's call for the Czechoslovakian people to hold firm and 'resist, if necessary, not only for the sake of Czechoslovakian independence, but also for the sake of liberty in Europe and throughout the world'.[21]

Those present at the meeting also heard more pessimistic reports from the war in Spain, as Franco's advances increased and the numbers of victims and people driven into exile were noted. Yet, in his chairman's closing address, Klugmann refused to be downcast about the situation. Buoyed by the revolutionary atmosphere he had experienced on his travels, he told his colleagues that 'there has never been so much activity throughout the universities'.

The expansion of the RME network was evident in the preparations for the Third – and what would be the last – International Congress of the RME, scheduled for August 1939. The urgency of the international situation continued to occupy Klugmann's time in the months before the Congress. At the RME International Council in December 1938, more front-line reports were heard from Spain, China and the Middle East, together with the situation of Jewish students in European universities and the victims of various fascist and Nazi atrocities.[22] His confidence in his own interpretation of the international political situation was evident in the Congress agenda. Long hours at the Bibliothèque Nationale, with his long-standing interest in the legacy of the French Revolution, were now innovatively applied to the dilemmas facing students in the impending fascist crisis in Europe. He found a way of drawing on his research under Mornet. In their joining instructions, alongside details of lodgings and venues, Klugmann informed international delegates that the 'theme' of the conference would be 'Democracy and Nation', with keynote sessions on 'The Universities in the Defence of Democracy and Nation' and 'The Value Today of the Ideas of the French Revolution'.

In his introductory letter to delegates which gave details of the conference, Klugmann explained his reasons for choosing the democracy and nation theme:

Students today, faced with the gravity of events throughout the world, take a more active part than formerly in the national and social life of their country.

[...] In face of these problems the students are becoming aware of the common aims and interests which bind them together, irrespective of their philosophical, political or religious opinions. An important factor has made its appearance in university life; the consciousness of solidarity between the students of each country and other countries in the defence of peace, of the nations of freedom and of culture [...]

Today when the liberty and independence of peoples has been ruthlessly suppressed when a war of aggression has continued for two years against the Chinese people, and the threat of world war daily confronts the whole of mankind, the responsibility of the students to the nation and to the international community has increased in proportion.[23]

His organisational plans were disrupted, however, as they had to move the venue from Nice to Paris because of the imposition of tougher travel restrictions. The Third International Conference of the World Student Association was held at the Maison des Centraux in Paris on 15–19 August 1939. The Maison des Centraux was a grand former townhouse from the Haussman period, situated between the Avenue Montaigne and the Grand Palais, in the heart of the Golden Triangle, just off the Champs Elysées. It was attended by 250 delegates from 35 nations. Klugmann called on his friend Jean Daudin, a physics research student and a member of the anti-fascist Action Universitaire pour la Liberté and Étudiants Communistes de France, the French student communist association which had been founded at the beginning of April, to open the Congress. Daudin started by telling delegates,

Today the revolution appears to us to be even younger and more full of life than ever before. The ideas of the French Revolution are not dead; its victories are additions to the total gains of humanity; its lessons still keep all their freshness in our present fight for peace and liberty.

Daudin set about rebuffing the explicit criticism made of the central ideas of the French Revolution in Nazi and Italian fascist propaganda – recalling that Goebbels had declared that 'the year 1789 would be blotted out of history'. Nazism promised the 'power of blood', a 'spiritual revolution' and an 'aristocracy of race'; it rejected claims to 'reason', the links between progress and human emancipation and the universal rights of men and women. He argued that the 'victories' of the French Revolution were now in danger, with the removal of 'the rights of man', racial and sexual inequality and the persecution of students, academics and intellectuals. Daudin ended by saying that 'what made the greatness of the French Revolution was that it did not remain an idea, but it lived and triumphed'. For Klugmann, in his role as revolutionary and intellectual, this was paramount.

'Who could pretend', Daudin asked, 'that this lesson is not applicable today?' 'To us Frenchmen', he concluded, 'our revolution has given among others the precious right to love our country and reasons to be proud of it.'[24]

The relevance of the French Revolution to the urgent international crisis remained a feature of the Congress – a testament, perhaps, to the success of a typical Klugmann strength of applying political ideas in imaginative ways to current problems. At the same time he was unyielding in presenting Comintern strategy as the rational and only conceivable alternative. Much of the conference, however, was taken up with messages of sympathy and solidarity to the victims of fascism, including what were now losing battles of the Republican supporters in Spain and Chinese victims of Japanese aggression. They heard moving testimonies from Spanish Republican students and Lithuanian Jewish students interned in concentration camps in the south of France and letters of support and defiance were sent to German, Austrian, Italian and Czechoslovakian students who were facing the daily reality of fascism and Nazism. 'As the lights go out in the universities and schools under fascism, must we not resolve that they shall burn more brightly in our institutions of learning', as Bert Witt of the American Student Union, put it.[25]

In his closing speech to the Congress, Klugmann sought to rally his charges. The occasion was well suited to his speaking style. The conference had demonstrated that the historical humanitarian ideals of the French Revolution needed to live on again in the broad popular front against fascism in countries as diverse as Spain, China and India. He had seen at first hand, on the ground, the struggles and sacrifices of students facing repression and had experienced the common purpose of an internationalist movement. He argued that the strategy of the Popular Front was now the only way forward. He announced further student conferences on 'Democracy and Nation' in the Balkan countries, which he saw as holding the most militant communist students, and a 'Pan-American Student Conference' in Cuba in December, as well as 'sustained anti-colonial work'. The expansion of the RME was now vital to step up the battle against fascism. To support him in this, the Congress elected a 12-member Executive Bureau. Klugmann himself, in the 'Last Act of the Conference' and 'by unanimous vote of the delegates', was re-elected as its secretary. He was at the top of his game.

His political ambitions for RME were to be unfulfilled, however. Three weeks after the conference, World War II was under way.

9

The Spy Circle

On a short break in London from his wartime service in August 1945, James Klugmann made an appointment to see Bob Stewart at the Party's King Street offices. Stewart, a veteran communist leader, was formerly the Party's representative to the Comintern and still had responsibility for clandestine connections between the Party and Moscow. Stewart was a foundation member of the CPGB, a working-class carpenter and teetotaller from Dundee, and was a figure regarded with much affection among Party stalwarts. Klugmann went to see him, partly to give a debriefing of his time in the Special Operations Executive. But he also wanted to get something 'off his chest', a matter that had been troubling him for the previous decade and for which he was now seeking some reassurance from Stewart. In the extracts from this interview, which revealed for the first time his reluctant espionage activities, Klugmann refers to his dilemma in working with Soviet intelligence for nine months, his fears of being found out, his distaste for 'mixing' two 'contradictory jobs', (espionage and public communist work), the sacrifice he would ultimately be prepared to make if asked to do so by Party leaders and even the initial 'subtle flattery', which made him and others involved in espionage feel 'incredibly important'.

Stewart, for his part, empathises with the dilemmas faced by his young comrade, vents his exasperation at the approaches made by the 'illegals' – as Arnold Deutsch and other NKVD agents who operated without the cover of diplomatic protection were referred to at the time – and of the unauthorised spying activities carried out by Dave Springhall, the Party's former national organiser, who had been imprisoned in 1943 for receiving classified information from Ormond Uren, another communist in SOE.

MI5 microphones recorded the conversation from Stewart's rooms in King Street:

James Klugmann: Can I – do you mind me talking of the case ... to talk of it to you?

Bob Stewart: As far as I am concerned you can talk of it just the same

JK: Fairly early in my career I was asked to do that job so …

BS; Yes, I know the buggers all right

JK: I got very very much mixed up in it. I don't mind you see. If I was told to do that and nothing else, I'm quite willing as much as anybody else. Anybody can be a hero, and six years gaol, if you think what you are doing is right, is six years gaol. But the thing that almost killed me – the only time I've been really unhappy in the Party …

[at this point the recording is inaudible as Stewart speaks over him]

JK: Nine months

BS: No, no, no, no

JK: It's the first time I've told anybody about it – but Harry knows what I mean. I did have sleepless nights.

BS: I quite understand that

JK: … if the man had come back I honestly don't know what I would have done …

BS: My impression – roughly my impression is if something interesting comes your way that is of intense importance …

JK: I quite agree

BS: Because those buggers. Bloody insistent

JK: They are out for themselves

BS: They just don't care one bugger what happens.

JK: I've had arguments with them before – for one thing they were coming to destroy something which was much more important. Of course I do get information …. I mean, purely in a personal capacity, nothing that

BS Then you can protect yourself

JK: Yes, first of all I didn't agree or disagree. Secondly I mean I – there's nothing written, and if it did come out, it's loose talk. I mean my friends there spoke to me and I spoke loosely. But that I think I should continue to do with you

BS: But there's nothing wrong with that

JK: It's the other thing

BS: I wouldn't enter into any other engagement

JK: If the other thing arises again, I would like to feel that I was being correct in not mixing with it. I mean when I come out I mean if I was ever told to do that and nothing else ok I mean that's the job and I'll do it. But I hope never to be told to do two jobs which are really contradictory.

BS: There's nobody has any right to ask you to do that. Honestly, if we had known that Springhall was doing that kind of thing he'd have been in for trouble. He concealed it. And it's just that same kind of thing. Sometimes you have the feeling that you're the hell of an important man.

JK: Well, it gets you, you know. I did some of it, and it gets you. It's a form of subtle flattery. In a way you feel incredibly important.

BS: Yes, yes I know

JK: The results are there because some of them are obvious

BS: But others are coming along for years

JK: Some of them are magnificent but others ...

BS: And some are perfectly ...

JK: I wanted to get that off my chest

BS: Yes I know your particular difficulty. I've had many people in the same position. It's all loaded on to one at times, when things begin to break down. But there it is

JK: Well, I wouldn't start on account of those things unless I'm instructed and then I will ...

BS: You won't be instructed from here

JK: Good

BS: Because the only people that we ever have any contact with are the responsible people.[1]

Klugmann, the intellectual mentor of Burgess, Maclean and Blunt, and international student leader, had got involved with espionage ('the other thing'), when he played the key role in the NKVD recruitment of John Cairncross, after he himself was recruited by Soviet intelligence to carry out the task. This was only completed on the authorisation of the Communist Party leadership. For his trouble he was given the code name 'Mayor'.[2]

Yet the story of his involvement in espionage has its roots in the political turmoil of the mid 1930s and the risks, choices, hopes and fears that confronted those who were drawn to revolutionary politics. One of these was Kim Philby. Though he had initially joined the CUSS in 1931 as a social democrat, Philby was increasingly drawn to Marxism during 1932–3, as the CUSS moved leftwards. This change in his politics had been less intense than the militancy of Klugmann, Cornford, Maclean and others and, like many other sympathisers, he never made the step of actually joining the Party. As he told Genrikh Borovik, a novelist and playwright, in a series of interviews conducted during 1985–8:

It took me a long time to decide to work for the communists, but the most important period was my last two years at Cambridge. [...] The study of Marxism and seeing the Depression in England. Books and lectures and the rise of fascism in Germany. Fascism was one of the deciding factors for me. I was becoming convinced that only the communist movement could resist it. Of course, there were doubts and unfounded expectations. But there was also dissatisfaction with myself. I kept asking myself – why not give yourself totally to this movement? I had only one alternative: either I told myself, yes, or I give up everything, betrayed myself, and dropped politics altogether.[3]

Philby had been taught by Dennis Robertson (who was a friend of his father) and had attended Keynes's lectures, but it was Maurice Dobb, Trinity's Economics tutor and the long-standing communist don, who cultivated his interest in Marxist economics and encouraged his political commitment. After graduating in the summer of 1933 with a 2:1 degree, Philby told Dobb that he wanted to work for communism. At that point he had no reason to believe it would involve secret work and, like others – including both those who became spies as well as others committed to open work – the initial attraction for him was to work for the Communist International.

Dobb, pleased with Philby's decision, provided him with a letter of introduction to the International Organisation for Aid to Revolutionaries (International Red Aid), a front organisation established by the Comintern in the 1920s. Philby met the agent in a Paris office, where he was provided with a further letter of recommendation to the head of the Austrian section of the Committee for the Relief of the Victims of German Fascism, one of the front organisations set up by Willi Münzenberg.

Dobb had warned Philby that the Communist Party in Austria had been made illegal under the fascist regime and its leadership had been forced underground. Once in Austria, Philby was sent by his committee contacts to the Kohlman household and there he met – and fell in love – with his landlord's daughter Litzi Friedmann, who was a communist involved in underground anti-fascist work. They returned to London together in April 1934 and were married shortly after, which enabled Friedmann to gain residency in London. On his return to Britain, Philby went to the Party's King Street offices, intending to join the Party, but was initially rebuffed – and in his view treated with some suspicion – and told to provide names of people who would support his application for membership. Despite this rebuttal, his commitment to the cause was undiminished in the weeks that followed and he was soon approached by one of his contacts in Austria who suggested there may be the chance to work for the international communist movement. It was through one of Litzi Friedmann's close friends from Vienna, Edith Suschitzky, that Philby was introduced to Arnold Deutsch ('Otto') in Regent's Park on a morning in June 1934. She accompanied him in a very long and circuitous journey of three to four hours, of the kind depicted in popular spy dramas, spread out over taxi, car and tube rides, doubling back, and eventually arriving at a destination close to where they had started. After walking the last few hundred yards in the park, Edith left him with Deutsch.

Edith Suschitzky was an Austrian Jewish communist whose family were persecuted after the Nazis took power. Her father was a bookseller and a social democrat but she had decided that the only way of working against fascism in Austria was by joining the underground communist movement. Edith, her husband Alex Tudor Hart, an English doctor whom she had met on an earlier visit, and younger brother Wolfgang had moved to London permanently in May 1934, following the decision of the Dollfuss government to crack down on communists in Austria.

Arnold Deutsch shared Suschitzky's Austrian Jewish communist background and had left Vienna shortly before Philby and Litzi Friedmann's return to London, to take a post-graduate psychology degree at London University, where he was part-sponsored by his cousin Oscar Deutsch, founder of Odeon Cinemas. In 1935, he moved to the Lawn Road Flats, (the 'Isokon' building) in Belsize Park, not far from the Klugmann family home, a newly built avant-garde 'minimalist' art deco block of flats which were popular among communist refugees, writers and intellectuals. As David Burke has suggested, the block was ideal for anyone involved in espionage, given that the flats backed onto woodland and the only access at the front was via an external staircase, which would prevent unobserved surveillance.[4]

Deutsch had been working for the Comintern in Vienna prior to his arrival, while he had also undertaken similar work in Greece, Romania, Palestine, Syria and Germany, during which time he had been noticed as ideally suited for espionage work. One of the first things Deutsch did on arriving in London was to recruit Edith and Alex Tudor Hart, whom he had known in Vienna.

As one of the Soviet NKVD 'illegals', Deutsch was not officially attached to the Soviet Embassy and had a degree of autonomy, under different superior officers. Nevertheless, he was crucial in cultivating the Cambridge spy network.

His wide-ranging intellectual interests included not only the works of Marx and Lenin, but the psycho-sex theories of Wilhelm Reich, and this put him on a similar wavelength to his younger recruits while he mixed seamlessly with the lifestyle of the Lawn Road bohemians.

Philby recalled pleasant memories of Deutsch, whom he described as 'a marvellous man', and found their conversations, often conducted in German, stimulating. He was struck by his warmth and empathy and remarked on his penetrating eyes: 'He looked at you as if there was nothing more important in life and interesting than you.' Deutsch, for his part, had been impressed by Philby's work in Austria and was aware of his intention to join the Communist Party, but told him:

> I respect your decision, but listen to what I have to say. You will be accepted in the Party. And you will become one of many thousands of communists. You will be a good communist. A loyal communist. You will have ties with the working class. But by background, education, appearance and manners you are an intellectual to your bone marrow [...] What will you do here in the Party? [...] Let's say you will hand out leaflets on the street. But anyone can do that, you don't need your education for that. You have a marvellous career ahead of you. A bourgeois career. And if you want to help the anti-fascist movement, the Communist movement, you have to help us in that way. The anti-fascist movement needs people who can enter into the bourgeoisie.[5]

Philby maintained in later interviews that it was not clear whether 'us' referred to Soviet intelligence or the Comintern. That ambiguity seemed to be a recurring initial dilemma for the others drawn to espionage, all of whom were excited by the opportunity of working for the Communist International, which they saw as fulfilling their revolutionary commitment. The attraction to Philby was the romantic one of joining an underground revolutionary organisation and finding his 'life goal'. He asked Deutsch if he was suggesting he become an 'infiltrator for the communist anti-fascist movement'. Deutsch's response was that as the British Communist Party did not occupy a significant role in public life, he would have the chance to serve the cause in more important ways. Within days, according to Borovik, a telegram was sent to the NKVD headquarters in the Lubyanka, informing them of Philby's recruitment. Deutsch also emphasised to his Moscow superiors the importance of the CUSS in Philby's move to communism, suggesting that there may be other possible recruits. We also know now that the NKVD believed that Philby's father worked for British intelligence, which would have made his recruitment even more attractive.

At the NKVD's request, Philby drew up a list of potential recruits, which numbered 17 in all. Donald Maclean was top of the list; ironically, he put Guy Burgess last. We do not know where Klugmann was on the list but given that he was following the precise career Deutsch had warned Philby against, he may not have been on it at all. Philby approached Maclean, who, like his friend Klugmann, was another communist with a first in Modern Languages. However, though Maclean had been initially interested in pursuing an academic career and had planned to spend a year teaching in Russia followed by an application for a fellowship, with a proposed thesis on Jean Calvin, he had not discounted the lure of the Foreign Office (FO). After all, his background meant he was suited to such a role, which would also have pleased his mother. Maclean's communism had deeper roots than Philby's. He had become a stalwart member of the Cambridge communist group and had a wider profile among the student body; his views variously appeared in *Granta* and the journal *Cambridge Left*. Now, another opportunity was floated before him.

During the 1934 Christmas break Philby invited Maclean to dinner at his place in London. He asked about Maclean's future career prospects and how he would resolve the dilemma of maintaining his communist principles if he went to the Foreign Office, the bastion of British imperialism. Did he really intend to sell the *Daily Worker* on the steps of the FO, he asked him? Philby told him there was a solution which would enable him to have 'a brilliant career and not despising himself for it'.[6] Maclean, according to Philby, then asked him if this was an offer to work for Soviet intelligence or the Comintern. In reply, Philby told him that he did not know for certain but thought it was for an anti-fascist organisation, with links to Moscow. Maclean asked for time to consider. He wanted to discuss it with Klugmann, who, since Gresham's, had been his close friend, political mentor and confidant. Philby told him that was 'categorically impossible' and that discussion with anyone else would jeopardise the whole idea.[7]

We do not know whether Maclean discussed the offer with Klugmann in the intervening two days before he agreed to Philby's offer. If he did not, then there is little doubt that Klugmann soon became aware of what his friend had become involved in. Did he approve? At one level, Klugmann was well aware of the importance of Comintern work and, since the meeting at his house in Hampstead in Easter 1932, knew that the Party had people in regular contact with Moscow. He himself, of course, in the same period Maclean was making his fateful decision, was being cultivated for his own Comintern role, at the founding RME Congress. The world of the Foreign Office, however, was a different thing entirely. Klugmann was an open communist who regarded such institutions with contempt, not only because of their role in international affairs, but as an institution which reflected the British class system; at the same time he remained suspicious of careerists and those who put their own interests above those of the Party. In this regard, he differed from his friend, whose stronger personal ambitions were reflected even in the role he sought for himself as a 'revolutionary'. Moreover, Klugmann had imbibed the ethos of the Party more readily than his friend and he was more comfortable with its class composition, routines and practices. He had hoped that Maclean would commit to more Party work, but he must also have been aware that he himself, following Gallacher's visit earlier in the year, had argued that communist intellectuals had a duty to serve the cause according to their specialist interests and in the most effective way possible. He could not have known then, however, the full implications of this argument, one that he had put forward with such conviction at Cambridge.

Working for the Comintern was therefore a much more attractive proposition to Maclean than the day-to-day work of the Party. As it did to Philby, it must have seemed then to the brilliant 21-year-old Cambridge graduate that he had his 'life goal' before him; though it was one to which he was never fully reconciled. Although it meant a public break with communism, such an action would have also appealed, as his biographer and Cambridge and FO contemporary, Robert Cecil, has written, to Maclean's intellectual arrogance.

> To go underground, to become a 'mole' (though the term was not used at that date), appealed to the elitist in him. He was not one of those who had gone to stay with coal-miners in his vacations; by entering a profession, such as diplomacy, he would have the satisfaction of serving the cause without abandoning the fleshpots of the society he was aiming to destroy.[8]

With Philby (code name 'Sonny' or 'Sohnchen' and 'Stanley') and Maclean (code name 'Homer') on board, Guy Burgess was the next NKVD recruit. Unsurprisingly, he was not an ideal choice, coming bottom of Philby's list of candidates, whose flamboyance, promiscuity and outspoken tirades at the Trinity dining table hardly constituted good material for an espionage agent. However, like Klugmann, he had grown close to Maclean through their student activism and was not taken in when his friend, on the orders of Deutsch, suddenly renounced his communism – 'Do you think that I believe even for one jot that you have stopped being a communist?' he allegedly asked him.[9] Either on Klugmann's prompting, or through his own reasoning, Burgess quickly came to the view that Maclean was engaged in some sort of underground work for the Comintern. Despite his often outrageous behaviour, Burgess did not take his communism lightly and he had played an important part in support of the anti-fascist movement, welcomed the hunger marchers to Cambridge, had got involved in the campaign against rising council house rents and helped organise a waiters' strike at Trinity. A brilliant history student and one of the 'Apostles ' – as the 12 members of the exclusive Cambridge Conversazione Society were known – he had not, however, achieved the degree he was expecting, though had managed to secure a research post. He too was attracted by the idea of working for the Comintern. From Maclean, Deutsch realised that it would be more dangerous to leave Burgess outside and, in any case, now thought his uncanny ability to make connections would be useful while the extremes of his personality would serve as a helpful cover. According to Anthony Blunt, Burgess 'went through agony' in pretending he had renounced his beliefs, as well as 'performing intellectual somersaults' and would have preferred to remain an open Party member, despite his evident difficulties in maintaining Party discipline.[10]

In fact, Burgess was becoming unreliable. He owed money to the Party; Klugmann, whose organising duties included fundraising and collecting membership dues, had begun to despair of his comrade's lapses. Maurice Dobb, who had inadvertently started the espionage journey by sending Philby to work for the 'international', was irked by Burgess's lack of discipline and, as an exchange of letters in early 1936 demonstrates, was apparently unaware of the real reasons for Burgess's exit from the Party the year before. In correspondence found in Burgess's belongings in Anthony Blunt's flat at the Courthauld Institute of Art, after the former's disappearance in 1951, Dobb makes clear his annoyance.

Dear Guy,

You may perhaps remember that you left Cambridge with a certain debt of 27/- which you have admitted + which you have on various occasions made promise to pay. I am not sure how long ago that was, but I believe it is now 12 months or more since then.

As I believe now that you have adopted a new political fashion, you are inclined to treat this debt with some flippancy. I am writing to point out that this happens not to be a debt in the ordinary sense of the word, but money paid to you by other people, to be handed on, which you have kept and used for your own purposes. For this there exists a very simple + direct word. May I also point out that a good part of this sum represents pennies collected from working men, who probably have less to spend on keeping a family in a week than you probably spend on gin, in the same time. I have hesitated for some time to write openly + directly to you in this way, despite the fact that this is the way in which a number of your former friends see the matter. Too long a time now seems to have passed, however, for it to be attributed simply to a well-intentioned defect of memory

Yours Sincerely

Maurice Dobb.[11]

We only get one side of the correspondence, but as the exchange of letters between Dobb and Burgess continue, it is clear that Burgess rejects the accusation and insists that he paid the money to Klugmann. Dobb becomes more conciliatory, though still aloof on account of Burgess's new political allegiances.

I am very sorry if you think this is an unjust claim on you and I do not quite know how at this distance of time the matter can be successfully arbitrated. I was careful to enquire pretty fully of all persons who had any knowledge of the transaction, including James and his sister who said that you had admitted to her that the money had been collected at some time. James is now in Paris [...] Certainly if you think the money, or some of it, was given to James, this should be gone into but I had no inkling of this before. For the moment I will lay the extra 10/- that you so kindly send to the Labour Monthly as you suggest, and the remainder I will hold for the time-being pending any further decision if such is possible. It looks as though some compromise solution will have to be found. I am sorry I was away + you had two fruitless journeys here. I should like to telephone you some day but during term mornings are unlikely to be possible.

Yours, Maurice.[12]

The correspondence gives some indication that Burgess, who by this time had found himself employment as parliamentary assistant to the right-wing Tory MP

'Jack' Macnamara, was not entirely comfortable with his new façade and had not forgotten his older Party loyalties. Klugmann, who was preparing to go to Paris at the time that Burgess had made his decision to work for the NKVD, had begun to see him as unreliable for the disciplines of Party membership – a view clearly held by Dobb in his letter. The letter demonstrates that Dobb was unaware of Burgess's involvement in espionage, while Klugmann almost certainly did know of the choice Burgess had made in following Maclean into underground work. His relationship with both would never be the same, but over the next couple of years he would also be drawn further into their new world.

Working for the Comintern was the rationale used by the Cambridge spies to explain their recruitment to the NKVD. These include Anthony Blunt, who was recruited between 1935 and 1936. Blunt had visited Russia with other Cambridge friends, including Michael Straight, Brian Simon and Charles Rycroft, and while he spent most of the time admiring neo-classical architecture while others visited factories, it was an important moment in his own decision to work for the Comintern. As he wrote in his autobiographical memoir, released in 2009: 'I came to believe that Marxism was not only a useful weapon for the study of art history but that it also supplied the solution to the political problems with which the world was faced in the mid-1930s.'[13]

This view was reinforced further following a visit to Spain with his friend Louis MacNiece at Easter 1936,

> the ivory tower no longer provided a refuge. It became imperative to take sides, and there did not appear to be any question which side one should take. The Chamberlain government was putting up no resistance to Hitler's demands but was seeking every possible compromise [...] Failure to resist the occupation of the Rhineland, the re-arming of Germany and the policy of non-intervention in Spain seemed to prove that nothing could be expected from the British or French governments, and that the only force really determined to resist Nazism was communism, based on Soviet Russia.

This, then, was Blunt's rationale for working for the Comintern when asked to do so by his close friend Guy Burgess. Burgess told him ('at a date which I cannot exactly pin down, but which must I think have been later in 1935 or early 1936'[14]) that he 'had orders to go underground', meaning effectively that he had to break all ties with the Communist Party, leave Cambridge and look for a position in government service or the media establishment, 'where he would be able to get information useful to the Third or Communist International from whom he had received those orders'.[15]

Burgess then, according to Blunt, used his 'extraordinary powers of persuasion' to convince him not to join the Communist Party as he had been invited to do by Klugmann, Roy Pascal and others, but instead to work in a clandestine way. Blunt's agreement to work for the Comintern was fuelled by the 'feverish' enthusiasm amongst communist students at Cambridge, notably Klugmann and John Cornford.

Blunt set out his task in his own words:

> My job for the Comintern in Cambridge was to find members of the Communist Party who might be expected to obtain good jobs in government service or other employment in which they would have access to information useful to the organisation. In fact I found three such people – one was John Cairncross, whom I did not myself recruit but introduced to Guy who in due course did so.[16]

Blunt's two other recruits were the American communist Michael Straight and Leo Long. Straight and Cairncross had both been talent-spotted by Klugmann for membership of CUSS and the Party, while Leo Long had been brought to Klugmann's attention on his arrival in Cambridge in autumn 1935 by comrades at the LSE, where he had earlier become a communist. Much has been written about Blunt's involvement in talent-spotting for the NKVD, variously citing predatory homosexuality and lobbying to become an 'Apostle' as his chosen techniques. However, as Miranda Carter, has shown, there is little evidence that the Apostles were a recruiting ground, given the declining influence of Marxists in their meetings in the late 1930s.[17] Rather, Blunt, in the absence of Klugmann, who had left Cambridge for Paris at the end of 1935, took the talent-spotting of left-wing undergraduates to a different level. As Klugmann had done, he had invited discussions with potential recruits but now raised the additional, undefined, tortuously insecure but still intriguing criterion of espionage work, which he continued to explain through the prism of working for the Comintern. Brian Simon, close friend of both Blunt and Klugmann, was thought to have been approached in this way by Blunt:

> The penny didn't drop. I thought the CI (Communist International) was a prestigious organization which stood up to the Nazis – Dimitrov, who stood up

to Goering at the Reichstag Fire Trials, was in the Communist International. It just seemed a rather good thing to be doing.[18]

Simon may have been the friend cited by Michael Straight who had rejected an offer from Blunt to work in espionage on account of not being mentally strong enough to work underground.

The circumstances of Straight's own recruitment to the NKVD have been contested. He himself, in his autobiography, *After Long Silence,* attributes some of the responsibility to Klugmann, albeit someone he regarded with the warmest affection. After moving from his lodgings to Whewell's Court in the autumn of 1935, Straight had become more involved in political activities, working in the unemployment centre, canvassing for the Labour Party, arguing against pacifism in Maurice Dobb's Anti-War Committee and selling the *Daily Worker* in town. He also became active in the Cambridge Union, impressing with his oratory and glamorous persona as a communist millionaire. Over the next two years, in the absence of Klugmann (who was in Paris) and Cornford (in Spain), Straight would take a stronger leadership role in the Cambridge communist group. His connections, intellect, wealth and charisma were much valued by the Party. He subsequently claimed that it was Keynes who provided the intellectual stimulation, while the comradeship of 'James and John' brought emotional 'dependency'.[19] 'It was the sense of brotherhood that had opened up a new life for me.'[20] After an evening spent in Whewell's Court with Klugmann, Blunt and Burgess in November 1935, Straight described in a letter to his mother this 'extraordinary sense of comradeship' and his 'inexplicable' love for James and John:

James in particular is so delightful. I've been with him, and Whitney's friend Guy Burgess and an art historian named Anthony Blunt all evening. Now at half past eleven I sit here and try to describe the terrible significance of it all.[21]

He described that evening as a memorable and critical moment in his recruitment to Soviet intelligence. He was stimulated by the brilliance of his friends, thrilled by the sense of common experiences and flattered by the interest they continued to show in him. Considering these events 50 years later, Straight pondered on the implications of that meeting and why he had used the phrase 'the terrible significance of it all' in the letter to his mother. Although he had been on the same Intourist trip to Russia that summer, he had barely known Blunt until that evening. Klugmann, who had introduced Straight to the Party leadership and from whom he had committed substantial Party funds, knew that he would do anything he asked for the cause. Looking back, Straight identified the meeting as the moment at which Blunt 'took a close interest in me', but adds: 'And James, whom I loved, did he know what was going on that evening? Was he part of the snare?'[22]

10

The Reluctant Spy

In his book *Their Trade is Treachery*, Chapman Pincher claimed that James Klugmann was 'an even more sinister Communist agent' than Anthony Blunt or Guy Burgess.[1] Michael Straight, looking back at his own recruitment to Soviet intelligence and from later discussions with other unnamed Cambridge contemporaries, seems to accept Pincher's assertion. This, Straight claimed, was due to Klugmann's role as a communist talent spotter, and his unwavering faith in the cause of international communism, and not due to a personality trait.

> James, we agreed, would have looked with distaste on deception in all of its forms. But in his gentle way, he would have justified it as a 'historical necessity'.
>
> 'Look comrades', he would have murmured, 'the historical era in which we live imposes hardships of many kinds upon those who participate in its decisive events. The roles to which we are assigned may seem questionable to us, but in the end, our actions will be measured by the general happiness that will be shared by all mankind.'[2]

Straight believed Klugmann would have rationalised Burgess's role as an NKVD agent. That November 1935 meeting in Straight's rooms in Whewell's Court also demonstrated that Klugmann knew something of Burgess's new role – Burgess had by that time already broken publicly with communism – as it was a couple of months before Dobb's letter to Burgess about money owed to the Party. While there is a distinction between talent-spotting for the Comintern and recruiting for Soviet espionage purposes, Klugmann had long argued that talented intellectuals could perform better roles by using their skills and connections in influential positions, and Burgess's decision could initially have fitted this logic. The important issue, as Klugmann himself made clear in his conversation with Bob Stewart in 1945, was not to mix two different kinds of work.

Straight's own actual recruitment to the NKVD took place a year later, after he was approached by Blunt. According to Straight, the art history don took advantage of Straight's distress at the death of Cornford in Spain in December 1936 – he had had to break the news to Margot Heinemann and Cornford's parents. He had also got himself into trouble earlier that year after organising a petition on behalf of Trinity College servants and had faced expulsion from the college, until Blunt and others came to his defence. Blunt had also offered Straight advice on his complicated love life; three or four different women were attracting his attentions. Straight argued that Blunt exploited his vulnerability in order to recruit him and, building on the sense of close comradeship and meeting of minds at that November 1935 meeting, took the probing a stage further in his rooms in Neville Court in January 1937, shortly after news of Cornford's death. Blunt asked him about his future career plans and, on hearing he only had a few vague intentions, told him that 'some of your friends [...] have other ideas for you'. Blunt informed him that the 'Communist International' had assignments for him, and suggested he return to the US and find himself a job in international banking. At the same time, he could use the excuse of the grief over Cornford's death, as precipitating an emotional breakdown and 'crisis of belief', to justify severing his links with communism.[3] Straight claims he lacked the willpower to resist Blunt's approach, but nevertheless pleaded with him to be excused this duty in a series of letters, the last of which promised to hand over all his wealth if he could be released from espionage obligations.

Blunt, however, had a different interpretation of that meeting and denied ever having received the final letter. When Miranda Carter, Blunt's biographer, pointed this out to Straight in 1996, he told her that 'it wouldn't have made any difference'.[4] She attributes his attempts to play down his political commitment and 'somewhat one-sided account of his recruitment' to his status as a public figure on the American left and opponent of McCarthyism, and the consequences that espionage revelations would have for his career.

Blunt stated that John Cairncross was recruited to Soviet intelligence by Guy Burgess, but he must have known who really played the key role. Cairncross was a very gifted, though introverted student, from a different class background to many of his contemporaries (his father was an ironmonger and his mother a schoolteacher). Though Blunt was part of the French teaching staff, Cairncross denies in his autobiography *The Enigma Spy* that he was personally taught by him and maintained that he held a lifelong dislike for him, though as a 'fellow-traveller' he did attend an economics group which met regularly in Blunt's rooms. Cairncross claimed he 'had drifted into communism' under the influence of Klugmann and Roy Pascal, his German tutor. He attended cell meetings, though – despite the lobbying of Klugmann and Cornford – never actually joined the Party. In 1936, after Blunt had assumed his talent-spotter role, Cairncross was targeted as a potential recruit for Soviet intelligence, particularly after he had left Cambridge and joined the Foreign Office.

On moving to London, Cairncross kept in touch with his Cambridge friends, notably Klugmann (whom he also visited in Paris), Professor Ashton and Roy Pascal. Soon after he started work at the Foreign Office as third secretary in the American Department, he met Pascal for lunch at a Lyons Corner House near Marble Arch. Over lunch, Pascal said he would like to put him in touch with a friend of his who would update him on 'political developments'. Cairncross feared such an approach but he assumed this was from within the British Communist Party's own intelligence section.[5] Nothing came of this suggestion, and it was not until Cairncross moved to the Spanish Section in February 1937 that he first met Donald Maclean, who was his 'immediate superior' and shared his office.

Cairncross and Maclean were very different characters. Maclean's class background and self-confidence enabled him to mix easily in the social networks of the FO, while Cairncross was more retiring and unwilling or unable to conform to some of the conventions. Maclean himself was not part of Cairncross's NKVD recruitment and, according to Cairncross, never discussed such matters with him. However, shortly after joining the Spanish Section, Cairncross met Burgess for the first time. Burgess, well aware of Cairncross's interest in literature, then invited him to meet the poet Louis MacNeice at a Sunday gathering in Blunt's rooms back at Trinity.

It was on the train back to London after this meeting that Burgess made the first of two extravagant attempts to recruit him. Burgess quizzed him on his views on the international situation and was sufficiently impressed that he later told his friend Goronwy Rees (whom he also recruited) that Cairncross was well on the way to working for the Comintern.

However, this had not yet been achieved and Burgess was forced to try again when, on hearing that Cairncross was visiting Paris, he suggested a rendezvous at Le Select, a homosexual café. Cairncross was not keen on that assignation and never appeared. He claimed that it was only afterwards that he perceived these two events as attempts by Burgess to recruit him and thought at the time that he was merely being patronised by introductions to exclusive social contacts. His non-appearance did not impress Burgess, and the NKVD, having identified him as an important potential agent, had to look for an alternative strategy.

James Klugmann had maintained a good friendship with Cairncross. They had many things in common. Although Klugmann came from a more affluent background than Cairncross, he was also an outsider from the conventional British class system and was not a confident or ostentatious socialiser. He was also, like Cairncross, a serious intellectual and they had many academic as well as political interests in common. Both maintained a passion for German and French literature, while the political cause of anti-Nazism was a recurrent theme in their conversations. They met regularly in London on Klugmann's visits back and also on occasion in Paris, which Cairncross knew well having previously studied there. The NKVD had asked their new Cambridge agents for their assessment of Cairncross and what they thought would be the best method of recruiting him. Burgess provided a detailed report to Moscow on Cairncross's character and capabilities and, concluding that the risks were too great for him or Blunt to take on his recruitment, recommended 'an open party member [...] approach him'.[6]

We know that Klugmann took on this clandestine work with reluctance. His own debriefing with Bob Stewart made clear his agreement to do it, but only if asked to do so by the Party: 'I mean if I was asked to do that and nothing else I mean that's the job and I'll do it.' This has been confirmed by the NKVD agents themselves. Theodore Maly, the senior illegal *rezident*, in a report to the Centre in March 1937 confirmed they had 'found a way of approaching C. without M. (Madchen – Burgess) and T. (Tony – Blunt). A former Party organizer in Cambridge who is now working in Paris will speak to him in such a way that we shall in no way be involved. His name is Klugmann.'[7] Deutsch's own notes to the Centre, written in 1939, confirmed that they approached Klugmann with this aim in mind in early 1937, but that Klugmann insisted that he would only take this role on the authority of the Communist Party leadership. Yuri Modin, the KGB controller who took over the running of the Cambridge Five after the war, and who had access to the prewar files, also confirmed Klugmann's reluctant role: 'From time to time, when he was asked to do something, he would say, "I will act only on the direct orders of the Party".'

This proviso made our relationship with Klugman [sic] somewhat awkward. To get him to act, Harry Pollitt, General Secretary of the British Communist Party, had to be wheeled out. Provided the order came from Pollitt, Klugman would comply [...] In this case, he was told straight out by Follitt that his duty as a communist was to recruit Cairncross – and he did.[8]

It is possible that Cairncross first met Deutsch ('Otto') in Paris through Klugmann on one of his trips in early 1937, though in his autobiography Cairncross suggests the main introduction was made in London. His sense of betrayal by Klugmann is evident in his description of their meeting in May 1937:

Klugmann had arranged for the two of us to meet in the evening at Regent's Park, a spacious and delightful spot close to the West End where, he probably calculated, we would not be recognised or disturbed. I had dined early in a small Italian restaurant in Soho and was looking forward to a pleasant stroll in a green setting. I arrived at our 7 o'clock rendezvous at one of the park entrances to find Klugmann waiting for me and we made our way into a part of the grounds with a fair number of trees. It was still light, but there were not many people around. I noticed that Klugmann was not his usual smiling, chatty self. My instinct of unease was not mistaken, for suddenly there emerged from behind the trees a short, stocky figure aged around forty, whom Klugmann introduced to me as Otto. Thereupon, Klugmann promptly disappeared without even daring to give me a furtive look – and I did not see him again until almost thirty years later, when I unsuccessfully confronted him with his deception.[9]

Cairncross claimed in his autobiography that he was recruited solely because of the 'crudeness and deviousness of Klugmann, who had acted as a catspaw, for the KGB would never have been able to catch me off my guard but for his trickery'. He also states that his recruitment was 'an abrupt leap from the academic discussions I had been enjoying with Klugmann' [10]

Klugmann's role in the recruitment of Cairncross was to torment him in his later life. Yet his own uneasy conflicts of loyalties, revealed in his debriefing with Stewart, were widely shared by communists of that period. This was true for several of the Cambridge spies and, despite those accounts which presented their spying activities as merely ruthless and cold-blooded treachery, they all remained troubled by it and had lasting moments of self-doubt. They justified their actions as 'working for the Comintern', which is how it was initially presented to them, and as a way of aiding the anti-fascist struggle, where loyalties were rooted in an international rather than national terrain. In his memoirs, Anthony Blunt recalled that faced with the most important decision of my life [...] it seems easy to say I should have refused, on the grounds that this meant working against my country, but [...] 'my country right or wrong' was not a principle that was deeply instilled into me. My loyalties were international as much as national, and above all, they were directed to causes.[11]

The difference for Klugmann, of course, was that he was an open Party member. Yet, as we now know from several sources, there was nothing unusual about British Communist Party members willing to provide information to the Soviet Union. Eric Hobsbawm, who worked for Klugmann as an interpreter in Paris in 1937, commented in his autobiography *Interesting Times* that if Moscow had asked him to work for them he would have done so:

We knew such work was going on, we knew we were not supposed to ask questions about it, we respected those who did it and most of us – certainly I – would have taken it on ourselves, if asked. The lines of loyalty in the 1930s ran not between but across countries.[12]

According to Hobsbawm, the 'key question' was 'who was giving authority to ask for intelligence work'. Communists were sometimes approached by illegal or unofficial sources, without the authority of the Party or the Comintern, which was a matter viewed with some concern. 'It was a big issue [...] who the hell are you. You've got no right.'[13]

Hobsbawm's concern at unofficial approaches mirrored that of his old friend, and was reflected in the fear that the two types of work could conflict. 'It was a bad principle', according to Hobsbawm, 'to mix Party work with espionage work.'[14] Similarly, Klugmann had told Stewart, 'I hope never to be told to do two things which are really contradictory.'[15]

Their friend and contemporary Victor Kiernan was another who was not prepared to reduce 'loyalty' to national terms. In the 1930s, when fascism was rising and Britain's privileged economic order was in serious decay at home, internationalism provided a logical solution. 'At such a time', Kiernan writes,

puntilios of 'loyalty' to things of the dying past seemed as archaic as the minutiae of drawing-room manners. And it was about the defenders of the old order that a strong smell of treason hung. We saw pillars of British society trooping to Nuremberg to hobnob with Nazi gangsters; we saw the

'National' government sabotaging the Spanish Republic's struggle, from class prejudice, and to benefit investors like Rio Tinto, blind to the obvious prospect of the Mediterranean being turned into a fascist lake and the lifelines of empire cut.

There was a sense of 'absolute divide'; 'Our watchword was Voltaire's *Ecrasez l'infâme*. Feelings like these were to carry a small number of our generation, from Cambridge and elsewhere, into acts of "treason", in the lawyer's meaning, not the only or best one.'[16] Kiernan took issue with the definition of treason as applied to the 1930s and justified the actions of his contemporaries on the grounds their cause was that of 'fighting absolute evil'.[17]

It would be misleading to assume, as many have done, that justification for taking part in Soviet espionage was confined to Cambridge intellectuals. In *MASK: MI5's Penetration of the Communist Party of Great Britain*, Nigel West uncovered details of major intelligence and radio interception surveillance by MI5 in the same period in which the Cambridge spies were recruited. MI5 was able to monitor a large amount of wireless traffic between the Comintern HQ in Moscow and British Communist Party representatives, operating from a clandestine transmitter in Wimbledon, south London. According to West, the Comintern was 'actively engaging' in espionage work and depended on the cooperation of Comintern members in different countries. In the case of Britain, this cooperation was coordinated and supported without question.[18]

West has revealed that the scale of espionage amongst British communists was much more widespread than originally believed and became part of the daily routine of the work of several communists. Douglas Hyde also recounted that in his time as news editor of the *Daily Worker* in the 1930s and 1940s, it was commonplace for ordinary communist members to pass what they thought was valuable secret material to Party leaders. He recalled how during the mid-1940s he was approached by a communist working as a civil servant in the War Office who felt the Party should be told about the preparations that were being made for hostile actions against Russia:

He promised to pass on anything which seemed significant. I passed him, as was our routine, straight on to a member whose job it was to keep in touch with such people. He was instructed to drop all local activity at once. 'This is far more important', he was told, 'than anything else you can do for the Party'. He had grown accustomed to the idea of passing on secrets 'for the Party'.

Now he was urged to remember everything in greater detail so that it might be of use to Russia too. Then he was passed to a colleague who was in touch with the Soviet Embassy.[19]

Despite the regularities of clandestine meetings, Hyde was aware that spying was a matter of great personal angst and that the spy in question 'never ceased to be scared of what he was doing'. Equally, he and others had no doubt they were doing the right thing.

At no point did the question of its being unpatriotic enter into our thoughts. We were, after all, agreed that a communist Britain would be a better Britain, that we should not see communism here in our lifetime if Russia was allowed to be crushed and that, therefore, in defending Russia from her class enemies and ours we were fighting for 'our' Britain. The conventional attitude to patriotism and love of country was easily dismissed with the question: 'Whose country – theirs or ours?'[20]

For James Klugmann, his duty was an uncomfortable one that could have lasted well beyond the 'nine months' he mentioned to Stewart. His NKVD recruitment took place in early 1937 after Percy Glading, acting on the authority of the British Communist Party leadership, introduced him to Deutsch for the purpose of recruiting Cairncross.[21] It occurred at the beginning of an intense period of espionage activity among the 'illegals' in which the Cambridge spies were the prize assets and only ended with the recall to Moscow of Theodore Maly, Deutsch's senior NKVD colleague in London, and of Deutsch himself.

During those nine months, Deutsch held occasional meetings with Klugmann in Paris, and the latter added espionage to his main RME and research work. Paris was the centre of espionage of various sorts, and also popular with Burgess and Blunt, while Maclean moved there with the Foreign Office in 1938. It seems that Cairncross was not the only candidate put Klugmann's way. Just after he had been recruited by the NKVD himself, Klugmann had dinner with Anthony Blunt and other guests at a restaurant in the Latin Quarter. As the artist Ben Nicholson, also present at the dinner, recalled in his diary for 10 April 1937:

Dined with Blunt [...] We sat up late in the Cafe de Cluny where Blunt had made an assignation with a full-blooded Marxist who controls four revolutionaries in

China and who seemed to know every fact about all advanced revolutionary activity in all countries. He was a German Jew called James Klugmann, heavy, spectacled and serious and refused to enter into any conversation except to correct other people's statements.[22]

The other guest at the dinner, in addition to Blunt, Nicholson and Klugmann, was Stuart Hampshire, a brilliant young philosopher who had recently been part of the Oxford student left and would go on to be an outstanding code-breaker in military intelligence. He was also at that time friendly with Guy Burgess. The significance of that intense political discussion in such convivial circumstances did not become clear until nearly 30 years later, when Anthony Blunt was being interrogated by MI5's Peter Wright. Blunt did not reject Wright's suggestion that Hampshire was being sounded out as being of potential use to Soviet intelligence and Wright subsequently visited Hampshire at Princeton University to ask him again about that meeting. Hampshire agreed that he may have been the target of a recruitment campaign by Blunt and Klugmann on behalf of Soviet intelligence.[23] That part of the discussion was almost certainly instigated by Klugmann, more politically experienced and able than Blunt.

During these nine months, as Klugmann got to know Deutsch, he was required to send in reports on his Cambridge comrades. This was a common practice among NKVD agents, but given his close friendship with Burgess and Maclean, this must have been an uncomfortable task, one which he achieved by writing as he might without prior knowledge of their espionage work (which he was not expected to have, as far as the NKVD were concerned). Thus, Maclean 'has broken off all relations with the party and even avoids old comrades as if he were ashamed of the fact that he has gone over to the bourgeoisie', while Burgess 'has distanced himself from us, because his family relations have enabled him to move in high society [...] It would be worthwhile to capture him because if he became an enemy he would be a dangerous enemy.'[24]

Deutsch's own report on Klugmann, however, was precise and uncannily accurate on his character and personality.

James is a party functionary who devotes himself entirely to the party. He is a quiet and thoughtful man. Modest, conscientious, industrious and serious. Everybody who knows him likes him and respects him. He exercises great influence over people. As a person he is honest and beyond reproach. Responsive and attentive to comrades. Ready to bring any offer for the sake of the party. A good organizer. Very careful with money. Never takes anything for himself. Outwardly shy and reserved. Strict in respect of women. Pays no attention to his appearance. He can do much for us if we are recommended to him by Harry Pollitt.[25]

It is also likely that Klugmann was one of the instigators in bringing a wider Oxford cohort to the attention of Soviet intelligence in the same period. He was in regular contact with Bernard Floud, who would accompany him to China the following year, and it was Floud, according to Jenifer Fischer Williams, who put her in touch with Soviet intelligence after she had joined the Civil Service. She had been an active 'open' communist at Oxford, but was now advised that it would be better to disguise her membership:

Student friends in the Party said I would be more effective by going into the Civil Service as a secret Party member. I was unclear what, if anything, I as a Civil Servant would do for the British Communist Party, but I think I supposed that I would occasionally pass them useful information.[26]

Although she met 'Otto' and an 'anonymous Party member' during her first year, she terminated the meetings without passing any material, as she was uncomfortable with her assignment.[27] The boundaries between helping the Communist International, encouraging communists to use their expertise on behalf of the Party and direct links with Soviet intelligence were tenuous at times. Peter Wright claimed in *Spycatcher* that there was a separate 'Oxford Ring', operating along similar lines to Cambridge. Certainly, there was the intention of setting up a 'second Sohnchen' (Philby) in the form of Arthur Wynn (code name 'Scott'), who had been recruited by Maly. Wynn was proactive in sending names of more possible recruits – excessively so, in the view of his controllers – and detailed reports on their activities. In fact, shortly after Wynn returned his detailed reports on student activism at Oxford in July 1937, the London *rezidentura* was closed down. The purges of Soviet intelligence were to follow, with Maly and Deutsch under suspicion.[28]

This accounted for Klugmann's fear, as he expressed it to Bob Stewart: 'If that man [Deutsch] came back, I honestly don't know what I would have done.' That he was not asked to do more was mainly the outcome of developments in Moscow. However, in the short term, it was an incident closer to home that terminated his espionage work. Deutsch and Maly had been operating a spy ring at Woolwich

Arsenal which involved extracting and copying secret documents. In order to do this they had used Percy Glading (code-named 'GOT'), the experienced Party organiser who had introduced Klugmann to Deutsch. Unknown to Deutsch and Maly, MI5 had their own undercover agent working in the Party's King Street offices. Known as 'Olga Gray' – and 'Miss X' in the subsequent trial – she had previously worked as a secretary to Harry Pollitt and had been a trusted courier on earlier assignments. Now she was given the task of leasing a flat for meetings of agents and the photographing of the secret documents and, as such, was able to brief MI5 as the work continued. Glading and his accomplices were arrested in Charing Cross Station in January 1938 and later convicted and given six-month jail sentences.

The previous autumn, before Glading's arrest, Deutsch had left Britain for Moscow. Prior to his departure he had experienced problems over his British residence status. He had intended to return to continue his work with the Cambridge recruits, but Moscow's closure of the illegal *rezidenza* put paid to that idea. Glading's arrest heightened fears in Moscow that the work was dangerous and the Cambridge group was put on hold. For Klugmann, the 'nine months' of espionage which started in April 1937 were over. Or so it must have seemed to him then. Deutsch, in his written report on Klugmann, had held out the possibility that 'he can do much for us'.[29]

Deutsch did not come back, but Klugmann would have many more 'sleepless nights' over what he told Stewart was 'too hard a question. It is, I think [...] it is the hardest problem.'[30]

11

A Communist Goes to War

Shortly before the outbreak of war in 1939, James Klugmann left his post in Paris as secretary of the Rassemblement Mondial des Étudiants and returned to Britain, awaiting call-up to the army. He left Paris after the RME had hurriedly wound up its activities as the likelihood of war increased – some of the professors he had got to know at the Sorbonne would later be arrested by the Gestapo – and he returned to Cambridge to stay with his comrades Ram Nahum and Freddie Lambert. Nahum, a brilliant young intellectual, would be killed by a stray German bomb in Cambridge three years later.

The war brought a political dilemma. Klugmann's work in Paris had focused on anti-fascist organisation in universities. He had helped mobilise opposition to the 'appeasement' of Chamberlain after the Munich Agreement. Now, the Molotov–Ribbentrop agreement – the 'Nazi–Soviet Pact' of August 1939 – seemed to throw in doubt his broad anti-fascist work. Many Communist Party members, including some who had joined in the mid-1930s, left the Party after finding the Soviet position incomprehensible and at odds with their anti-fascist principles. Others, like Philip Toynbee, left when more news of the Soviet show trials emerged. For Klugmann, who had joined the Party as Hitler came to power and had embraced the politics of the Popular Front, the Soviet position would have been difficult to understand.

In fact he did not have to compromise his principles at this point. As he later told Bob Stewart, 'with agreement from the Comintern, I volunteered through my normal source, which was the Cambridge University Recruiting Board'.[1] His idea was to join the army, contribute in the battle against fascism, and continue to make the case for communism. He had to wait a year to be called up, spending the intervening period helping out at Sir Ernest Simon's Association for Education in Citizenship, in its Victoria Street offices in central London. The Association had been set up to educate young people in the virtues of democracy and citizenship, for which Klugmann was well-qualified, and Sir Ernest, the father of his two Gresham's friends, might well have had him in mind for a future role in the organisation, though by now was wary of his communism.[2]

After a year Klugmann was finally called up by the Royal Army Service Corps (RASC) in November 1940 and told to report at Aldershot, before being sent to London on an army clerk training course. Here he was put up at the Belmont Hotel, Highbury, from where he updated his former Cambridge tutor George Kitson Clark in a cheerful letter in February 1941. After conveying his hope that 'warden duties have not been unduly troublesome, and that the college is continuing to function as of old', he carries on:

I have been in the RASC for the last 3 months, having a very good time indeed. They have apparently decided to turn me into an army clerk, and I was confronted by a clerks' test on arriving at Aldershot some 3 months ago. What with an Intelligence Test (apparently devised by a Cambridge professor) and an examination in arithmetic, including compound interest and the area of the garden path [...] it was altogether the strangest exam I have ever had to sit but the habits of bluff that I had learned at Cambridge enabled me to scrape through, even the garden path.

After a month on the square at Aldershot I have been sent back to school in London to learn shorthand and typing and army organization for 3 months which I am very much enjoying. Again Cambridge education is extraordinarily useful, as I seem to be able to sleep in lectures with an eye open more successfully than any of my colleagues.

I expect to be here for another 2–2½ months before being posted.

Up at Aldershot I enquired about the possibilities of a Commission. It seems that in the RASC itself it is quite possible, but might need to be waited for, for a long period, but that there is some more chance in various other regiments. The Cambridge Recruiting Board Recommendation did not seem to impress them very greatly and I was given another large form (Army form B2617) to fill out, and will have at some future date to go before another Army board. I have filled in the bulk of the form but need a 'certificate of moral character' to go with it. I explained to them that I had not been at Cambridge for the past 4 years but they suggested 2 signatures – 1 from the university and 1 who knew my work during the last few years. I hope you will be able to sign the enclosed form re 'moral character' and I will send it to Sir Ernest Simon for a 2nd signature.

He ends by saying: 'Army life seems to agree with me as it is very pleasant to be at school again.' Two days later, Kitson Clark gave a brief reply, confirming he had signed the certificate and hoping that 'you will get work worthy of you'.[3]

At the same time that his old Cambridge tutor was certifying his 'moral character', MI5, which already had a file on 'Norman John Klugmann' and had followed his movements in China and India, stepped up their monitoring and authorised Special Branch to keep an eye on him. However, once he enlisted, an extraordinary series of delays and mix-ups meant that for the next few years he was always a step ahead of his papers. In reality, a suspected communist and Comintern representative should not have been let out of the country on army work, but in May 1941 he found himself on an RASC troopship heading for Cairo with other privates, many of them clerks and fitters. The conditions on board for this eight-week journey were harsh, with poor ventilation on deck and, as he put it to Stewart later, 'nothing to do except talk'. Talking was his forte, however, particularly with a political mission in mind, and he set about converting his colleagues. As he told Stewart:

> I formed legally – I was a student and a private – a sort of boat university and we had French, German, Arabic, Geography and English lessons. We got several hundred people coming to these, and a great deal of discussion. Only in the course of the journey – June 22 – it happened that the Soviets came into the war and you can imagine there was a tremendous amount of discussion on that.
>
> We were able to orientate this boat university to discuss this under any pretext. As a result, at the end of the eight weeks, there were some very valuable contacts made with the fitters – these young chaps – about five or six.[4]

On arrival in Egypt, Klugmann and his colleagues were sent to a training depot in a desert base near the Suez Canal. Conditions here were 'very bad', and there was 'low morale' and 'discontent' among his colleagues. In July, however, he was sent to the British HQ in Cairo to work as a clerk. Over the next six months he worked in comfortable conditions; Cairo was a 'luxurious' city, food was plentiful and he had regular free afternoons. He clearly regarded his army work as only one part – his official work – and unofficially he continued to work for the wider political struggle. He made contacts with like-minded people and initiated discussions about the future and the role of the Soviet Union now it had entered the war. He put his free time to good effect by gaining a certificate in colloquial Arabic. Inevitably, this 'most peculiar private', with a double first from Cambridge and a talent for languages, soon attracted the attention of his brigadier, who after putting word round to various branches of intelligence, finally found him a place in SOE, through a colonel friend who had been a pupil at Gresham's School. Klugmann then received a visit from a major – 'to the excitement of the lads' – who:

> went through the usual rigmarole that they have for recruiting for Special organisations – 'would you jump out of an aeroplane with a parachute or go in a submarine, sign a blank cheque; have you any dependants?'. I said yes to all the questions. And without any check of dossier as far as I could plainly see I was posted as a private to this intelligence organisation.

That was how he found himself in the Special Operations Executive, the organisation committed to sabotage behind enemy lines, or, as he described it to Stewart, the 'organisation of the British Fifth Column'.[5] When MI5 finally caught up with his whereabouts, they sent a letter to Cairo instructing further observation. The letter never arrived, and so not only had MI5 allowed someone they had first noticed in 1934 to leave the country, but crucially were unable to prevent his entry into SOE, in which he was to have access to sensitive 'top secret' military intelligence.

SOE recruited Klugmann on the strength of his intellectual qualities and his talent for languages – and apparently without any knowledge of his communist convictions, though his left-wing views were never a secret. To his interviewers he gave a selective view of his work for the RME in Paris where, in addition to postgraduate research, he had been gaining 'considerable experience organizing and lecturing [...] as secretary of the international Student Association'.[6] Procedurally, in January 1942 SOE asked for clearance from MI5 to appoint Klugmann. MI5's warning that he should not be employed on secret work was considered but rejected by SOE on the grounds that his abilities were continuing to impress and that his knowledge of the politics of the Balkans would be invaluable. In February 1942 Klugmann was sent as a private to look after the secret foreign agents and, after impressing in this role, he was given an emergency commission. By August 1942 Klugmann's friend Gabriel Carritt was able to tell his brother Michael, then a Communist Party organiser in Yorkshire, that 'James has jumped from the lowest clerk to Lieutenant. They just couldn't get on without him, as he was the only one who could make himself understood to the native masses.'[7]

Klugmann had been put in the section dealing with Yugoslavia, under German control since April 1941. Here, his knowledge of Serbo-Croat and experience of dealing with Yugoslav students was put to good use.[8]

I used to have to prepare the Yugoslavs, teach them their codes, get their equipment ready, take them for the parachute course and go with them – fly over Yugoslavia, and push them out of the hole. Push them out if they didn't want to.[9]

From his time in the RME, Klugmann had good contacts in the Yugoslav Communist Party, and had regarded its student section as 'the strongest Party influence in the world even including Moscow'.[10] Its leader, Lolo Ribar, had become a close comrade to whom, over the next couple of years, 'through some liberal and friendly offices in my organisation, whom we infiltrated to Tito's Headquarters, I was able to send personal messages'.[11]

There was now a growing tension between MI5 in London and his SOE superiors who held him in high esteem, recommending his rapid promotion from private to lieutenant, captain and finally major. SOE robustly defended him and even recognised the value of having someone who was sympathetic to communist views. Brigadier 'Bolo' Keble, chief of staff at SOE Cairo, despite his conservative politics, described Klugmann in a reply to MI5 in January 1943 as:

> thoroughly reliable, most painstaking, hard-working, absolutely trustworthy, loyal and secure. We are not really interested in Klugmann's politics [...] and any Communist tendencies he may have had, he would appear to have grown out of [...] In any case, are we to stamp on Communism when probably our largest ally is a nation composed of nothing but Communists?[12]

Through his contact with Ribar and others, and in what he called his 'concerted political work', Klugmann certainly played an important part in moving the SOE strategy away from support for the Royalist General Mihailović's Chetniks in favour of Marshal Tito's left-wing Partisans. His role was to select agents for missions and decide how arms and other resources were to be distributed, as well as monitoring incoming intelligence. Some historians have claimed that it was Klugmann's manipulation of reports and deliberate subversion of agents which was responsible for the shift in policy. However, while he admitted to giving a more favourable interpretation of the Partisans' strengths, the situation was more complicated than that. First, policy decisions over whether to support Tito were taken by higher government bodies than SOE. Secondly, Klugmann's objectives as a communist happened to coincide at this particular moment with the strategy of the Allies. Indeed, as Roderick Bailey, the intelligence expert, has pointed out, 'the fact that he managed to join and stay for so long inside it reflects well on his compatibility with SOE's needs and unique line of work'.[13]

It was a visit by Winston Churchill himself in January 1943 which proved crucial to the change in policy. Up until that point, SOE had been supporting Draza Mihailović's Chetniks, the Royalist Nationalists and the first of the resistance groups to be formed, which had repeatedly clashed with the left-wing Partisans of Marshal Josip Broz 'Tito', and had been suspected of collaboration with Nazi forces. Now, German intelligence reports intercepted by British intelligence had confirmed that Partisan positions in Yugoslavia were strong while the Chetniks in some locations were found to be collaborating with Germans.

Churchill's arrival enabled Bolo Keble, who had by now established an unusual friendship with Klugmann (even reportedly bundling him into a lavatory on one occasion to avoid a security check), and Captain William Deakin, the newly arrived SOE intelligence officer and friend of the British Prime Minister, to make the case that the deputy head of SOE Yugoslavia had been making. Klugmann had a crucial role. He knew Tito from before the war and had the trust of the communist Partisans. Tito, for his part, also needed to trust Churchill and it is likely that Klugmann was a key figure in these meetings, in the Partisan mountains of Yugoslavia as well as in the Cairo offices.

Churchill, who had also received favourable reports on the relative superiority of the Partisans in Ultra decrypts from Bletchley Park, was won over and from this point gave support to Tito, a decision which caused much debate at SOE, in the BBC and subsequently among historians. By the end of 1943, following a mission to Yugoslavia by his 'personal liaison officer', Fitzroy Maclean, 'to find out who was killing the most Germans',[14] Churchill became further convinced that exclusive support for Tito was the best strategy in harming Nazi forces.

Klugmann's influence in making the Partisan case owed much to his teaching skills, his intellect and his political acumen. In his 'boat university' he had earned the nickname 'The Prof' from the unofficial 'language' classes he organised on fascism, the causes of war and the case for socialism. Once in Cairo, according to Basil Davidson, his immediate head of SOE Yugoslavia, he was the centre of attention and would give lectures in a villa by Mena House, an old palace near the Great Pyramid of Giza. His audience was mainly Yugoslav (Croatian) miners who had emigrated to Canada and were now being recruited by SOE for parachute missions to establish Allied support in their former homelands. They had been recruited by Basil Davidson with the help of the Canadian communist leadership, and their revolutionary politics meant they would only take advice from Klugmann. According to Davidson, the big political changes from the end of 1942 at SOE could have been called the 'Klugmann period'.[15] It was his finest hour.

In the villa by Mena House, he combined stirring political lectures with practical instructions to the Canadian-Yugoslav miners as they awaited their mission. According to Davidson, at the critical moment in the lecture Klugmann would pause

> and consider his audience with an especially owlish stare, meanwhile raising his right hand and extending the well-known index finger until it pointed, slowly and deliberately, straight ahead. Nobody in that stubbornly argumentative gathering was ever heard to speak at this juncture. They watched that elevating finger; I watched it myself [...] Suddenly the pointing finger stabbed forward, transfixing the dilemma, the classical dilemma, while the left hand and arm swept up and round and down again, enclosing in sorrow not in anger all those revealed to be upon its horns.
>
> 'You see, don't you? If we refuse to help the Left in Europe, that leaves us with no resistance worth helping. But if we do help the Left, what about our dearly beloved kings and governments in exile?'

Davidson went on:

> Clasping his hands together with the cigarette between his lips, he demanded greater mental effort: 'No, you've got to see beyond that, haven't you? You've got to see that this war has become more than a war against something, against fascism. It's become a war for something, for something much bigger. For national liberation, people's liberation, colonial liberation'.[16]

For the Canadian-Yugoslavs it was dangerous work; they were asked to go into very difficult situations, with many killed as a result. Klugmann's own work, according to Michael Barratt Brown, one of his SOE colleagues, 'was very brave', even if he himself was not engaged on assignments. He had to brief them and convince them of the importance of the work, knowing many of them would not return.

His bravery, according to Barratt Brown, was also evident in the work he was doing making the case for the Partisans in a divided SOE office. Some of his opponents there knew his communist allegiances and tried to make things difficult: 'He was brave because he stuck his neck out when he was trying to defend Tito against all sorts of criticism. He was behaving very bravely. He was in danger of being sacked. James went on fighting.'[17]

During late 1942, Klugmann's political justification for allying with Tito's Partisans might have seemed unpalatable to the conservative ranks of SOE. Following Churchill's visit in January 1943, however, he could claim his argument had been vindicated. He was supported by Bill Deakin, Basil Davidson and others, but it was his devotion to his work that won him friends as much as his sophisticated political analysis of the situation. He was an experienced strategist and propagandist and had charm and guile, with a proven record in winning converts, notably among privileged people of liberal opinion. He thrived in this environment, benefiting from the fact that SOE had recruited other intellectuals so that 'amongst the people I found myself were some first class contacts'.[18] This political work did involve undermining Mihailović and selective use of material at his disposal but, as John Earle makes clear, this was not unusual: 'In everyday office work Klugmann presumably selected and manipulated material in favour of one side and against the other. What bureaucrat, to a certain degree, does not?'[19]

On his own admission to Stewart, Klugmann's first 'political aim' was to promote the interests of the Partisans, to win sympathy for their cause among colleagues in the SOE office and ultimately to win formal recognition for their campaign, at the expense of Mihailović's troops. His next political objective was to get agents to the Partisans. As an experienced talent spotter, his control of the selection of agents was important in the overall strategy. Next, he had to get the agents into Serbia, a Chetnik power base. Of course, not all agents were communists or left leaning. John Earle was not a Marxist but was impressed by the attention to detail in Klugmann's briefing, which he thought 'could have come straight out of a boy's adventure book'. For his operation, code-named 'Demagogue', Earle would be dropped to the Partisan HQ in Serbia, in a hilly district just outside Belgrade. Earle was given street plans, a set of handkerchiefs with a map of the Balkans, and ten gold napoleons 'to gird round my waist and thus bribe my way out of any unforeseen situation'.

Above all, I was instructed to seek out Kika, and attach myself to her. She was said to be the woman commander of the Kosmaj Odred, a small Partisan detachment named after a 628 metre hill in the Samadija and believed to be about 300 strong. She was reputed to be a bold and daring amazon; whether she was also beautiful was not the sort of detail to interest Klugmann.[20]

The final element was to gather data and (as Klugmann put it) 'skew' intelligence reports to show that the Partisans were in the front line against the enemy while the Chetniks were making little progress. Klugmann later admitted to Stewart that he used intelligence which supported the policy of the former and either suppressed other intelligence more sympathetic to the Chetniks or produced intelligence detrimental to their cause. He ensured that the best agents were sent to Partisan areas and less able ones to Chetnik locations. After SOE moved to Bari at the end of 1943, Klugmann, along with other 'pro-Partisan' colleagues, 'acted as a sieve' in order to distribute information that was beneficial to the Partisans.

This 'concerted political work' was driven by his communist beliefs, helped enormously by his political experience. He clearly felt his work was some kind of continuation of what he had been doing in Paris: galvanising broad support to defeat fascism while at the same time keeping an alternative future on the horizon. This work was much valued by his Party, as it was no doubt by the Comintern, the higher authority which he had served since 1935 and whose permission he sought before joining up. This, and from August 1944 his work in the United Nations Relief and Rehabilitation Administration (UNRRA), where he was assistant to the Soviet head of section in Belgrade, was to lead to his rapid promotion to the Party leadership on his return in 1946.

Despite MI5's protestations, his objectives coincided with the military ambitions of the Allies at a certain stage, a situation which did not alarm his SOE superiors. The only scare he encountered along the way was in the immediate aftermath of the arrest of Dave Springhall, the communist apparatchik who had helped set him on his way as a communist student leader. 'Springie' was convicted in 1943 after it was found he had obtained classified material on anti-radar devices from an Air Ministry official and passed it on to the Russians. Following Springhall's trial it was discovered that he had obtained classified material from Captain Ormond Uren, another communist in SOE. Both he and Uren were sent to prison. As a result of these trials Klugmann was given a four-hour interview at the SOE offices. The main line of attack was his supposed 'double loyalty' to the Russians and the British. 'They were trying to catch you', he told Stewart. Such a claim was 'ridiculous', he went on. 'We're supporting the Partisans and the Russians and there is no question of divided loyalties.'[21]

That was not the view of MI5, however, after their microphones picked up his conversation with Bob Stewart. Nor was it the opinion of some of his former SOE colleagues.

6 James Klugmann and Bernard Floud arrive in China on the World Student Association delegation

7 Speaking at a student rally in China

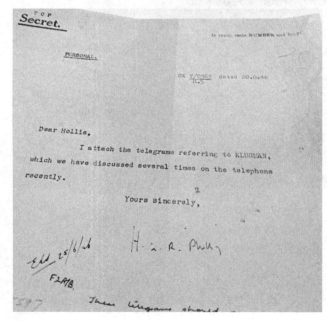

8 Kim Philby's memo to Roger Hollis after MI5 were alerted to Klugmann's SOE activities

9 A communist at war

12

Comrade or Conspirator?

Klugmann's admission that he manipulated reports to give more favourable impressions of Partisan strength has been the basis for the later claims that he was acting on behalf of Soviet interests. In 1999, the Crown Prince of Yugoslavia, in an interview with the historian Hugh Thomas in the *Spectator*, described Klugmann as the 'determining influence' in winning over Winston Churchill and Allied support for Marshal Tito's communist Partisans. According to him, Klugmann's role was crucial in 'ensuring pro-Tito' reports and by implying that Mihailović's Chetniks were involved in German collaboration. In the ensuing discussion in the *Spectator* former SOE officers and historians debated Klugmann's role. Richard Lamb claimed that Klugmann had 'bamboozled' SOE leaders as well as Churchill and others in doctoring reports and manipulating information, omitting evidence of notable Chetnik resistance and sending the best agents to Tito. Moreover, it was implied that this was done on the orders of Moscow to aid the Soviet cause.[1]

Many of these arguments were shaped and constrained by the remnants of the Cold War and its aftermath and some revisionist accounts of that period. However, as early as the end of 1943, George Orwell, in a proposed preface to his book *Animal Farm* entitled 'The Freedom of the Press', commented on what he saw as misleading pro-Soviet reports in the British press.

A particularly glaring case was that of Colonel Mihajlovic, the Jugoslav Chetnik leader. The Russians, who had their own Jugoslav protégé in Marshal Tito, accused Mihajlovic of collaborating with the Germans. This accusation was promptly taken up by the British press: Mihajlovic's supporters were given no chance of answering it, and facts contradicting it were simply kept out of print. In July of 1943 the Germans offered a reward of 100,000 gold crowns for the capture of Tito, and a similar reward for the capture of Mihajlovic. The British press 'splashed' the reward for Tito, but only one paper mentioned (in small print) the reward for Mihajlovic; and the charges of collaborating with the Germans continued.[2]

Some of those who served with the Chetniks in SOE would have endorsed Orwell's concerns. Major Archie Jack, for example, worked as a sabotage officer with the Chetniks and was involved in operations against German forces which he later claimed were either ignored by SOE and BBC reports or wrongly attributed to the Partisans. He argued that the SOE hierarchy went along with all Tito's main arguments. Rejecting claims that Mihailović was a traitor or collaborator, he maintained that the Chetniks were the strongest resistance movement throughout 1943, but that someone at SOE had 'cooked the books' and was sending out fake reports. He and Jasper Rootham, a former private secretary to Neville Chamberlain who was also serving with Mihailović forces, visited the SOE offices in Bari and were astonished to find a wall map of the relative resistance forces dominated by the red Partisan pins in areas they knew to be Chetnik strongholds. Rootham 'lost his temper and swept the pins to the floor'. Archie Jack then invited Klugmann, whom he remembered as a contemporary of his at The Hall prep school, to his and Rootham's hotel room to 'explain this extraordinary situation' in the company of 'half a dozen' of his friends. Klugmann, he says, offered only 'lame excuses' that there were 'policy changes at a higher level', and 'overworked personnel', which he found 'terribly unconvincing'. He had no idea that Klugmann was a communist, or 'a Soviet mole', as he put it. He also blamed the alliance of Keble, Deakin and Fitzroy Maclean and the 'extremely left wing' Basil Davidson.[3]

Following the release of SOE intelligence documents, others have pointed to a more conspiratorial role played by Klugmann. David Martin in *The Web of Disinformation* holds him responsible for a political shift of historic proportions for the future of Yugoslavia. Martin makes connections between Klugmann's links to the Cambridge spy circle in explaining his role in manipulating material, which, he argues, had a wide-ranging impact on not only the policy of the Foreign Office, but BBC reports and even MI6 strategy.[4]

In his book *The Rape of Serbia*, the former SOE officer Michael Lees, who had spent a year serving with Mihailović's Chetniks during 1943, also claimed that Churchill's decision to switch support from Mihailović to Tito was because of the communist infiltration and disinformation within the intelligence services and the actions and recommendations made by SOE officers. The pivotal role, according to Lees, was played by Klugmann, who 'was doing his utmost to paint Mihailović as a collaborator and replace him with his communist rival Tito'.[5] In one case this involved omitting information that Mihailović's Chetniks had destroyed five railway bridges, in order to dampen their impact in anti-Nazi resistance. Klugmann, according to Lees, was able to exert this influence as one in a troika of SOE leaders sympathetic to Tito, along with Davidson and Captain Bill Deakin. Lees pointed to Klugmann's role in compiling reports, making recommendations and as mentor to the Canadian-Yugoslav communists. Unlike Davidson, whom Lees regarded as complicit, and whose description of the 'Klugmann period' he interpreted as a 'eulogy', Lees has a more sinister interpretation of Klugmann's role in looking after, briefing and politically educating the 30 Yugoslav agents. 'The freedom given Klugmann, a known leading communist, to read the secret MO4 signals, to brief and debrief agents, and to wander off in the evenings holding political meetings with the Croats recruited through the Communist Party is amazing.'[6]

Lees argues that the decision to recruit the Canadian communists was the result of communist influence in the British Secret Services, SOE and the Foreign Office and maintains that this decision was crucial in the 1942–3 period in increasing the optimism of Soviet strength behind Tito. Klugmann's role, he argues, was therefore crucial in supporting the development of 'Soviet imperialism'. Klugmann, according to Lees,

> was not only an overt communist, he was also a central figure in putting together the covert communist organization that penetrated the British secret agencies and even the Foreign Service [...] He was a professional, totally dedicated and enormously hardworking. He may have been the best man the Soviets had, even including Philby, because he had no weak spots. He was outwardly charming and human, but inwardly he was a hard man.[7]

For his critics, Klugmann's deference to his Soviet masters implicated him in another tragic and controversial episode in the history of SOE, involving his friend Frank Thompson. Thompson, the elder brother of Edward (with whom Klugmann would clash in 1956), was drawn to communism while a student at Oxford, where he was recruited to the Communist Party in 1939 by Iris Murdoch. Like Klugmann he was a brilliant linguist. When he arrived in Cairo in January 1943 the two men would have had much to talk about on the terrace at Shepheard's Hotel – Christopher Caudwell's 'Studies in a Dying Culture' among common interests. They were both committed to the politics of the Popular Front. Thompson had experienced the Oxford by-election when Sandy Lindsay, Master of Balliol, drew support from dissident conservatives, liberals and communists in his failed attempt to defeat the Chamberlain candidate

Quintin Hogg. While they both had faith in the Partisan struggle, Klugmann, the older, was the more politically experienced, and it is likely he became a mentor to his young friend, though Thompson, as his biographer Conradi put it, was the 'least doctrinaire of Communists'.[8]

Thompson agreed to lead a mission code-named 'Claridges' to Bulgaria in January 1944, which would provide a base for an earlier mission, 'Mulligatawny', headed by Mostyn Davies. The purpose was to establish links with Partisan groups on the ground, bring down weapons and supplies and provide detailed reports on operations. This was new territory for SOE, which did not have a Bulgarian expert: it was regarded as a mere 'sub-set of the Yugoslav' brief.[9] Nor were the Bulgarian Partisans keen on SOE dropping agents. Hugh Seton-Watson, a former schoolfriend of Thompson, was one of the most well-informed SOE officers on the Bulgarian situation and he and Klugmann clearly felt that a similar strategy to that of Yugoslavia was possible.

According to Stowers Johnson,

Klugman [sic] was deeply interested in events in Bulgaria. This was new ground and dangerous [...] Bulgaria was a country which offered the same first-in-the-field appeal to the adventurer and the ideological type, of which Frank Thompson was a combination.[10]

However, Bulgaria was in a very different situation from Yugoslavia: the Partisans were nowhere near as well organised and, crucially, unlike Yugoslavia there was no occupying force. As a result the plan was 'ill-conceived and ill executed'.[11] After arriving in Dobro Polje in Serbia in January 1944, Thompson and his mission spent the next few months evading Bulgarian and Royalist troops, losing comrades, including Mostyn Davies. Thompson also lost contact with Klugmann and other colleagues in SOE – who had moved offices from Cairo to Bari, Italy, during this time – because of a mix-up whereby the new wireless operator and codebooks were dispatched to different places. When Thompson did finally get messages through, he had little joy in receiving requested supplies because of the number of SOE missions operating at the time. Eventually, in May, before receiving any confirmation from SOE, he and the Bulgarian Partisans, after many near misses, were finally captured. After several interrogations, he was executed on 10 June in the village of Litakovo, near Sofia. Before his death he had made a heroic speech of defiance and led his other officers, fists raised, on their final journey.

In 1981 Thompson's younger brother Edward, by now a leading social historian, gave a series of lectures questioning the politics surrounding that mission. He noted the differences between the Comintern's view and that of communist Partisans on the ground, as well as the position of the Allies. He also pointed to the very different representations of this mission in Cold War ideology, where at different times Frank Thompson and his colleagues were seen as 'imperialist allies' or 'Stalin stooges'.[12]

Although Thompson exonerated Klugmann from any culpability in his brother's death, there has been much discussion over the reasons for the mission failing so badly. Some attribute it to the different tactical interests of the Comintern and the Western Allies as they attempted to win over the Bulgarian Royalists, resulting in the abandonment of the mission. Others, like Lees, argue that it was 'evidence of the freedom enjoyed by Klugmann, Seton-Watson and others to operate their own private policies'.[13] Kenneth Sinclair-Loutit, Klugmann's former Cambridge recruit, who had become disillusioned with the CPGB while serving in a medical unit in the Spanish Civil War and would meet Klugmann again in UNRRA, speculated in his memoirs that there may have been a more sinister role played by Klugmann, in sabotaging communications on the orders of Moscow. However, there is no evidence or apparent motive to support it.[14]

Klugmann himself must have been concerned about the fate of his younger comrade during the spring months of 1944, and he did not have the same expertise and insight on the Partisan strength in Bulgaria to match his knowledge of the missions in Yugoslavia The movement of SOE offices did not help communications, with lack of aid to the mission at crucial moments. Losing Thompson, a few years after Cornford and Guest had died in Spain, came as a further blow.

Yet there has been no evidence that Klugmann was implicated in some political conspiracy or sacrificed Thompson out of political dogma. Moreover, his political support for the Partisans in preference to the Chetniks seems to concur with the testimonies of many former SOE officers who maintained that support for Tito's Partisans was justified on the grounds of military strategy and likely success. Captain Robert Wade, SOE liaison officer with the Chetniks in Serbia, was among several former officers who questioned the military strength of Mihailović's forces.

The army of Mihajlovic was completely peasant-based and they hadn't got much discipline, whereas Tito's lot, ruthless though he was, they behaved like the Brigade of Guards by comparison. I mean. No drilling, but when they were told to keep their distance they kept their distance and they were properly led and you could see the difference.[15]

Captain Charles Hargreaves, another SOE officer working with the Chetniks, recalled similar experiences:

After one had been living with them for some time, you did notice that they were often very depressed because, so far as I could see, their main intention was to secure control of the country after the war. They were more interested in that really, than in fighting the Germans.[16]

He continued: 'Often when one went into a village or a town the local commander would get all the people together and address them against the partisans much more than against the Germans.'[17]

Basil Davidson recalled that Chetniks had collaborated with the Germans, and he came across 'commanding officers [who] were determined not to risk lives against the Germans'. He also thought it 'extremely offensive' and 'absolute rubbish' to suggest there was a 'communist plot' in SOE, 'however subversive Klugmann might have been'. In fact everyone in the office knew that Klugmann was a communist – he was open about it – and it was inconceivable that the policy of the British Army could be decided by his actions alone. According to Davidson, Klugmann, whom he promoted from lieutenant to captain, 'did his duty very well and understood the situation extremely well'. He said that Brigadier Bolo Keble, who had quite different politics, 'developed an affection for James'.[18]

Klugmann's actions were consistent with his ideological commitment to communism. After all, since Cambridge his communism had incorporated the Popular Front strategy, with the aim of establishing the broadest possible coalition against fascism. This had been evident from the 1930s and was crucial to him remaining a communist. It was what drove his work in Paris in support of the Republican side in the Spanish Civil War and which enabled him to form a close working relationship with colleagues in SOE. It is clear from his lectures at Mena House that he was focused on a future objective, but this did not take away the importance of the immediate tactical battles on the ground. In this regard, Tito's forces were the stronger and therefore the military strategy combined with the political strategy of the Popular Front, as it did in many other parts of Europe. It also meant working with the Soviet Union at this particular moment, not because of covert operations, but because of the common objective of defeating fascism.

For these reasons we can exonerate Klugmann from claims that he acted as a Soviet agent and conspirator who subverted the just causes of the Chetniks in shifting Churchill to support Tito. His secret Soviet links were not a deciding factor and, as Roderick Bailey has shown in his detailed research into his involvement in SOE, there were sound reasons of military strategy behind the decision to align with the Partisans.[19] As Klugmann made clear in his conversation with Bob Stewart, he did not welcome aproaches from Soviet agents as they threateneded to 'destroy' the good political work he had started. His political convictions at this moment enhanced rather than obstructed the wider Allied military strategy. Klugmann's ideological convictions included a romantic belief in what the future might hold. This romantic side no doubt contained illusions and was what others depicted as two sides to his personality: being 'hard' inside, while 'warm' and 'engaging' on the outside.

Among those who viewed Klugmann in this way was Evelyn Waugh, who was shocked that a British communist could get to such a senior position in the army. His friend, the writer Anthony Powell, who also worked in military intelligence during the war, had told Waugh that the decision of the Allies to shift support from Mihailović to Tito was based on 'dubiously reliable advice [...] I have myself read reports circulated on the situation applauding the Yugoslav Communist irregulars in a tone more suitable to an adventure story in the *Boy's Own Paper* than a sober appreciation of what was happening.'[20]

Waugh had been recruited to SOE by Randolph Churchill in June 1944 and they were both briefed by Klugmann in Bari, before embarking on their liaison mission on the Croatian island of Vis, where Tito had temporarily moved his HQ. Michael Barratt Brown remembers Klugmann being put out that the whisky supply he had sent to Randolph had fallen from the parachute and eluded him.[21] The plane carrying Waugh and Churchill crash-landed and they had to recuperate in a former brothel requisitioned by the Partisans for military convalescence. Waugh, who had the proofs of *Brideshead Revisited* with him, was concerned at the treatment of the Catholic Church and its likely future fortunes under a communist government and later made clear his reservations in a personal appeal to Klugmann, tinged with a note of sarcasm. He complained that the local Catholic seminary had been closed down as the seminarists were all enlisted for military service by the Partisans. He added: 'If it is a piece of private initiative (by the garrison commander) a word from the Archbishop of Zagreb – at whose well-being we all rejoice – to his chum Broz might help.'[22] Waugh later compiled a report entitled *Church and State in Liberated Croatia*, which was suppressed by the Foreign Office, keen to placate Tito.

However, he did not forget what he saw as Klugmann's duplicity in promoting Tito, which he attributed to his misguided romantic illusions and sinister manipulation of British intelligence. Klugmann's lasting impression on Waugh is apparent in two of his later books.[23] In the last novel of his war trilogy, *Unconditional Surrender*, the character Joe Cattermole, the 'Hazardous Offensive Operations' officer responsible for briefing agents, was loosely based on Klugmann. Cattermole, like Klugmann, was an amiable donnish figure who had become utterly committed to communism and who worked tirelessly for the Partisan cause. According to his commanding officer,

> Joe's a queer fellow, some sort of professor in civil life [...] But he works like the devil. Takes everything off my shoulders [...] Joe likes everyone – even the Jugs. Awfully good natured fellow Joe; always ready to stand in and take extra duty.[24]

In Bari, Joe Cattermole had the role of briefing Guy Crouchback, based on Waugh himself, before he was dropped on a mission into Croatia. Cattermole gave him a 20-minute 'exposition', identifying 'liberated areas', routes taken by Partisan brigades and delivered in his 'precise donnish phrases'.

> Until quite lately those men in Cairo were sending arms to Mihajlovic to be used against our own people. We're doing a little better now. There's a trickle of supplies, but it isn't easy to arrange drops for forces on the move. And the Russians have at last sent in a mission – headed by a general. You can have no idea, until you've seen them, what that will mean to the partisans. It's something I have to explain to all our liaison officers. The Jugoslavs accept us as allies but they look on the Russians as leaders.[25]

Waugh's narrator sums up the Cattermole-Klugmann political trajectory:

> When major Cattermole spoke of the enemy he did so with the impersonal, professional hostility with which a surgeon might regard a malignant, operable growth; when he spoke of his comrades in arms it was something keener than

loyalty, equally impersonal, a counterfeit almost of mystical love as portrayed by the sensual artists of the high baroque.[26]

Cattermole's commanding officer, rather like Bolo Keble, had the utmost respect for his work, while disagreeing with his political analysis, as he explained to Guy Crouchback:

Joe Cattermole's a first class chap. He doesn't tell anyone, but he did absolutely splendidly over there. The Jugs love him and they don't love many of us. And Joe loves the Jugs, which is something more unusual still. But you have to take what he says with a grain of salt.[27]

Waugh's view of a more sinister side to Klugmann's politics is evident in his earlier short dystopian satire on socialism, *Love Among the Ruins*, which he called a 'romance of the near future'. Clara, Waugh's ballerina heroine, a beautiful and promising dancer, was subject to the 'Klugmann Operation' – effectively sterilisation – to enable her to fulfil her bright future as a dancer without the burden of childbirth. Inevitably, 'performing a Klugmann' has risks, goes wrong ('they had two or three cases at Cambridge') and instead of fulfilling her future dreams Clara ends up with a long, golden beard.[28] Written at the height of the Cold War, and based on his experiences with Klugmann in Yugoslavia, this was Waugh's interpretation of what happens when you follow the prescriptions of a communist intellectual.

Waugh's concerns would not have worried Klugmann – who regarded him as 'insufferable'[29] – when he returned to London in August 1945 for the first time in four years. He had reached the peak of his influence and his career as a leading communist intellectual was about to take off. By this time he had left SOE and since the liberation of Yugoslavia that spring had been working for the UNRRA mission in Belgrade. This gave him much insight into the work that was being done on the ground at the beginning of the reconstruction of the country. It also brought him into closer contact with both Yugoslav and Russian communists and he felt a 'good bit freer' as special assistant to the chief of the UNRRA Yugoslav mission than in his previous role.[30] Much of his work at UNRRA was to help ensure Belgrade had a fair allocation of food and other resources. He told Stewart it was a 'fight' to get adequate supplies to Belgrade as more was going to Greece. During this work, he was able to build up a picture of the transformation taking place throughout the country, as well as the political changes under Tito. He had more opportunity to meet fellow communists and sympathisers in UNRRA (which included Dr Eleanor Singer, a communist doctor friend from Hampstead) and he held weekly meetings of the group, which found him in the familiar role of coordinator and educator. His Cambridge recruit, Kenneth Sinclair-Loutit, however, was by now 'shaky' and unreliable, in Klugmann's estimation.[31]

Although he was officially in London on an UNRRA mission, he made sure he found time to visit King Street and provide a political debriefing of his work to the Party leadership. It was this King Street conversation with Bob Stewart, when he explained his actions in SOE, admitted being involved in earlier espionage work and indicated that he had been further approached by Soviet intelligence while in UNRRA, that set alarm bells ringing at MI5, which immediately put him under close observation. Klugmann made it clear during his visit that he was sounding out the Party leadership over a future role with the Party. Emile Burns, a leading CPGB intellectual, had already told Maurice Cornforth that the Party leadership had been considering Klugmann's future career prospects. Burns had hoped that in his UNRRA role Klugmann would expand his contacts with Eastern European communist leaders. They hoped that, on his permanent return, he would take on the task of improving the circulation and influence of *World News and Views*, which they planned to relaunch on the back of the new interest in international affairs. Cornforth thought him ideal for the role. 'The only snag was that James had become such a "swell" that if a Labour government got in he might be offered a job in the foreign office.' They both concluded that if such an offer was made he should accept it.[32]

Normally Klugmann would stay with his mother on his visits to London, but on this official UNRRA visit he put up at the Hyde Park Hotel. MI5 tapped his phone conversations and had put a tail on him as he travelled between the hotel, UNRRA offices in Portland Place and the ABC Restaurant off Regent Street, and on his visits to the Communist Party offices in King Street. His mother, whose phone was also tapped, told his close friend Margot Heinemann, who had not seen him since before the war, that her son 'was most elusive'. Heinemann, who made several attempts to meet Klugmann during this time, told Tamara Rust that he was over on a 'short stay', on an 'hour to hour basis', 'and he never knows when he is going to have time' to meet. For Heinemann, it all sounded 'frightfully interesting and exciting'.

During this trip Klugmann visited Michael Carritt, with whom he would have discussed the tragic death of their mutual friend Frank Thompson; he also went to Hugh and Joan Faulkner's house, a short distance from his mother's in Belsize

Park Gardens, where he had kept a suitcase containing details of his Communist Party contacts and materials. Hugh Faulkner was working in a hospital in Bari, along with several Yugoslav Partisans, and was one of Klugmann's communist friends in the forces. 'He is smashing', Joan Faulkner described Klugmann to Margot Jefferies over the phone. 'Came in like a whirlwind and dashed to my cupboard, where his case has been for about four years, dished it out and wanted to contact all sorts of people.'[33]

After Klugmann's disclosures to Stewart on 8 August, David Petrie, director of MI5, informed MI6, SOE, the War Office and the Foreign Office of Klugmann's 'most unforgiveable offence'.[34] As well as following him each time he left the Hyde Park Hotel, MI5 also authorised a break-in at the Faulkner home to locate his suitcase and found a locked card index in Joan Faulkner's bedroom. There were further implications: after Klugmann's conversation with Stewart, Anthony Blunt, then working at MI5, who heard about the conversation involving his former pupil, alerted Moscow to the news that King Street had hidden microphones.[35] For Klugmann, the conflict of loyalties between his commitment to the Communist Party, his intellectual integrity and increasing pressure from Moscow was only just beginning.

13

Great Expectations

James Klugmann arrived back in Britain from UNRRA in 1946 full of optimism and expectation that a new role in the Communist Party leadership awaited him. This was not mere personal ambition on his part. His work in SOE had made an important contribution to the war effort and to his superiors shown the Party in a good light. His 'concerted political work', in making the case for Tito and channelling support for his Partisans, was seen as an exemplary demonstration of what communist leaders could achieve as well as a justification for the Party's strategy. His work with UNRRA, however, was also significant, enabling him to appreciate the situation on the ground, as well as gaining a wider appraisal of the international situation and the immediate outlook for Eastern Europe. He had proven his worth as an international student leader, and as a notable political organiser and propagandist; he had an exceptional grasp of languages, and through his increasing number of international contacts it was clear that he could be of much value to the Communist Party leadership. The Party was clearly aware that he was someone who had built a good reputation and would be in demand; the possibility of a role in the new Labour government – a destination for some of the fellow student leaders he had known in RME, like Michael Young – was briefly mooted. However, his commitment to the Communist Party was by now irreversible.

A new political world was emerging which would test to the limit his loyalties as a communist intellectual. From being wartime ally, the Soviet Union was now the perceived enemy of the West. In his famous speech in the company of President Harry Truman in Missouri, in March 1946, Winston Churchill, Tito's former ally, gave his prophetic warning: 'From Stettin in the Baltic to Trieste in the Adriatic, an iron curtain has descended across the continent.'

One inevitable consequence of the growth of the Cold War which followed was the British Security Services' renewed interest in the Communist Party leadership. After becoming aware of his SOE activities, which they had on record and had been the basis for a major internal inquiry, MI5 increased their surveillance of 'our clever and dangerous young friend James Klugmann'.[1] He was the first of the Cambridge communists recruited by Soviet intelligence to come under serious suspicion. His admission to Stewart that he had worked for Soviet intelligence before the war, had been approached by Soviet agents while working for UNRRA and that he would reluctantly carry out further work again if necessary (as long as it had been authorised) might have been expected to lead to further interrogation by British Security Services. In fact, MI5 decided instead to keep him under close surveillance. It is likely that Kim Philby, by now head of counter-espionage at MI6, who had had several phone conversations with MI5's Roger Hollis in June 1946 about the Klugmann case, acted to protect him from further inquiry.[2]

From his return to Britain on 20 July 1946 until the early 1950s – that is, the peak years of the Cold War – Klugmann was the subject of regular surveillance. This amounted to MI5 obtaining a Home Office warrant to open mail sent to his home address, phone checks and transcripts of incoming and outgoing calls at the Party HQ in King Street and copying letters and correspondence. Occasionally, at particular times, notably when he was meeting Eastern European representatives of embassies or addressing Party meetings on what were considered important international questions, this included observing and trailing his movements, with Special Branch officers secretly attending meetings and providing detailed reports of his talks. They saw him as 'an experienced and able conspirator'[3] with a 'bad security record' who was on a rapid rise to the top of the Party leadership on the back of his expertise on questions of international politics and foreign affairs; this interest intensified when it became clear he was regarded as a Party expert on Eastern Europe. There was regular correspondence on Klugmann's activities between the offices of Roger Hollis at MI5 and MI6's Colonel Valentine Vivian (vice-chief) and Sir Stewart Menzies, head of MI6 ('C'), throughout the late 1940s and into the early 1950s. In addition, MI5 also enlisted the help of some ex-SOE colleagues of Klugmann, who encountered him at SOE Old Comrades' Club or who met him for lunch, though MI6 had some reservations about how far this could be taken:

> After a certain amount of uncomfortable thought we have decided that it would be rather tricky to warn our ex-SOE officers about him or attempt to ascertain which of our purely SIS [Secret Intelligence Service – MI6] officers had come across him in the Middle East. 'C' has, however, asked me to enlist your assistance in bringing to notice any connection with any of our officers that may come your way.[4]

They were concerned to know which SIS officers had come across him in Cairo and, for this reason, Kim Philby, Klugmann's old Cambridge comrade, was kept in the loop.

The close interest of British intelligence helps provide further insight into his daily routines, Party friendships, moral dilemmas, intellectual interests and the shifts in his political allegiances as the Cold War unfolded. On his immediate arrival back in Britain, Klugmann went back to his mother's house in Belsize Park Gardens, but ten days later moved in with his sister and brother-in-law to 61 Talbot Road, Highgate, which Kitty had bought for £2,100, taking on sitting (non-communist) tenants on the ground floor, making the first floor their own living quarters, with James on the second floor. He would live with Kitty and Maurice for almost two decades. Here, over the next few years, he settled into a life dominated by the Party, writing for its publications, speaking at its schools and meetings, presenting reports for its committees. It was a commitment that involved at times great stress, notably in the late 1940s and early 1950s, when the demands imposed on him proved damning for his health, political judgements and intellectual credibility.

His first job with the Party on his return was on *World News and Views*, its weekly journal, where he contributed a regular European news page; more widely, the Party leadership promoted him as an expert on Yugoslavia, while making him a candidate for several Party committees. His first task, however, was to put together his own analysis of the current situation in Yugoslavia, based on his 15 months there with the UNRRA commission between April 1945 and July 1946. His 'Notes on Yugoslavia' was circulated amongst Party leaders (and also found its way, via MI5 to Kim Philby at MI6). He described this, rather modestly, as 'some rough impressions on recent developments in that country', rather than a 'co-ordinated survey of the Yugoslav Resistance Movement [or] of the formation and achievements of the [...] People's Republic of Yugoslavia'. Nevertheless, his view on what was taking place was clear.

> The traveller who passes today by car from Yugoslav territory on the eastern side of the Churchillian curtain to Trieste on the western side, with its occupying British and American forces, will feel that he is passing from a real democracy, from a free land of the free peoples of Yugoslavia to a zone of oppression, foreign occupation, where the most rudimentary democracy is denied.

On the Yugoslav side, he reported, 'peasants feel they own and administer the villages in which they live'. The origins of this 'new democracy' were to be found in the war with

[the] new state, the new social advances, and the new cultural developments [...] based on the achievements of the partisan army, and the National Liberation Movement, which, under the inspiration of the Yugoslav Communist Party accomplished so much in the course of the war.

For Klugmann the social background of the new leaders was testament to the genuinely democratic and grassroots nature of the new leadership, including 'Marshal of the Yugoslav army, head of the Yugoslav government Josef Broz-Tito, [who] was a Zagreb metal-worker'.[5]

'The visitor to Yugoslavia', he reported to the CPGB leaders, 'sees everywhere the signs of reconstruction. Everywhere you go people are building, digging, cleaning and clearing.' He had witnessed the first state elections in November 1945, held within six months of the liberation, which he regarded as a major triumph for democracy; it was an election which involved more than twice the number of voters of any previous election, with every party having the right to submit candidates. Around 90 per cent of those entitled to vote did so, voting overwhelmingly (by 90 per cent) for National Liberation Front candidates. The new constitution incorporated equal rights, people's assemblies and committees, with the duty of all citizens to work according to their skills. The constitution, he argued, was a historical document which 'should be studied by all communists and progressive people'.

Klugmann ends his 'Notes on Yugoslavia' with suggested tasks for his Party:

I consider that the CPGB has certain deep responsibilities to our comrades in Yugoslavia and to the Yugoslav people of which the most essential are:

To popularise the story of the Yugoslav movement of resistance to fascist aggression and of the development and achievements of the new democracy.

To refute the falsehoods spread by the reactionary press concerning the new Yugoslavia.

To make known the details of the recent Mihailovic trial and in particular to make known in Great Britain the reactionary role of British imperialism in support for the Cetniks and émigré government against the Partisans at the beginning of the war which were made known in the course of the trial.[6]

He also said that the Party should 'fight for economic aid'.

Excitement over developments in Yugoslavia took up much of his time during his first months back, with meetings and lunches with old SOE friends, while other contacts updated him on the latest developments. He settled into the routine of working on editions of *World News and Views* and continued to espouse the positive developments there in his regular European page.

His insight on Yugoslavia was much valued, but the Party had a grander role in mind for him. This was the editorship of a new journal which would seriously engage with the changing international situation, notably the emerging 'new democracies' of Eastern Europe. The journal's particular focus was to be informative rather than agitational, with the need to present the British people with a factual corrective on developments in Eastern Europe to counter the propaganda of British and American imperialism. It would be a supplement to *World News and Views*. Initially, Klugmann was asked to use his wide international contacts, many of them made during his time in the RME or SOE, in the search for sponsors. In this task he enlisted the official help of Harry Pollitt, who wrote to Maurice Thorez, the French Communist Party leader, with a request for articles and factual material from 'specialists' who could provide informed analyses of developments in the international situation.[7]

Pollitt went on to promote Klugmann as the prospective editor of the journal, pointing out to Thorez his previous role at RME in Paris. Klugmann himself wrote a few days later to the Agit Prop Department of the PCF, explaining the Party's concern at the British Labour government's foreign policy and the difficulties in countering US propaganda about Eastern Europe.

> The reactionary press widely circulates the greatest distortions and misrepresentations of true developments in the Soviet Union, the new democracies and the colonial countries, but the progressive press has not been able adequately to explain and inform the British people of real developments in the world today.
>
> In this position in Great Britain, many people are confused and demoralised. Many do not understand the nature of the events that are taking place.[8]

Klugmann's new project brought him more contacts and status in the Party and he now directed his energies towards the international situation. He divided his time between writing articles at home at Talbot Road and meeting international contacts at King Street, Colletts, the left-wing bookshop in Charing Cross

Road, or Lawrence and Wishart, the Communist Party publishers. He remained deeply optimistic about Yugoslavia, while increasingly hostile to the US. In a closed Party meeting held in the Garibaldi restaurant in central London, prior to the Party Congress in November 1976, he echoed the view of the American Communist leader James Allen, that the US was headed for a major slump, while talking up Tito's leadership as an example of the new democracies.[9]

His enthusiasm for Yugoslavia was also a regular talking point in conversations with his friends. The 'united trades union movement in Trieste', where Yugoslav and Italian trades unionists were working together, 'really is a very big step forward', he told Margot Heinemann, 'and you know it really takes the bottom off all sorts of reactionary attitudes to that question. It's a very good thing indeed.'[10]

The Party took the new journal proposal seriously and set up new offices in Bloomsbury, under the auspices of World Books Publishers Ltd. Klugmann initially worked alongside two assistants, Peter Wright, whom he had known in Cambridge and SOE, and Alwyn Birch, with the help of a secretary, Helen Smith. Wright and Birch, along with Margot Kettle, were the directors of the company. Klugmann updated Emile Burns, head of the Party's Propaganda Department, on the progress of the journal at regular Thursday meetings, with the early expectation that it would come out monthly from spring 1947.

The new journal, which was to be called 'Changing Epoch', needed publicity and financial backing beyond what the Party could provide, and to this end Klugmann called on Tom Driberg the Tribunite MP (and friend of Guy Burgess), Gordon Schaefer of *Reynold's News*, and Aylmer Vallance of the *New Statesman* for support. He also circulated information about the journal through the Czech Friendship League, the British-Yugoslav Association and Eastern European embassies.

At this time Klugmann and his Party enjoyed a reasonable relationship with others on the Labour left, both in critical support for the new Labour government and in shared enthusiasm for Tito's Yugoslavia, exemplified by *Yugoslavia Faces the Future,* a pamphlet published by the British-Yugoslav Association, jointly authored by Klugmann, Betty Wallace, Doreen Warriner and Konni Zilliacus. This reflected the cooperation that then existed between parts of Labour's Bevanite left and the Party over Yugoslavia. This unity, and indeed, the British-Yugoslav Association itself, were not to last for much longer, however.

Despite Klugmann's efforts, it was clear that the journal was having difficulties finding a circulation and there was concern about prospective sales. At the same time Klugmann's rise in the Party meant he was much in demand as a speaker on Yugoslavia, Eastern Europe and US foreign policy, including the Marshall Plan and the Truman doctrine.[11] He gave an opening talk on 'The Problem of the USA' at the Party's International Committee meeting in July 1947, where he argued that the Party needed to be as 'thoroughly equated with the nature (internal + external) of US imperialism in the same way as with Hitler's fascism'.[12] This was followed by a series of meetings over the next few months on the Marshall Plan and US power, including a debate with the Fabian Society.[13]

He was also called on to write frequently for the Party press, and invited as a tutor and speaker at Party schools. This was all physically draining as well as intellectually demanding – 'the traffic of the Klugmann telephones has continued to be heavy', MI5 reported in July 1947[14] – and he had little spare time outside the Party, with lunchtime trips to bookshops and occasional cinema visits his main recreations. This did not detract from his good humour, and he accepted his many invitations with his accustomed cheerfulness. He had won the esteem of the Party leadership, none more so than Harry Pollitt, its general secretary, who now called on him for help with the Party's political strategy.

The previous year, Harold Laski had led a Labour delegation to the Soviet Union, where Stalin had told them there were two roads to socialism: the Russian way and the British version, which could be achieved through parliamentary means. This provoked some discussion in the British communist leadership, keen to distinguish a parliamentary road to revolutionary change from the reformist Labour Party. They had even issued a *Daily Worker* leaflet entitled *The British Road to Socialism*. The most thoughtful contribution on the debate, however, was from Klugmann's sister Kitty, who argued in an article for *Communist Review* that the model of the 'new democracies', combined with the changing 'balance of forces' in Britain, opened up the possibility of a new road to socialism. British capitalism faced crisis, she argued, with a 'sell out to Wall Street' on the cards. The only conceivable alternative strategy was for a

> reconstituted Labour government which will end the policy of surrender to capitalist interests [...] for a more effective control over economic life by the Labour government backed by new forms of participation in control by the working class from the factories up.[15]

Pollitt wanted to take this idea of a British road to Socialism further in a chapter for a book he was writing, which would later be published as *Looking*

Ahead. He enlisted the support of Klugmann and Margot Heinemann, his 'favourite duet', and asked the former to draft a chapter on 'The Road to Socialism in Britain':

> The aim in this chapter will be to introduce a number of new thoughts, and you James, being familiar with the Marxist literature of the ancient and moderns alike, as are now to be found in the Soviet Union and the New Europe, are just the man for the job.

In a long letter, which gives a flavour of Pollitt's down-to-earth wit, he lists points he would like Klugmann to take up, notably on how 'British socialism' can appeal to the British people's everyday experiences and 'How do we see the way to Socialism in Britain?'

> Just ask yourself a simple question, what was it that prompted for example Tom Mann to do what he did in his early years every Sunday? What was it that prompted Morris to go to the street corner? What was it that prompted Will Thorne to go every Sunday morning and never miss, wet or fine to speak at Beckton Road in Canning Town extolling his conception of the gospel called Socialism. And do not be afraid of being sentimental in your approach even if you did go to a university [...] How do we see the way to Socialism in Britain? [...]
>
> All the past theses of the CI [Communist International] on the violent character of the revolution were written after the Russian Revolution and when no other nation in the world had won through to power.
>
> But precisely as a result of the Russian Revolution and the strength of the Soviet Union, the last war saw a series of revolutions take place during the course of the defeat of fascism the most reactionary etc etc, you know the classic definition of fascism –
>
> In other words the new democracies have gone through their revolutions, with an enormous difference in the balance of forces, so that the old isolation of nations as far as their labour movements are concerned is ended, and in my humble judgement ended for ever.
>
> Have not enormous changes taken place also in the colonial countries, and does not the sum total of all this show that the prerequisites for the peaceful transition towards Socialism in a country like Britain now exist.

Pollitt asks Klugmann 'to get cracking' with his own ideas; 'I think the time has arrived, when bearing in mind what has been said in other countries, we now need to say something new.' Signing off, he wishes Klugmann and Margot (whom he calls 'the Coal Queen' on account of her work on the mining industry) 'a good holiday in France. Do not let the lady's charms get you down.'[16]

The contributions made by Klugmann and Margot – no doubt with Kitty's input – made a substantial contribution to the founding idea of the 'British Road to Socialism', which later became adopted by the Party in 1951 as its first official political strategy since 'For a Soviet Britain' in 1935. However, in the intervening years, its credibility was to be seriously dented by its Cold War allegiances, while the document itself was only published after receiving a formal endorsement from Stalin on Pollitt's Moscow visit in 1950.

Klugmann's holiday with Margot in July was a much-needed two-week break. It was the first time he had been abroad since his return from UNRRA, and he was keen to catch up with some old friends, including Penelope Brierley, who had been interned during the war, but was considering returning to England with her French-born son, to take up a teaching job. More difficult to trace was André Victor, though by the end of the visit Klugmann had received news that he was alive, had fought with the Greek partisans and was now writing for the French communist press.[17] The holiday was combined with a stint teaching with his friend Yvonne Kapp at a Party school. It was also an opportunity to consider a new job offer.

The new journal *Changing Epoch* was struggling, while in the meantime, Arthur Clegg, the editor of *World News and Views* had left and Klugmann was thought by the Party leadership to be the best person to take over. This would give him a more central role in influencing foreign policy and bring him closer to the Party's core propaganda department at a time when tensions in foreign politics were sharpening. Klugmann became editor of *World News and Views* in September 1947. The timing was significant as it marked the beginning of the Cold War. His own politics would become increasingly defined by the Cold War, and his writings and speeches already demonstrated an unyielding loyalty to communist orthodoxy. He warned of Wall Street domination and colonisation, while at the same time arguing in the *Daily Worker* that the Soviet Union was keen on trade with the West. The 'true democracies', he told a packed Dulwich Communist Party meeting, in a speech entitled 'The World Situation Today', amounted to the 'greatest concentration of democratic forces today than any time after the First World War'. The US, by contrast, was heading for a major economic crisis which would affect all Western countries attached to its foreign policy and military strategy, while engaged in a 'witchhunt' against individual communists.[18]

Though his accession to the hierarchy was rapid and impressive, his career in the Party was now in danger of succumbing to the trajectory taken by other intellectuals, notably Emile Burns and Rajani Palme Dutt. Certainly there are more similarities with Burns, an earlier graduate of Trinity College Cambridge, the Party's propaganda chief and the author of introductory books on Marxism. Burns was also chair of the National Cultural Committee and involved in Party education work. He had formed a close association with communists working in anti-colonial movements, notably Kwame Nkrumah, who was studying at the LSE in the late 1940s. Dutt, the long-serving editor of *Labour Monthly*, was the defender of Party orthodoxy, the prototype Stalinist intellectual, who was unwavering in his support for the Soviet Union. He would clash with Klugmann in later years. That Klugmann, from a different generation, became a stalwart of Party orthodoxy is a reflection on the constraints imposed by the Cold War, with little room for manoeuvre for communist intellectuals. Setting out the intellectual case for the Party's policy increasingly took the form of delivering Party propaganda, through its vehicles of opinion and theoretical debate. For Klugmann, such a shift was to prove disastrous for his later intellectual credibility and marked a significant departure from the role as an intellectual he had sketched out for himself in 1934. Then, his intellectual pursuits informed his evolving principles as student organiser and he saw no contradiction between his research, private reading and political leadership. Meeting with potential recruits and allies was partly a testing ground of his own ideas as the chance to impose his own interpretation of the political situation and he had always enjoyed wide intellectual interests. In short, he was not a dogmatist by nature.

Klugmann had long advocated communism as the progressive culmination of all that was best in democracy and liberalism – 'Forward from Liberalism' was his defining political strategy, which was broad enough to recruit widely at Cambridge, to sustain the Popular Front against Fascism and War in Paris, and to inspire the vision of national liberation in those who attended his lectures in Cairo. His endorsement of the 'new democracies' in Eastern Europe reflected some of that, notably when describing the transition from partisan campaigns in the construction of new societies. Following the drafting of the chapter for Pollitt, he addressed several meetings on the 'road to socialism in Britain', including a whole day at the Hornsey Borough School in September, but his judgements now remained dependent on the Soviet Union.

This helps explain why he shared the sectarian turn in the Party's politics and outlook from 1947, notably in its growing hostility to the Labour left, at a time when the Labour government was pushing through significant domestic reforms. Though the Party continued to support the major social and economic reforms like the National Health Service and the nationalisation of coal and transport, its hostility to the Marshall Plan put immediate constraints on how far this could be extended. Even before the split over Tito, there were signs of growing tensions between the Party, the Bevanites and others on Labour's left. He viewed the reformism of Labour's left as little better in practice than right-wing social democracy: both maintained the illusion that real progress was being achieved under the Labour government. Growing discontent with the scale of nationalisation was now overshadowed by the Communist Party's attack on the Labour Party's foreign policy, which the communists saw as increasingly subservient to the US.

The Cold War was taking its toll and the Party's own troubled relationship with the Labour Party, now trying to rebuild Britain, did not help matters. The Communist Party had difficulty in convincing the British public that Labour's allegiance to the US would lead to economic ruin, while its attempts to argue that the 'new democracies' were anything other than satellites of the Soviet Union were unconvincing. Moreover, the projection of the Party's own political strategy was thwarted by confusion over what its real relationship to Labour should be, including whether to stand candidates against a party with which it had until recently enjoyed joint membership. This also meant that its 'Leninism' was the subject of debate within its own ranks, both on account of its own parliamentary road and its reading of the international situation.[19]

Klugmann's life with Kitty and Maurice had taken on a familiar routine since the three of them had set up house together. As experienced Communist Party organisers, his sister and brother-in-law had themselves become absorbed in the life of the Party. Kitty was chair of Highgate Branch, which also included Klugmann's close friends Margot Heinemann and Yvonne Kapp, and Sigmund and Connie Seifert. Their home became a regular rendezvous for Communist Party meetings and gatherings of the Party's Social Philosophy Group, which Kitty ran on Sundays. During the day Kitty and James often worked at home together, writing articles, talking about the political situation and preparing meetings. They were devoted to each other, and Klugmann remained dependent to a degree on his elder sister. Like her brother, Kitty was an able organiser and communicator, used to talking to Party audiences and public meetings on questions such as the Marshall Plan and US power or British social policy. She was not as prolific as he was, but her writing carried conviction and originality, and on occasions – such as her article on a 'British Road to Socialism' – had some influence on the Party's political strategy. Kitty took a part-time job lecturing at Morley College and often helped in the Party offices at King Street.

Like his wife and brother-in-law, Maurice Cornforth had strong intellectual interests and preferred to be in the sort of work which also gave him time to write. As assistant editor at *Soviet Weekly* he made daily trips to the paper's Trafalgar Square offices, travelling on the Northern Line from Highgate. Like Klugmann, he had sacrificed an academic career to work for the Party, initially as its organiser in the eastern counties in the 1930s, before requesting a job more suited to a philosopher; he had, after all, been a protégé of Ludwig Wittgenstein. His role at *Soviet Weekly* was to commission articles and act as liaison between the journalists and King Street, and as such he was an important source of information for his brother-in-law. Until 1949, when he found the demands of this role excessive and engineered a move to the Party publishers Lawrence and Wishart to allow him to embark on a philosophical study of dialectical materialism, Cornforth was kept busy by developments in Eastern Europe. As a household, therefore, their social lives were inseparable from their work, and it is difficult to disagree with the intelligence service observation that 'The Cornforths are full-time communists with, apparently, no other interests in life'.[20]

Subsumed by his Party work, Klugmann was still much in demand and Kitty would frequently take messages for him at the house and sometimes stand in for him at meetings. It seemed that he had arrived at the point that Arthur Koestler had already reached by the mid-1930s, where his allegiances had isolated him from life outside and his intellectual energies were vested in internal Party and Comintern projects.

I no longer had any friends outside the Party. It had become my family, my nest, my spiritual home. Inside it, one might quarrel, grumble, feel happy or unhappy; but to leave the nest, however cramping and smelly it seemed sometimes, had become unthinkable. All 'closed systems' create for those who live inside a progressive estrangement from the rest of the world. I disliked a number of people in the Party but they were my kin. I liked a number of people outside the Party, but I no longer had a common language with them.[21]

On the now rare occasions he met old acquaintances and colleagues, his growing sectarianism did not go unnoticed. Kenneth Greenlees, his ex-SOE colleague, now working as a stockbroker for Laing and Cruickshank, met him for lunch and found him 'indiscreet to say the least of it'. Greenlees reported back to MI5 that Klugmann made it quite clear which side he would be on in any war between the US and the Soviets.[22]

14

Cold War Intellectual

Klugmann's rise in the Party had been rapid and demands for speeches, articles and keynote talks were unrelenting. By the end of 1947 he was not only editor of one of the Party's flagship publications, but also a member of the Party's International Committee, its Middle East Committee, on the editorial board of *Labour Monthly* and on the Hornsey Borough Committee. More importantly, he had the ear of Harry Pollitt and, as the Party's acknowledged expert on Yugoslavia and most of Eastern Europe, he was not only sought after by branches and districts but constantly pursued by various embassies and press attachés – enquiries that would increase as Cold War tensions mounted.

Indeed Klugmann had some difficulty meeting all his demands, and in his hectic schedule his intellectual pursuits were the first casualty. 'I'm afraid I got badly caught out by this article – found it impossible to say all the things I wanted to', he told Robin Page Arnott, at the *Labour Monthly*. 'In the space of 2,500–3000 words or so I'm afraid the result is a mess – saying everything or nothing.'[1] Margot Heinemann told Kitty that she thought he took on too many things, with the result that the quality of his work was suffering. Heinemann, who knew as well as anyone his intellectual potential, was also aware that he had been planning a book – probably on Yugoslavia and the new international situation. 'It is time he really learned to write', she told Kitty, who agreed that the commitments were taking their toll and that his articles were not up to scratch. She told Margot that he intended to take a break to get on with the book; Heinemann, however, was sceptical about whether he would actually find the time to do it.[2]

Klugmann's rise as a prominent Party intellectual at this moment meant there was no escape from the worst aspects of Stalinism, and in the Cold War atmosphere of polarised opinion and counter-accusation, he was required to justify Soviet purges of former anti-fascist and communist leaders who had fallen out with the official Soviet-backed line. As editor of *World News and Views*, he had a key role in reporting and explaining the trials. Those on trial included Nikola Petkov, the Bulgarian anti-fascist leader who had been jailed in the 1930s before helping to organise the broad front which brought the communists and their allies to power, subsequently becoming a minister in the first Fatherland Front government of 1944–5. There he represented the Bulgarian Agrarian National Union and then became leader of the United Front, which provided parliamentary opposition to the Communist Party. It was for his role in defending parliamentary democracy, which was perceived as 'counter-revolutionary' by the communist authorities who were then seeking to impose a one-party state, that he was arrested in June 1947, charged and put on trial. After what was widely believed to be a 'show trial' he was hanged on 23 September 1947, for which the Bulgarian government was severely denounced by the West, including the British Labour government.

Klugmann discussed the trial in an article in *World News and Views* entitled 'The Petkov Pattern'.[3] It took him further down the road of sectarianism and revealed his now-entrenched position as defender of Soviet orthodoxy against all critics. On the trial itself, he started by roundly denouncing the 'violent attacks on the Bulgarian government' by the Western press, including 'a number of liberal or even Labour papers'.[4] Despite Petkov being allowed neither legal representation nor to give evidence, Klugmann regarded the trial as fair, largely on the grounds that no evidence was presented by the court in support of Petkov.

However, as others debated the merits of the trial, Klugmann suggested there was a wider strategy – the 'pattern of treachery' – at stake. He saw it as further evidence that Western intelligence was working with reactionary groups, including those discredited by fascism, in 'plots and conspiracies' to undermine the 'new democracies' in Bulgaria, Poland, Hungary, Romania, Czechoslovakia and Albania – countries which he had been given the responsibility of monitoring for the Party press.

> The pattern is only too clear. US and British reaction, operating through every sort of agent and agency, open and secret, official and unofficial, made contact with the discredited remnants of East European reaction, offered them every encouragement, a good foreign press, contact with each other and the outside world, money, equipment and instructions. This is the pattern of treachery that has been revealed by recent conspiracy trials in Eastern Europe.[5]

Ignoring the fact that Petkov and others had been part of the anti-fascist struggle, Klugmann persisted with the line that the conspiracy had its origins in the fascist period: 'The firm attitude of the Eastern European government in ferreting out and suppressing these conspirators should be welcomed by all those who thought that the war against Hitler and Mussolini was just. It is a logical continuation of that war.'[6]

He ends, as editor of the Party's weekly newspaper, with what is a very rhetorical and defiant attempt to rally the readership with a statement of intent:

> The task of British progressives is to make known the true character of these conspiracies and *World News and Views* in the coming weeks will publish detailed reports of these trials. But above all it is to fight against continued British intervention through obscure agencies against the new popular democracies. The 'Petkov Pattern' is in the first place a fight to end US and British intervention which is directly responsible for these conspiracies and to purge the British state of those undesirable agents and agencies who carry on in the plot against European progress and who detest, as much as they hate, the popular movements of Eastern Europe, the Labour movement in this country.[7]

It was the developments in Tito's Yugoslavia which propelled Klugmann further into a mire of Cold War tangles, from which he never fully recovered. The first inklings came in the months after the first meeting of the newly formed Communist Information Bureau (Cominform) in September 1947, held in Yugoslavia. Tito's stated intention in January 1948 to employ troops in Albania, on the pretext that not enough was being done to support the Greek communists and that the internal Greek conflict could spill over into Albania, was a trigger for the dispute, as was the claim that he intended to merge Yugoslavia with Bulgaria. Yugoslav communist leaders were called to Moscow to explain their position, and an increasingly hostile series of communications followed over the next couple of months, in which Tito's criticisms of the Soviet leadership were met with the accusation that the Yugoslav Communist Party leadership had betrayed the principles of Marxism-Leninism. This culminated in Yugoslavia's expulsion from the Cominform in mid-June 1948. However, the scale and implications of the split took Klugmann and the British Communist Party by surprise. They were clearly not prepared for it and Klugmann, the Party's Yugoslav specialist, was given the unenviable task of delivering the intellectual justification for the change in line.

On his return from another short holiday in France in June 1948, Klugmann had to deal with the consequences of Yugoslavia's expulsion as news spread in the

British Communist Party. Kay Beauchamp of the London District Committee (LDC) was one of many keen to get 'background stuff' on the Tito split ahead of their forthcoming aggregate meeting. Before that the Party's Political Committee at its 1 July meeting endorsed the Cominform line unanimously, based mainly on what Klugmann could tell them and without any inclination to seek further clarification. This statement did not make the 3 July edition of *World News and Views*, however; instead Klugmann's editorial included an apology that 'owing to conditions of printing [...] it has not been possible this week to publish the full text of the statement of the Communist Information Bureau'.[8]

At the London District aggregate meeting on 7 July, Pollitt, relying on what Klugmann had managed to pass to him as well as what he had gleaned from official statements in *Soviet Weekly*, was not much clearer in his explanation of the reasons for the expulsion of Yugolavia. His main vindication was the testimony of communist leaders who had sacrificed long years to the cause. 'Men like Rakosi, never out of prison for 15 years, men like Slansky, who was tortured in Dachau, are not men who turn when Joe says turn,' he told concerned delegates. The loyalty of the British Communist Party to the Soviet Union remained overwhelming at this point and, whatever private concerns members may have had, the resolution supporting the Party's position was supported by 100 votes to 2 with 20 abstentions.[9]

Nevertheless Klugmann found himself in serious trouble. The news had come as a 'shock', he admitted to members of the Belsize branch, while warning those present – in the familiar bourgeois streets of his childhood – that 'capitalists are rooting round, looking for trouble and discovering Tito'.[10]

He had consistently championed the Yugoslav case as a shining example of the new democracies throughout his voluminous writings, as well as talks and classes. He had enthused endlessly about the democratic qualities of the People's Councils, the inspiring leadership of the Yugoslav communists in the National Liberation Movement – comrades he knew well – and the model constitution which embodied its new democratic structure: one, he had maintained, that should be studied by all communists and progressives. Moreover, he had argued that their democratic struggle had been in defiance of the reactionary elements of British imperialism, which had initially opposed the Partisans during the war and resumed hostility after it.

The split had severe consequences for the Party in Britain. The British-Yugoslav Association, which counted a broad range of pro-Yugoslav individuals and groups among its spokesmen, headed by Hugh Setor-Watson and Fitzroy

Maclean (friends and colleagues from Klugmann's SOE days) and Konni Zilliacus, was irredeemably split from that point on, until its eventual implosion in November 1949. Zilliacus had been a close ally of Klugmann's for some time. Only the previous year, they had been co-authors of *Yugoslavia Faces the Future*. Zilliacus had contributed to Party publications and was considered to be a fellow traveller (he was later expelled from the Labour Party in May 1949). The links with the Bevanites, which had already been strained by the Cold War, were now irretrievably broken, thereby thwarting further political alliances with groups which in other times would be seen as potential allies, such as those who produced the *Keep Left* statement (including Michael Foot, Ian Mikardo and Richard Crossman); Aneurin Bevan himself remained a strong supporter of the Tito leadership.

The split over Tito was the spark for further divisions with the Labour left. Klugmann attempted to explain the divisions between the CPGB and the Labour left in two articles for the Party monthly *Communist Review*, in December 1948 and January 1949. His argument was unconvincing and tainted by a sectarian tone indicative of the Cold War; little doubt, though, that it was what the Party membership at that time wanted to hear. The Labour left's 'democratic socialism' – a term he could not bring himself to use without inverted commas throughout – was no different in reality to the 'social democracy' of Labour's right, in its belief in a neutral state, a peaceful transition 'within the framework of capitalism', and capable of extracting only 'minor reforms' when capitalism could afford it. The British workers, he argued, had brought a Labour government to power in the expectation that the 'anarchy of capitalism' would be replaced by socialist economic planning. What they got instead was nationalised industries run by a capitalist class that had never left power, thereby making real socialist planning – as was being practised in the Soviet Union and elsewhere – 'impossible'.[11]

In his regular articles, now long on rhetoric and interspersed with long quotes from the Marxist classics, he held an air of lofty sarcasm towards his opponents, as he set about their theoretical flaws and reformist illusions. Whatever he said in public, however, in private the tension was mounting. He had cultivated Yugoslav communists in his time as a student leader and had known Tito better than anyone else in his own Party and, of course, in his extraordinary wartime role in SOE, had played a major part in securing Allied support for the Yugoslav Partisans. He had worked with Tito and colleagues in UNRRA and spoken passionately in their cause from the time he first embarked on full-time work at King Street. He documented their achievements as the shining light of what would be known as the 'new democracies'.

Now, as Geoff Eley put it,

Condemning Tito became the litmus test of communist loyalty [...] It was an excruciating test of Klugman's faith in communism; of his intellectual integrity, of his moral courage. He chose, what certainly could not have been the easy way, to prove himself a steadfast communist by denouncing the object of his past ardour.[12]

To Victor Kiernan, recruited to the Party by Klugmann after long hours of political discussion in his room at Cambridge, 'Tito's sudden excommunication seemed inexplicable'.[13]

In early January 1949, Klugmann spent a frenetic week attending meetings trying to make sense of the fast-changing situation in Yugoslavia; he was 'in a jam', he told Lazar Zaidman, on the phone. The British-Yugoslav Association, after remaining neutral throughout 1948, had now endorsed Tito's policy at its January Executive Committee. By the beginning of February Klugmann had fallen seriously ill and on the advice of the Party doctor, Angus McPherson, was promptly taken to Archway Hospital. According to intelligence files, visitors were restricted to his mother and Margot Heinemann, his closest friend. The illness, clearly brought on by stress and overwork, was in all likelihood worsened by fear of his developing predicament. There was certainly evidence of panic on behalf of those who were caring for him. McPherson was told by Joan Faulkner that 'James Klugmann is one of the most valuable people in the Party and that all red tape must be cut through or else he would be moved somewhere else'.[14] There were suggestions that outside nurses were sent to the hospital to care for him.

What are we to make of his illness? His asthma was a growing problem, not helped by years of smoking, and he was clearly overworked. However, the psychological demands of having to adopt a new position on Yugoslavia and to work closely with Eastern European embassies and representatives in providing information against former allies, including former friends at the Yugoslav Embassy, must also have been overwhelming at times. His illness was probably precipitated by what we would now call a panic attack or a minor breakdown. The paranoia of the time − evident in some of his remarks, and underpinning some of his articles − was indicative of the constraints on intellectuals required to produce propaganda on a regular basis at the height of the Cold War. The Party was very concerned and after Klugmann's recovery he was given two months of convalescence.

On his return to work at the beginning of April, the divisions within the British-Yugoslav Association were widening, and Klugmann was now regularly consulting Pollitt, Bob Stewart, Palme Dutt and others. Part of his and the Party's dilemma was to try and maintain good relationships with ordinary Yugoslavs while remaining hostile to the government. Tito still had many supporters in the UK, in the British-Yugoslav Association, among the Bevanite left and in the embassy and on other official bodies. Konni Zilliacus, Klugmann's long-time ally, had remained steadfast in his support of Tito and now openly agreed with the stand he took against Stalin. Zilliacus had visited Yugoslavia in September and on his return quoted Tito approvingly: 'If socialism does not mean humanism, if it does not mean human dignity, more respect for freedom, truth and justice, it would not be worth working for'.[15] Those words must have rankled with Klugmann.

The British-Yugoslav Association Annual General Meeting was set for November 1949, when the divisions would come to a head. By this time Soviet troops were already on the Yugoslav border. Although the association was under the leadership of pro-Tito Hugh Seton-Watson, its president, who was supported by Fitzroy Maclean, many rank-and-file members were communists and adopted the pro-Soviet position. In the event, two alternative slates of 15 candidates for the Executive Committee were nominated, and counter-motions, pro- and anti-Tito in nature, were proposed. The results of the election, carried out by postal ballot, were announced on 17 November. All 15 pro-Cominform candidates were elected, and the anti-Tito resolution passed by 72 votes to 57. The long-standing communist fellow traveller D.N. Pritt was elected president. Konni Zilliacus and the pro-Titoites promptly resigned and founded a rival organisation, the British-Yugoslav Friendship Society.

November 1949 was an important month for Klugmann. He had to prepare for the CPGB's National Congress and now had the responsibility of delivering the new Party line that was emanating from the Cominform: that Titoism was like Trotskysism in the 1930s and had been bolstered by British intelligence and Anglo-American imperialism. There was also the question of the next British general election and how the Communist Party, deeply entrenched in Cold War propaganda, would present itself electorally at a time when the Labour government was fighting for survival.

In January 1950, as part of the Party's general election campaign, Klugmann gave a talk at a public meeting of the Hampstead Communist Party, where he told an audience of around 60 people that the Yugoslav liberation movement had been 'betrayed', that Tito had won new allies in Churchill and the US media and within the intelligence services and that the Tito regime had 'planted' spies and agents-provocateurs. This, he admitted, was 'hard to believe' and the 'big change' in attitude towards Tito had come as a shock. Moreover, the betrayal of the Titoites, he argued, also needed to be viewed in light of wider betrayals such as those of Traycho Kostov, the Bulgarian Communist leader, and Laszlo Rajk, Hungary's former foreign affairs minister, both of whom had been executed during the previous three months for various alleged anti-Soviet positions, 'nationalist' loyalties and pro-Titoist sympathies.[16]

His talk in Hampstead was received by a loyal Party audience, who by and large went along with the Party leadership's position and maintained their faith in the Soviet Union. The Party's performance in the general election, however, was a disaster. The entrenchment of Cold War positions and divisions with the Labour left, together with the Party's own ambiguous political strategy, had come at a price. Its arguments on Tito were lacking credibility. Klugmann was in open conflict with former allies. His criticism of Konni Zilliacus, now one of his major opponents, for 'inexplicable inconsistency' (as he put it in a letter to the *New Statesman*) could easily have been turned on him and his Party.

Klugmann's Hampstead speech made clear he was not merely delivering the new line on Tito but endorsing support for the trials of Rajk and Kostov as part of a wider denunciation of betrayal and spies. In order to do this effectively he was obliged to meet officials from embassies and security services. This, he was warned, by a phonecall to King Street, was 'dangerous' work, and there was 'no going back' once he had done so.[17] Others noted the pressure he was under at Party centre: 'Someone told me of having seen him at headquarters, about to face the leadership over some question, looking distressingly nervous.'[18]

He clearly felt, however, that meeting embassy officials was the only way to get the information he needed. There was particular interest from the Bulgarian Embassy, given the claim that Tito's objective had been to try and absorb Bulgaria within his political orbit, as part of a 'Balkan Federation'. Since the development of the Popular Front, Klugmann had held a long-standing admiration for Georgi Dimitrov, Bulgaria's Communist leader, and his death in 1949 had come as a blow. Dimitrov had been close to Tito, which was a further issue of concern for Klugmann, as he was required to respond to constant queries from the Bulgarian Embassy and press attachés for meetings. This situation was getting serious, and he was alarmed at the 'tactless' habit of the Bulgarians calling him at King Street.

Things were also getting more serious for him in other respects. British intelligence was renewing its interest in him, and the purge of communists in the British Civil Service was well under way, coming on the back of the 1950 conviction of atomic scientist Klaus Fuchs for passing information to the Soviet Union, and in the midst of 'McCarthyism' in the United States. Following the CPGB's poor showing in the election, when they lost their only two sitting MPs, Willie Gallacher and Phil Piratin, the time seemed ripe for clearing out communists from the trade unions. On 29 March 1950, in introducing a House of Lords debate on 'Communists in Public Service', Lord Vansittart outlined his concern at communist influence in the Civil Service, the Church of England, the BBC and the education system. He was particularly alarmed at what he saw as the role of the Cominform Bureau in Bucharest in 'direct[ing] the activities of diplomatists and agents in the non-Communist countries – including, of course, here'.

Vansittart was clearly worried that not enough was being done to win the propaganda war, and that Eastern European communist diplomats and agents had been allowed to gain a foothold through regular meetings with British communists, under embassy and diplomatic shields:

> This country has been infested by hostile missions, masquerading as diplomacy, and by all the agents that radiate from them; and it has been plagued by bogus friendship societies which exist mainly for spreading sedition; and it has been infiltrated by a whole host of fellow-travellers and double crossers, who present the greatest problem of all.[19]

On the penetration of British intelligence by communists, Vansittart named Klugmann, along with his comrades from his Cairo days – Peter Wright, Betty Wallace and Kenneth Syers. He was at pains to point out their recent and current political activities as indicative of the wider problem. For its part, British intelligence was becoming convinced that Klugmann was a key contact for the 'hostile missions', 'agents' and 'bogus friendship societies' alluded to by Vansittart in his House of Lords speech. These meetings with Eastern European representatives produced speculation that he could be reunited with former Soviet intelligence agents whom he had encountered when in British intelligence during the war. They had discovered that one of his confidants was 'Egorov', a member of the Russian secret police whom they had been closely monitoring for some time. In mid-April, MI5 'watchers' followed Egorov to Collett's Bookshop, where he had a lunch rendezvous with 'A' (later identified as Klugmann). They were followed to the Restaurant de Paris in nearby Dean Street, where they spent an hour chatting over lunch. According to the MI5 watcher sitting at a table behind, 'A' explained his regular daily schedule and 'office routine', and commented that 'these meetings are useful to both sides'. However, 'he seemed somewhat ill at ease throughout' before agreeing to further meetings. After lunch MI5 followed Klugmann back to Talbot Road, which also provided another glimpse into his solitary existence: a film at the Berkeley Cinema in Tottenham Court Road, a meal at Fortes restaurant in Charing Cross Road, before returning home alone.[20] While it is likely that his solitary visits to the restaurant and cinema were purely for entertainment, he may also have been checking to see if he was being followed.

Klugmann was clearly concerned about what he was getting into but it was now something he had long accepted as part of his role as a communist. In public, at least, he was defiant in the face of Vansittart's remarks and the purge of communists from public bodies. In a speech the following month to the Muswell Hill Communist Party, entitled 'Who are the Traitors?', he delivered a robust response six weeks after the House of Lords debate. Dismissing 'Vansittartism' as another form of 'McCarthyism' which saw red spies in the way others spot 'flying saucers', he claimed anti-communists were the real 'traitors to peace and the people': 'We communists see a new Britain and a new world of peace, co-existence and liberty', 'Fight with us!'[21]

He continued to hold regular meetings with Bulgarian Embassy officials throughout the spring of 1950. Nevertheless, he was tired and his health was not good. He had aged considerably, was prematurely grey with a receding hairline, he was putting on weight and was still smoking heavily. It wasn't just intelligence reports which described him as 'looking around 50', when he was in fact only 38. He was given to joking about his own appearance, cheerfully suggesting to an organiser who had invited him to speak that his introduction might point out that 'this comrade in spite of his hair is under sixty'.[22]

It must have been something of a relief when an opportunity arose to become head of the Party's education department in July 1950 after the existing incumbent, Dougie Garman, decided to leave his post. At first John Gollan was earmarked for the job, but he chose to stay at the *Daily Worker* and so Klugmann was offered the role, which he took up following another two-week holiday in France that summer. His close friend Margot Heinemann replaced him as editor of *World News and Views*.

This was the position that Klugmann had coveted, and he was the ideal candidate. He was highly regarded as a tutor and lecturer and was one of the most popular speakers at Party schools and conferences. He might have expected that it would provide him with more time to do serious writing. It kept him in the leadership of the Party but without the pressure of having to bring out a weekly paper. Given the stress and conflicts he had endured, the post offered some release and the possibility of greater intellectual freedom. It was a role he was perfectly suited for and one which he would make his own. He remained a renowned and inspirational Party tutor for the rest of his life.

Much as he enjoyed his new role, however, he could not get away from the Cold War conflicts. In fact there would be little respite for the next decade. A reminder of the predicaments faced by communist intellectuals at that time can be seen in the treatment of the renowned scientist J.B.S. Haldane, who withdrew from the Party over the Lysenko affair, though he did not officially leave the Party until 1956. Trofim Lysenko, a Soviet scientist who claimed to have discovered a system of genetics and evolution which was in advance of Western scientific discovery, had divided opinion among British scientists. Many thought his ideas suspect and driven by ideological dogma, as was subsequently demonstrated. Stalin had instituted harsh penalties for dissenters from Lysenko's theories and put pressure on the communist movement to bring its scientists in line. Though some did, Haldane, its leading scientist, did not share Lysenko's theory which, as a geneticist himself, he considered lacked intellectual credibility. He could not contemplate giving support to such a flawed theory. However, as Haldane was a loyal Party intellectual, his 'exit from the Communist Party was reluctant, slow and agonised'.[23] It did not help that his eventual departure was confirmed by a Sunday newspaper, which was the basis for a backlash from the Party hierarchy towards someone they had previously revered. This was a further warning to intellectuals who dissented from Soviet orthodoxy.

Yugoslavia remained at the forefront of the Party's political dilemmas, and Klugmann's role in the whole affair was to have one final decisive and disastrous twist. Moscow was increasingly hostile to Tito and his allies and was demanding that other parties demonstrate their allegiances. Under pressure from Moscow, the British Communist Party leadership gave Klugmann, the acknowledged expert, three weeks' leave at the beginning of 1951 to write a short book on it. He had only been at his new role for a few months and it was a task he did not relish. After a 'splendid' education conference in Manchester in the third week of January, he told Gladys Brooks that he felt 'a bit under the weather with this Tito thing'.[24] By that time he had written 40,000 words, with another 12,000 to do by the end of the week.

Nevertheless, he completed it on time and *From Trotsky to Tito* was published later that year. This short book starts by making the connection between 'Titoism' and other examples of betrayal in the communist movement, then goes on to the critique of Tito and the Yugoslav Communist Party by the Cominform at its meeting in June 1948 – a gathering that was, he reminded his readers, attended by 'twenty of the world's leading communists'. He spelled out again the specific criticisms: namely the breach with Marxism-Leninism on the transition to socialism (he compared the Yugoslavs to the Mensheviks and Ramsay MacDonald), its denial of Leninism in failing to see the 'class differentiation' in the peasantry and by deviating from the view of Marx, Engels, Lenin and Stalin 'that the working class is the only consistently revolutionary class, and that only under its leadership can the transition to socialism be realised'.[25]

He also reiterated the Cominform's further criticism that 'bourgeois nationalism' had replaced 'internationalism' and that Tito and the other leaders had made 'concessions' to 'western imperialism' which 'can only lead to Yugoslavia's degeneration into an ordinary bourgeois republic'.[26]

Though admitting that the news of Tito's betrayal came as a shock and accepting that 'most of us made the mistake of confusing the achievements and sacrifices of the Yugoslav peoples with the actions of the group of leading Titoites', he needed to find a stronger explanation for what occurred in Yugoslavia. The story he concocted – which fitted with the official explanation from the Soviet leadership – was all the more preposterous given his own role in British intelligence.

At a certain time, and exactly how and when history has to disclose, the British political and military leadership, on a very high and top-secret level, must have received information, some of which it may have had all along, that there were leading elements inside the Partisan forces, inside the Yugoslav Communist Party, spies and provocateurs, Gestapo elements, Trotskyites, who could be 'trusted' (from the point of view of British imperialism) and could be used to betray the Yugoslav people's liberation movement *from inside* and carry out an Anglo-American imperialist policy.[27]

Yet, he knew better than anyone that this did not happen, as he himself was party to the negotiations between the British and Partisan leaderships. Moreover, he had played a major part in influencing British policy in favour of Tito; indeed that work was partly the basis for his quick rise in the Party. Writing the next sentence, therefore, must have been particularly irksome.

This was the basis of the change of British policy from Mihailovic to Tito in the period of 1942–43. It was carried out with the maximum secrecy and with that great measure of cunning and deceit for which British imperialism with its long and unrivalled experience of cunning and deceit, has become notorious throughout the world.[28]

That he was now effectively denying his own 'concerted political work' in order to present a palatable explanation to British communists which matched that of the Soviets is an indication of how far he had surrendered his own political integrity. In the remainder of the book, he made further connections between the Titoites and Trotskyites, and other 'spies' and 'traitors' at other times in the history of the British Labour movement. Following the line he had taken in his article 'The Petkov Pattern', he made links to the Rajk, Kostov and Xose trials and the wider threat to communism from within. His dismissal of the arguments of former friends, notably Konni Zilliacus, and the overtures made to British communists from the Yugoslav Embassy in supporting a 'new kind of communism', a term he derided, was equivocal and seemingly final. His book not only made the possibility of any alliance with the Labour Bevanite left more unlikely, it contributed to the Party's political isolation. For Klugmann personally, it capped an intellectually and politically disastrous turn of events.

15

Trials and Tribulations

The ordeal of being a Cold War intellectual had not diminished Klugmann's enthusiasm for teaching, and he was ideally suited to lead the Party's education department. He had a strong academic background and unfulfilled promise to be a history teacher. Moreover he had a growing reputation as a brilliant tutor and lecturer who had the capacity to hold and inspire an audience and to put across complex Marxist concepts in a way that could be understood by ordinary members. For this reason he was loved for a non-patronising and empathetic teaching style which put those new to Marxism, including many working-class members, at their ease in his classes. On his part he knew, like all Party intellectuals, that 'middle-class comrades', had to make extra efforts to demonstrate their worth to the Party; they were still often regarded with suspicion and could never hope to share the status of the 'industrial comrades', those Party militants who were leading the political battles in the unions. The CPGB was not only an overwhelmingly proletarian party in its social composition, it imbibed the culture of the skilled working class in its ethos and outlook. This did not detract from an attitude which valued the contribution of intellectuals and the importance of learning, which continued to set it apart from the labour mainstream. This was reflected in the regular Party schools and the key role of the 'Lit Sec' (literature secretary) in replenishing branch educational material.

Klugmann's education role was also bound up with the direction of policy and propaganda. His important contribution to Harry Pollitt's *Looking Ahead*, and his pamphlet on Wall Street, had impressed the leadership and Pollitt now consulted him when ideas needed to be adapted to immediate policy priorities. "'Here,'" he used to say to Klugmann, handing him some draft or other, "now you put the Marxism in that.'"[1]

His meticulous speaker notes, always handwritten in fountain pen in A5 notepads, with clear subheadings, were constructed with current policy and prospects in mind. In fact his talks at public meetings were partly educational events. Typically, they would start with a reference to the current situation, often with a question or humorous aside, then move on to the bigger picture before returning to the tasks ahead. One of his gripes with the Labour Party and the British socialist tradition was their aversion to theory; this was something he would address in his new role.

Now he could put this experience to better effect in the more formal day schools and weekend schools, with residential schools in the summer months. His predecessor, Dougie Garman, an aspiring writer and poet and member of an artistic and literary circle that included the bohemian art collector Peggy Guggenheim and the war poet and critic Edgell Rickword, had left to pursue his writing interests. Garman was a passionate lecturer and teacher, 'erudite and thoughtful'; yet his style was 'not ideal for working class students', and the organisation of the education department in 1950 was thought to be close to 'collapse'.[2] Klugmann was a popular choice as his successor. Margot Heinemann thought it was a 'marvellous idea', while he himself acknowledged that it was the job he really wanted. He was looking forward to 'going back to school', he told Emile Burns, and promised to 'overhaul' the education material on offer to branches and districts and revive the ailing structure of the Party schools.[3]

After five intensive and stressful years justifying the Party's changing policy on Eastern Europe at the height of the Cold War, Klugmann would now get more time to do what he knew best. He had built up a formidable library of some 4,000–5,000 books since his time as a student, partly financed by his army pension, but had not had as much time to study as he would have liked. His intellectual interests remained inseparable from his political commitment as a revolutionary. Indeed, to 'be a revolutionary is a very full-time occupation', he had told the Recent History Group in February 1950. His intellectual work was now invariably tempered by politics and the realisation that it is 'very hard (impossible) to study a revolutionary movement without participating in it'. Quoting Lenin approvingly, he pointed out that 'when you are making history you have less time for writing it'. He broached a question that was to occupy much of his time over the remainder of his life. 'When will communist history be written?' he asked, also warning any prospective historians in the audience that 'if you write Party history without understanding [the] context it will be worthless'.[4]

Klugmann made a positive start. By October 1950, the Party's Executive Committee noted the 'radical improvement in the education work of the Party' evident in the number and type of schools – day schools, weekend schools, summer schools – as well as the more rigorous and up-to-date content. Yet, for all his determination to give his attention to the Party's education needs, he could not escape the continuing constraints of the Cold War and its effect on his status as an intellectual.

He also had something else to worry about. In May 1951, Guy Burgess and Donald Maclean, both close friends and political allies of his at Cambridge, had disappeared, leaving behind a political storm and a wave of publicity. MI5 had been alerted by the Soviet intelligence defector Walter Krivitsky as early as 1940 that there was a leak in the Foreign Office from someone 'who was the son of some titled individual'.[5] This was confirmed by leaks from the British Embassy in Washington in 1944 and 1945, and by April 1951 MI5 had narrowed the search for two people, one of whom was Maclean, the son of a former government minister. Serious inquiries were made into Maclean's activities, and his movements were observed by MI5 watchers from mid-April and throughout May, during which time his heavy drinking and state of unease were evident.

Nevertheless, MI5 was slow to act, and Guy Liddell, then MI5's deputy director general, responsible for counter-espionage, noted in his diary on Monday 29 May that:

> The Watchers failed to pick up Maclean since his departure for the country on Friday, and we now learn from the Foreign Office that he was given a day's leave on Saturday. He has not apparently been seen since and TCS [telephone checks] indicate considerable anxiety in the family.[6]

Liddell was informed of Guy Burgess's disappearance on the same day. This clearly came as a shock. He knew that Burgess had been sent home from the US by the Foreign Office because of three motoring offences, but it became clear that he had accompanied Maclean in his flight. It took MI5 considerable time to come to the conclusion that Burgess, like the suspected Maclean, could be a Soviet agent – and Liddell himself apparently refused to believe this for several months – but as the search continued at airports and ports, colleagues and friends of the two were called in for questioning. These included Anthony Blunt, a personal friend of Liddell, Goronwy Rees (who had received a call from Burgess in which the latter indicated he would not see him again for a long time) and, of course, Philby. They were all interviewed several times and, as the investigation into Burgess and Maclean's disappearance continued, both Philby and Blunt came under suspicion, though again Liddell continued to reject the idea that Blunt and Burgess were likely agents. Philby was eventually forced to resign from MI6 after failing to give satisfactory answers to enquiries about his links with Burgess. Goronwy Rees also came under suspicion after he had revealed that Burgess had told him in 1937 that he was a 'Comintern agent'.[7]

Inevitably, as the questions over the reasons for their disappearance grew, MI5 looked into the two men's political backgrounds at Cambridge. At the beginning of June, Special Branch were asked to keep a close eye on Klugmann and his movements to be 'discreetly recorded and notified during office hours to Mr Reed or Mr Skardon of MI5', the two officers who were investigating and interviewing the Burgess and Maclean circle. Skardon, in particular, was known for his subtle interviewing technique. Arthur Martin, the MI5 officer who would later interrogate both Bernard Floud and John Cairncross, was asked to investigate whether Klugmann 'might have been the means of effecting the escape from Paris of Donald Duart Maclean and Guy Francis de Moncy Burgess'. However, Martin reported:

> there is no evidence that Klugmann was in Paris at the time of the disappearance of Maclean and Burgess [. . . and] although there is no positive evidence that he remained in London during the intervening period there is nothing to suggest that he went abroad.[8]

Some suspicions remained, however, and on 11 June over dinner with Tess and Victor Rothschild, Guy Liddell was also warned about Klugmann, as someone they knew from their Cambridge days.

> They were as confused about Burgess as we were. Tess, however, thought that it would be worth our while to keep an eye on James Klugmann, who was at one time a fairly close friend of Burgess and the moving spirit of his group at Cambridge.[9]

Both Rothschilds had worked for MI5 during the war, as had Stuart Hampshire, another friend of theirs, and of Blunt, whom Klugmann had allegedly attempted to recruit to the NKVD in Paris in 1937, though this did not become fully apparent until later. Over a weekend in late June Hampshire and the Rothschilds had discussed the case at length, and the latter approached

Liddell again, strongly convinced that former left-wing acquaintances of Burgess and Maclean should be persuaded to meet MI5 officers to help the investigation, and if they were not prepared to do it, they 'would have to take the matter into their own hands'. However, Liddell took the view that early confrontation would provide any of those who may have carried on with espionage activity to clear themselves at an early stage, and that a better strategy would be to make more enquiries.[10]

Klugmann resisted all approaches from MI5 at this point, as he would continue to do for the next two decades, but his unease at his own position can only have increased as he became aware of the growing crisis surrounding his two former comrades. Over the coming weeks it was not just MI5 who wondered if he knew of their whereabouts. Mrs Klugmann, no doubt surprised to see pictures of her son's closest schoolfriend blazoned all over the front pages, rang him in exasperation: 'James, *where is* Donald?'[11] Although proud of her brilliant son, she had never really understood much about his communism or where it had taken him. He also received a call at King Street from Donald Maclean's mother enquiring about her son's disappearance.[12]

Other acquaintances of the two 'missing diplomats' (as they were referred to) were called in for interview. These included John Cairncross, now under suspicion after a note in his handwriting was found among Burgess's possessions. Though kept under surveillance and interviewed by Martin and Skardon, Cairncross did not then admit to the espionage he had carried out when at Bletchley Park in passing German decrypts to the Soviet Union, and they did not prosecute. He was, though, obliged to resign from the Treasury, and shortly after left Britain for Rome. Klugmann must have feared that Cairncross might implicate him and it is likely that some of his former Cambridge acquaintances may have urged him to offer information to protect himself. However, as a leading communist, collaborating with MI5 was clearly out of the question, particularly at the height of the Cold War. His fear of being hounded by British intelligence was to remain with him over the following years, as he was considered by MI5 to be one of the main candidates for the 'fourth' or 'fifth' man' up until the mid-1970s.

The publication of *From Trotsky to Tito* in late 1951 coincided with the final act of 'Stalinisation', starting with the Slansky trial and ending with claims of anti-Semitism in the case of the Jewish doctors arrested at the time of Stalin's final illness. These were followed, after Stalin's death, by the beginning of a *rapprochement* with Tito and Yugoslavia, Khrushchev's Secret Speech and the

Soviet invasion of Hungary, which would spiral the communist movement into turmoil. In Klugmann's case, the extent of his collusion and his inability to give any hope to growing critics, among them friends from the Historians Group and former student comrades, had severe consequences for the remainder of his career in the Party.

Shortly after the publication of *From Trotsky to Tito*, Rudolf Slansky, who, as general secretary of the Czech Communist Party after World War II and second to Gottwald, was one of the leading instigators in helping bring communists to power in Czechoslovakia, was arrested. Earlier, he had gained much respect for his clandestine work in the country before the German occupation in 1938, whereupon he left for exile in Moscow, where he witnessed the resistance to the German offensive and continued to build support for Czech resistance. The respect he had within the international communist movement was such that Harry Pollitt, in defending the new Moscow line against Tito, had singled him out. Pollitt had, as mentioned, told London communists after the Tito–Stalin split that 'Men like Slansky are not men who turn when Joe says turn'. The arrest and subsequent trial of Slansky in 1951, along with other leading communists, was an extension of Stalin's purge against those threatening to pursue more independent socialist roads. There was rivalry between Slansky and Gottwald (who may have felt threatened himself) but the depiction of Slansky as a 'spy' in the service of Western imperialism was now a familiar, if absurd, claim of the Soviet leadership, but one accepted unquestioningly by the British communist hierarchy. By this time, however, the Party leadership, slow on the uptake, losing support at home and declining in status and influence among their international communist allies, adopted the changes in Moscow positions without being overly troubled by the need for detailed explanations.

For Klugmann, there were several reasons to feel uncomfortable over the move against Slansky. First, the nature of the charges must have tested credibility and put his own role as exponent of the anti-'Titoite' charges in *From Trotsky to Tito* in more serious light. Secondly, among those facing charges alongside Slansky was Otto Katz, his former boss in Paris and another communist he had worked with in the cause of anti-fascism. He would also have had some understanding of the situation in Czechoslovakia from his close friend in the RME Blaho Hruby, and more recently through his friendship with Pavel Kavan, press officer and chargé d'affaires at the Czech Embassy. Kavan had worked in the underground resistance movement against fascism. While in London he got to know Klugmann and they would often meet at Collett's Bookshop before going for lunch and would sometimes travel back to Highgate together. However, in 1950 Kavan was called back to Prague, with his British wife Rosemary, and he himself was charged in the same trial that indicted Slansky.

Nevertheless, Klugmann had remained loyal to the Party in the trials of Slansky, Katz and others, and accepted their executions. He was still delivering the Moscow line on Titoite and imperialist agents. For some time, former close colleagues had warned him of the growing evidence emerging from the Soviet Union on the trials that had taken place. Victor Kiernan was one of those who urged him to reconsider.

I and a friend, who had spent some time in Prague on scientific work, went to see him privately – we had known him well at Cambridge – and tried to make him see that some of the tales told at the trials, as at the earlier ones in Russia, were quite incredible. They meant that men who had risked their lives for years as revolutionaries had been wearing traitors' masks all the time, ready to be thrown off at a given signal. We could make no impression whatever.[13]

His renunciation of Slansky was set out in 'Lessons from the Prague Trial', an article for *Communist Review* in which he essentially put across the same line he had adopted in *From Trotsky to Tito*, justifying the trial and the execution on similar grounds that they were agents of Western imperialism. The article was published in the month of Stalin's death, while at the same time there were major disturbances in East Germany with demonstrators calling for free elections.[14]

Despite his loyalty, Klugmann must have had some concern over the strong anti-Semitic element in the charges against Slansky and other defendants. Slansky's perceived 'rootless cosmopolitanism' had been a factor in the attacks made on him. In the British Communist Party this was the beginning of a major rift with its Jewish membership, many of whom had occupied leading roles in the Party hierarchy. The Party's National Jewish Committee (NJC), set up in 1943 as a sub-committee of the International Committee, remained loyal to the line on Moscow. Its leading members, Chimen Abramsky and Lazar Zaidman, both of whom had lived in Eastern Europe, were close to Klugmann and had shared his view at that time that the 'Jewish question' in the Soviet Union would be resolved through social and economic equality and universal citizenship, on the back of socialist victories. The Party had long demonstrated its anti-fascist commitment at home in the Battle of Cable Street and political activism against Mosley, which had helped bring Phil Piratin to parliament. Even after the

Tito split, the Jewish Committee followed the line which linked Titoism and Zionism to Western imperialism; the defence of the Soviet Union was crucial to safeguarding the Jewish community. The Slansky trial, however, took the charges of anti-Semitism in socialist countries to a new level.

Suspicions of anti-Semitism went back to the late 1940s, when members of the Soviet Union's Jewish Anti-Fascist Committee, several of them Yiddish poets, were arrested and subsequently charged, tried and executed for espionage and treason in August 1952. On the back of this and the Slansky trial, more fabrication of evidence by Stalin and others within the leadership concocted the story that there was an attempt to poison the Soviet leadership by doctors who were serving the interests of Zionist imperialist agents – a story which Stalin, in his last months, embellished in increasingly preposterous forms. This provoked a wider purge of Jewish cultural institutions and the closure of many institutions. The newspaper *Pravda* and news agency TASS carried a series of articles indicting the doctors, and charges were subsequently brought in January 1953, which were only halted by the death of Stalin two months later. The doctors were subsequently cleared of all charges. However, the growing evidence of anti-Semitism in the Soviet Union would make many British communists reconsider their political loyalties and

> led to much soul-searching and to an admission on the part of the NJC that it had not taken seriously the possibility of anti-Semitism in the Soviet Union. There were numerous debates and heated arguments between people who had been comrades for decades.[15]

There had long been criticisms within the wider Jewish community, for example among the British Board of Deputies and World Congress of Jews, but this was the first real indication of unease within the British Communist Party.

Klugmann's own identity as a communist had always allowed him to overcome conflicting identities. Initially, calling himself a communist was his response to his sense of being an outsider, an 'oddity', at Gresham's School. It was partly his way of assimilating into British life and culture, as an 'emancipation' 'from the narrowness of a religious environment', as Raphael Samuel has written of Jewish communist identity.[16] He fits the example of what Isaac Deutscher called the 'non-Jewish Jew', or what Alfred Sherman, himself an ex-communist, described as the communist identity of a 'de-judaised Jew'.[17] Like many British Jewish communists, Klugmann's faith in the Soviet Union stemmed from communist internationalism – in particular the sense that he belonged to a broader communist fraternity with Moscow as its head – and the sacrifices it had made in the cause of anti-fascism. This would explain why he was not immediately deterred by these events.

Following Stalin's death, investigation into the so-called 'Doctors' Plot' was discontinued, and others took the blame initially to shield Stalin's role. The arrest of Lavrentiy Beria, whom British Communist Party delegates had met as recently as the previous autumn, on grounds of treason, terrorism and counter-revolution took attention away from the case. Unease among some leading Jewish communists in the British Communist Party had been planted, however, and would lead to the departure of several leading members of the National Jewish Committee over the next few years.[18]

Stalin's death was followed by predictable eulogies from the Party leadership. For Harry Pollitt, Stalin 'was the greatest man of our time. As he died [...] a world transformed was the living monument to his greatness.' His tone was defiant and unyielding in its attitude to critics of Stalin's leadership:

> How unutterably stupid and degrading were the hopes of the imperialists and their spokesmen who thought to profit by the death of Stalin! They hoped for disunity and panic. They got unity and strength. Stalin was dead, but the work of Stalin lived on.[19]

Following Stalin's death, events moved too quickly for the British Communist Party leadership and along with the rest of the international communist movement would soon descend into crisis. The culmination of the Korean War provided a distraction from what was becoming a serious crisis ensuing within the Soviet Union, as disclosures of repression under Stalin's regime were gradually becoming clear. Lavrentiy Beria was soon charged and executed for treason and terrorism. By 1954, this concern had reached beyond Beria with the first public indication that there was unease with Stalin's 'cult of personality', as it was expressed among the Soviet hierarchy.

In May 1955, Stalin's successor Nikita Khrushchev visited Belgrade and the following month a joint declaration was agreed between the Soviet Union and Yugoslavia on the acceptance of 'different forms of socialism' according to particular national conditions. This was a major step towards the rehabilitation of Tito, the possibility for new trade agreements and the recognition that principled and innocent communists had been killed on the basis of false testimony. 'What's all this about Tito?' Peter Fryer asked Klugmann at a Party education school on philosophy. 'I haven't had a postcard you know,' Klugmann replied.[20]

Despite these signs of change, the British Communist Party and its ageing leadership was very slow to recognise the scale of the shift that was taking place. They were therefore quite unprepared for the impact of Nikita Khrushchev's Secret Speech and even less ready for the upheaval in Hungary towards the end of the year. Both these events would have a catastrophic effect on the British Communist Party, as elsewhere in the communist movement; for James Klugmann, it was to be another burden to be borne as the Communist Party's house intellectual and a further, seemingly irreparable, rift with fellow intellectuals of his generation who had looked to him for leadership.

As in the past, the British Party leadership sent representatives to the 20th Congress of the Communist Party of the Soviet Union, held at the end of February 1956. On this occasion Harry Pollitt was joined by Rajani Palme Dutt and George Matthews, the 39-year-old assistant general secretary who was to play a key role in the clashes with British Communist Party intellectuals as events unfolded. Khrushchev's keynote speech, where he criticised the 'cult of the individual' and revealed that a large percentage of the Communist Party of the Soviet Union (CPSU) leadership had perished in the show trials of the 1930s, was held in secret at the end of the Congress, and the British delegation was not invited. (Harry Pollitt was being shown around a Soviet condom factory at the time of the speech.) This hardly explains the slow process and defensive postures of the Party leadership, who picked up early reports of the speech either from the Soviets themselves or its sister parties. In fact, Sam Russell, the *Daily Worker*'s Moscow correspondent, knew about the speech straight away and told Harry Pollitt about its contents over lunch, while the British delegation were still in Moscow. Russell also sent in a report on 18 March, which the *Daily Worker* and the Party both suppressed.[21]

Two weeks later, the British Communist Party held its own Congress. A few days before, *Pravda* had published an attack on Stalin, and the rehabilitation of leading purged communists like Kostov and Rajk was already under way. There had been no mention of the speech in the traditional pre-Congress discussion which closed on 12 March, and in an article in *World News and Views* on 17 March George Matthews epitomised the defensive position, making clear 'mistakes have been recognised and put right', while, in what became the leadership line in the months that followed, claimed that criticisms of Stalin's 'mistakes' did not detract from his many achievements.[22] The Congress itself did not formally discuss the speech, despite the concerns of some delegates; the *Daily Worker* staff, for example, had been made aware of the severity of the speech from Sam Russell's reports, and intense meetings and discussions were going on at its offices.

Elsewhere, details of the speech had already been more readily available; in Italy, for example, the Italian Communist Party leader Palmiro Togliatti had attended the secret session and in mid-April the American Communist Party revealed the extent of Soviet anti-Semitism and the destruction of Jewish culture and the attack on Jewish intellectuals. It was not until 21 April, nearly two months after the CPSU Congress, a month after *Daily Worker* staff were made aware of it and several weeks after the Soviet leadership had officially released details to its fraternal parties, that Harry Pollitt discussed the speech in an article in *World News and Views*.

The Party leadership was clearly unprepared for the implications of Khrushchev's speech; it showed little urgency in addressing the growing voices of dissent among its own ranks. There was a growing crisis within its own leadership, which was bound up with the end of Harry Pollitt's long tenure as leader. Pollitt had been leader of the Party since 1929, and was much loved by ordinary members. He was retiring from the leadership on grounds of ill-health, following the discovery of a blood clot behind his left eye which made reading difficult and the need for a six-month rest on doctors' orders. It seemed that the decline of his own status as a leader mirrored the wider crisis at the heart of communism; he found himself ignored by Khrushchev and Bulganin during a reception on their London visit at the end of April, while the dismantling of the Cominform at the beginning of that month, a body which had become synonymous with the Stalin–Tito split and the Slansky trials, further signified the end of an era.

Pollitt had found it difficult to come to terms with the revelations against Stalin and was at the point in his career where he could not make the leap of imagination needed to take the Party through it. In fact John Gollan, his protégé whom he had identified as his long-term successor, and George Matthews, the rising apparatchik, had agreed with Pollitt's decision to resign and take on the role of Party chairman. Pollitt was to regret his resignation over the coming months, as the Party's crisis in the wake of Khrushchev's speech intensified. As events developed, it became clear that neither Gollan, a dour and unimaginative leader, nor Matthews, already a conservative defender of the faith, were up to the task.

Matthews showed himself to be particularly inept when dealing with the intellectual critics, led from early spring by the two historians and adult education tutors, John Saville and Edward Thompson. Klugmann, on the other hand, was in a much better position to engage with them. His failure to find common ground was to prove very costly.

16

The Party Functionary: 1956 and After

As news of Khrushchev's speech seeped out from the *Daily Worker* and elsewhere during March and April 1956, the serious concerns over the lack of information and public discussion from the Party leadership provoked the historians John Saville and Edward Thompson, both members of the Party's Yorkshire District, into making their concerns public. On 15 March, Thompson wrote to Klugmann in response to an invitation to speak at a Party school on labour history. Thompson, of course, was the younger brother of Frank, who had served under Klugmann in SOE. Edward Thompson had got to know Klugmann in various Party history gatherings. His wife Dorothy, herself at the beginning of a distinguished career as a historian, was even closer to Klugmann. She played a more prominent part in the Communist Party Historians Group and she and Klugmann would spend hours together rummaging through second-hand bookshops in the search for Chartist or other labour history literature. In his letter to Klugmann, Edward Thompson made clear his growing frustration with the lack of self-criticism from the leadership. It was a frank exchange, partly played out in a discussion of the programme of the labour history school to which he had been invited. Thompson proposed replacing 'Lessons of Labour History' with 'The British Democratic Tradition' or 'The Free Born Englishman' – an early indication of themes he would later take up in his seminal work *The Making of the English Working Class*.
'Lessons of Labour History', he wrote,

is of course very worthy and what one would expect from King Street. You are quite clear on what the lessons of our history are, the need for a Communist Party etc. I think this a rather dusty answer, out of all these years; should we not also ask; why the British people have not seen this need as clearly as we do? Why the British Communist Party has formed its vast and shadowy branches of lapsed members? Why the British Communist Party, struggling heroically on the main questions of principle, has also marched triumphantly from mistake to mistake in its tactics and propaganda? Why the *Daily Worker* is the [...] least inspired paper in Labour History?[1]

In their ensuing exchanges over the next two months, it was not only the divergence of their views that became clear but the contrast between Thompson's restless radicalism and Klugmann's cautious conservatism. In his reply, five days later, Klugmann was clearly a bit put out.

> You seem to be rather cross with King Street and take it for granted that all communist officials are a bit dim, dull, dusty or doctrinaire. Is this your personal experience? Or a more theoretical presumption? Anyhow perhaps we could just meet sometime and discuss it.

Two days later, on 22 March Thompson replied: 'My comments on King Street are political and not personal. As you know, we have the greatest affection for you.'

He continued: 'I am appalled at the lack of shame of the deeper implications, of serious self-questioning, with which up to now the 20th Congress has been received.' Then, in a passage which must have hurt his old friend, 'I have been re-reading your own "From Trotsky to Tito", and am alarmed (both personally and politically) as to how you can correct certain statements in this book without loss of intellectual integrity'.

Though Thompson was clearly sceptical of Klugmann's capacity for self-criticism, he held some hope of enlisting his support and continued to use the discussion of the school on labour history as a bargaining tool with which to try and shift his friend's position.

In April, Thompson proposed a motion to his own Halifax Branch, which set out its criticism of the 'totally inadequate reaction' to Khrushchev's speech. The motion called on the Party's Executive Committee (EC) to convene a Special National Congress and to

> take the lead in initiating during the coming months the fullest discussion within the Party upon the implications of this new information upon such questions as the transition to socialism, democratic liberties, the Popular Front, the role of theoretical work, democratic centralism in theory and in practice and socialist principles in questions of truth and morality.

It ended by calling on the Committee to open a 'frank public self-criticism of our Party's errors'.

Shortly after this motion was passed, Thompson wrote to Klugmann again. By this time he was already considering his position in the Party and, with Saville, was weighing up future strategies and looked for some assurances.

Our future action will of course be determined very much by how far we succeed in budging you. If you are prepared to loosen up, encourage real discussion in World News and elsewhere, and make some self-criticism to help the comrades who are arguing the political toss up and down the country in very difficult circumstances, then we shall feel much more cooperative.

If, on the other hand, you want to string us along in your wake and refuse to permit people like ourselves to express our real views and criticisms in Party journals, then you will find that we are definitely not in a mood to cooperate with that sort of circus and indeed will think some of our time better spent in getting a fitter leadership for a British Communist Party.

That is the position, James. I bear not the least personal ill-will towards you. But I find the attitude of our EC inexplicable. Bert (Ramelson, Yorkshire Disctrict Secretary) actually argued at our Branch meeting that the reason why the EC has issued no self-criticism as yet is that it hasn't met since the revelations. Well, what the hell ARE you doing?

If you were real communists you would have called an extended emergency meeting weeks ago.

Thompson ended by asking his old friend: 'Do you want the work of 36 years to be chucked away for simple fear of your own positions being threatened?'[2]

Thompson's direct questioning of the Executive Committee's actions and by implication of Klugmann's own abilities and motives, did not elicit the response he was seeking. Klugmann had no inclination to 'loosen up' and engage in 'self-criticism'. On 21 April, Pollitt had officially withdrawn publication of *From Trotsky to Tito*, a move many considered should have come at least a year earlier, and which cast further doubt on the Party's capacity for honest appraisal while undermining Klugmann's own credibility among his peers. On the steps of Battersea Town Hall, as delegates arrived at Congress at the end of March, Gerry Healy, the Trotskyist leader, had been quick to goad the Party leaders with the implausibility of their position. 'Hey Johnnie! What about that book, eh? From Trotsky to Tito?' he called out to J.R. Campbell, editor of the *Daily Worker*.[3]

In his response to Thompson on 26 April, Klugmann could only point to another forthcoming article by Pollitt and offer the view that 'the new EC will doubtless issue a statement'. He was more concerned with the forthcoming Party school: 'I don't know whether or not you will be satisfied with the statement but I am afraid I must press you both for a reply on whether you or Dorothy are prepared to take the Labour History School.'

On 2 May, Thompson wrote to Klugmann, finally declining the invitation to speak. He told him that he had received 'no satisfactory answer' to the questions raised on a need for frank discussion and saw no signs of self-criticism.

> If we had received a satisfactory answer to these questions (and gave you an opportunity to discuss them) then of course there could be no question of our very gladly taking part in the summer school [...] But you are in fact demanding a much more serious political decision from us than your chatty evasive letter suggests. By agreeing to take part before any statements have been made on these matters, we are being in effect asked to pledge ourselves to active support of Party policies, whether or not we have the right to present any effective challenge to these policies.[4]

Klugmann refused to be drawn into further public discussions with Thompson and for the duration of 1956 would remain a largely acquiescent, if uncomfortable, member of the Political Committee, disappointing those who had turned to him for support. At the beginning of April, he had appeared sympathetic to the concerns of the Communist Party Historians Group at their Annual Meeting, reporting back to the Executive Committee their main concerns.[5] Passing on criticism, however, was as far as it went for him. The Party leadership opened a debate in *World News and Views* in May but only one of the letters sent by Saville and Thompson was published, reinforcing their view that the leadership was not in the mood to relent and that the differences were now irreconcilable. At the end of May, Thompson wrote to Bert Ramelson, Yorkshire District Secretary, to resign from the District Committee. In his letter, he was scathing about the failures of the existing Party leadership: 'Gollan, Dutt, Matthews, Burns and co have in fact been acting as High Priests interpreting and justifying the Holy Writ, as emanating from Stalin.' There was a need for 'new blood' in the leadership, Thompson warned Ramelson, to 're-establish confidence in the Party'. His hope that Klugmann could help further a new direction was diminishing, and he was more candid to Ramelson in his comments.

> I believe that JK has very many qualities. But he above all is compromised. Who will believe his propaganda? Who can trust his educational direction? Without any explanation or self-criticism on his own part? Anyone who could write 'From Trotsky to Tito' must either have an element of dishonesty or of irrational dogmatism in his intellectual make-up.[6]

By June, when the *Observer* published full details of Khrushchev's speech to a wider public, in Saville's view 'it had already become clear that no serious debate was ever going to be permitted'.[7] At this point Thompson and Saville, by now in daily communication, started to think about making their opposition to the leadership more public.

> By about the beginning of June [...] we had agreed first, that the Party leadership were deliberately curbing and confining discussion, and second, that the most obvious way to force an open debate was probably to publish independently of the Party press.[8]

They decided to establish a new journal, the *Reasoner*. The hastily printed first edition in mid-July sold several hundred copies quickly and attracted 300 letters. On the masthead of the new publication was a quote from Marx: 'To leave error unrefuted is to encourage intellectual immorality', an undisguised address to the leadership. The publication of the *Reasoner* inevitably brought Thompson and Saville into conflict with Party authorities – it was after all an unauthorised publication – and at two Yorkshire District Committee Meetings in August they were instructed to 'cease publication'. The second motion contained a recommendation that the matter be forwarded to the Party's Executive Committee and as a result the two were invited to attend a meeting with Pollitt and others at King Street on 31 August, prior to the September Executive Committee Meeting.

A fortnight after publication of the *Reasoner* and before the motions at the Yorkshire District Committee, Thompson had gone to see Klugmann in London in a last attempt to win him round. It was an attempt on Thompson's part to offer a

> gesture of conciliation, hoping that some informal proposal or hint of proposal might result from our discussion in the direction of compromise. [...] I thought that if any member of the Pol. Committee at that time in England would have authority to open up such a discussion – however informally – it would be James. But not one suggestion of this character came from him.[9]

By this time, the crisis in the international communist movement intensified after riots in Poznań had seen the return of the rehabilitated Polish communist Gomulka, and culminated with unrest in Hungary. In October, news came from Budapest of Soviet intervention to quell large unrest which had broken out in favour of the former communist leader Imre Nagy, whose 'new course' of socialist reform between 1953 and 1955 had brought him into conflict with Soviet authorities and led to his removal from office. Now, he was reinstated by popular demand of the Hungarian people on 24 October, by which time Soviet troops had gathered to resist the demonstrators. On 1 November he declared Hungary had left the Warsaw Pact and sought support from the United Nations and other bodies to accept Hungary as an independent and neutral state.

Feelings were running high in the offices of the *Daily Worker*, where the staff were already divided over the implications of Khrushchev's Secret Speech. Its foreign correspondent, Peter Fryer, had earlier written an orthodox account of the 1949 trial of Laszlo Rajk, the catalyst for the anti-Tito purges, in which the Hungarian leader had 'confessed' to being a spy and agent of Western imperialism. He now wanted to know the truth. Rajk's rehabilitation and reburial in October had attracted an audience of over 200,000 and Fryer, traumatised by the memory of his earlier reports, was determined to give an accurate picture of what was now happening on the streets of Budapest. His reports of the Hungarian uprising in November – save a heavily edited first one – were refused publication, largely because he reported it as a genuine uprising of a discontented people rather than the official line that the demonstrations aided the West and were counter-revolutionary. This led eventually to Fryer's resignation on 16 November, shortly after his last dispatch was refused publication in the *Daily Worker*.[10]

The Party was now in turmoil. The British bombing of the Suez Canal on 31 October had brought members on to the streets in an offensive against the Eden government, no doubt seeking respite from their own unanswered questions. However, despite the attentions of the Party leadership – Gollan placated the Young Communist League Congress at the end of October by urging them to 'Look at Eden' – the events in Hungary were leading to widening divisions in branches, and even among families. At an anti-Eden demonstration on 4 November, Alison Macleod reported, 'The banners were all about Suez; the arguments among the banner-bearers were all about Hungary.'[11]

The *Reasoner* remained the main focus of dissent, with an expanding range of supporters and contacts. The second issue had been published in September just before the Executive Committee instructed its editors to 'cease publication'. Now, the third and final issue was finished as the Soviet troops entered Budapest. In their editorial, Saville and Thompson wrote:

In this crisis, when the Hungarian people needed our solidarity, the British Communist Party has failed them. We cannot wait until the 21st Congress of the CPSU when no doubt the attack on Budapest will be registered as another 'mistake'. The International Communist movement, and also the World Peace movement, must exert its full moral influence to effect the immediate withdrawal of Soviet troops from Hungary; at the same time demanding the neutralisation of Hungary and resisting all Western attempts to turn the situation to their military and political advantage.[12]

The editors called on their supporters to reject the CPGB leadership, believing by this time that there was little chance of change. They were subsequently suspended from Party membership for three months, though both decided to resign. They were not alone.

On the Party's Executive Committee, only Arnold Kettle and Max Morris voted against the Soviet action in Hungary. Klugmann himself was said to be concerned at the developments and was only too well aware of the discontent, particularly among intellectuals. This did not translate into action, though. After a promising start as education organiser, Klugmann had become haunted by his past duplicity. He may have been instructed by Pollitt and Moscow to write *From Trotsky to Tito*, but it was his intellectual credibility that had been eroded. Moreover he was dependent on a failing leadership. Pollitt was finished; his contemporary, John Gollan, was unconvincing, while George Matthews had become the *bête noire* of the intellectuals; his anti-intellectualism was growing more sectarian as the perceived threat from the *Reasoner* increased. Palme Dutt was now barely taken seriously, with his own muddled attempts to explain Soviet actions a cause of derision among some Party members. Yet whatever Klugmann's reservations about his colleagues, he clearly felt he had nowhere else to go. He did not have the choice of leaving his full-time work for an academic career, as did his historian friends, nor did he have an alternative journalistic career in prospect like Peter Fryer. However, the question of whether he had somewhere else to go politically, *in the Party,* was more debatable. His brother-in-law Maurice Cornforth had some sympathy for Fryer's predicament and supported the idea of the *Reasoner*, sending it a £50 cheque after hearing of Nagy's execution, though he wanted the intellectuals to stay in the Party.[13]

This was Klugmann's position too. He had lost the Thompsons. He and Dorothy Thompson had spent time together over many years, discussing labour history and organising teaching materials at summer schools, and would often have a meal together after meetings of the Historians Group. Following the crucial meeting which discussed Khrushchev's speech – 'one of the most tense and emotional that I have ever attended', according to Dorothy – they went to eat together as usual. On the top deck of a London bus, Dorothy reported a story she had heard from her husband that day at the Yorkshire District Committee that Stalin himself had authored part of what came to be known as *The British Road to Socialism* and had even disagreed with aspects of the CPGB's own contribution. Klugmann, who was one of its original authors, was so upset at being reminded of Stalin's intervention that he 'went pale, got up and got off the bus, and I never saw him again'.[14]

Nevertheless, he still had two further opportunities to keep some of the leading critics on board. The first was the commission set up to examine 'inner-party democracy' (IPD). The IPD Commission was made up of 15 members, nine appointed by the Party's Executive Committee and six by the Party regions. Klugmann was one of ten full-time Party officials on the commission, which was chaired by John Mahon, with the formidable Betty Reid as its secretary. Also on the commission were leading critics, including the historian Christopher Hill, Malcom MacEwen, who had recently resigned as the *Daily Worker*'s features editor, Peter Cadogan, from the South-East Midlands District and Kevin Halpin, the one industrial worker. It met for the first time on 11 September 1956 and for the last time on 6 December 1956, convening every Friday evening and occasionally at weekends. Its remit was to report to the 25th Party Congress in May 1957, but as the critics on the commission pointed out, this gave very little time for prolonged discussion or to receive substantial evidence from Party groups or individuals. The concern at the lack of discussion in the Party following the Khrushchev speech, and the general inadequacy of the Party's response to unfolding events in Eastern Europe, was the starting-point for the critics. MacEwen's opening paper called for an investigation of the Party's response to the expulsion of Yugoslavia from the Cominform, the electoral system at Party Congresses and the functioning of the Party press after the CPSU's 20th Congress.[15]

However, according to MacEwen, the commission did not consider 'real evidence' or attempt the examination of any witnesses. The tight time-scale, composition of the commission and political priorities of the full-timers decided that. In the event, the majority saw the minority (which initially also included Halpin and Joe Cheek in addition to Hill, MacEwen and Cadogan) as threatening the Party leadership because of its criticism of democratic centralism – that is, the system which reconciled accountability of leadership to rank-and-file members with the need for Party discipline and unity. The majority argued that it was not democratic centralism per se but an abuse of it that had been the problem in the Soviet Union, while accepting the need for improving and extending discussion within its own ranks. This 'oiling and tinkering', as the critics saw it, however, was a long way from what they felt it should be: namely, the 'democratic spirit and method of working, from above downwards and from below upwards'.[16]

This gulf on the commission resulted in the submission of 'majority' and 'minority' reports, but only after the suspension of Peter Cadogan for writing a letter to the *News Chronicle* critical of the Party leadership on its policy towards Hungary. This event seemed to reinforce the leadership's position, as Cadogan's actions were regarded as a breach of Party discipline and Betty Reid refused to sit at the same table as a 'traitor'. It also increased the isolation of Hill and MacEwen – Halpin and Cheek having been won back to the majority view, albeit with some reservations.

Klugmann's own role on this commission might have promised a different outcome. Paired with Christopher Hill, whom he had known since their student days in the 1930s, he had joint responsibility for drafting the section on Party discussion. Klugmann's belief that communism was an extension of all that was best in the British democratic tradition might have produced a coming together of minds at a critical moment. In the event, his role as Party functionary and his fear of expressing any public disagreement with Party orthodoxy shaped his outlook. His offering, in draft form, of the boundaries of Party discussion offered little hope to the critics:

> Normally, discussion should be terminated by Party decisions and the adoption of Party policy which is binding on all members, but in some cases as on problems of art and literature, there is a basis for continued discussion and debate without decision.[17]

According to MacEwen, Klugmann and Hill 'were only able to produce a joint draft by offering alternative passages on the key points or, in one case, by Hill inserting the word "not" before a Klugmann verb'.[18]

Both the majority and minority reports were published, though only the majority report was discussed at the Party's 25th Congress. By this time, MacEwen was in the process of being expelled, and Christopher Hill resigned shortly after a forlorn attempt at Congress to win support for reform, He was one of around 7,000 members who left the Party in the wake of 1956.

It was significant that the most open and serious challenge to the Party leadership in 1956 came from the historians Thompson, Saville and Hill. The Communist Party Historians Group was the most intellectually stimulating and notable of all the sub-groups of the National Cultural Committee. First established in the late 1940s, it brought together the best of the 1930s generation of intellectuals, many of whom would go on to distinguished academic careers or play a major part in the British New Left. The Historians Group always had influence well beyond the confines of the Party, stimulating interest in social history and 'history from below', inspiring new journals like *Past and Present* and having a pivotal role in the development of a British Marxist historical tradition. The Communist Party was crucial to its activities, and participants regarded it as fundamental to their commitment as historians. Moreover, despite the tensions of the Cold War period, relations between the group and the Party were good before 1956, and Klugmann, along with Jack Cohen, John Gollan and other Party full-timers, played a key role in the group's activities.

The group met at weekends at Marx House or the room above the Garibaldi restaurant in Clerkenwell. Discussions flourished in an atmosphere of 'physical austerity, intellectual excitement, political passion and friendship [...] "History" recruited us as individuals', as Eric Hobsbawm, the group's chairman recalled. 'Where would we, as intellectuals, have been, what would have become of us, but for the experiences of war, revolution and depression, fascism and anti-fascism, which surrounded us in our youth?'[19]

The group grew rapidly under a large and active committee with sub-groups on ancient, medieval, sixteenth- and seventeenth-century and eighteenth- and nineteenth-century periods. They were an impressive milieu, counting Victor Kiernan, Christopher Hill, George Rude, Rodney Hilton, Dorothy Thompson, Eric Hobsbawm, John Saville and a young Raphael Samuel, and several conferences were organised with the support of the Party.

Klugmann, who chaired the most stimulating of these gatherings, normally held in the convivial surroundings of Netherwood Guest House in East Sussex, must have relished the opportunity to draw on his interests in British labour history, to coordinate the proceedings and cajole the participants into getting their research into written form for a Marxist history of the British labour movement. This book would have been the pinnacle of his achievements as education organiser. The conferences were also much appreciated by the participants. 'For us as historians it was a memorable, and instructive experience,' Hobsbawm recalled.[20]

But it did not allow us to write the planned book. The gap between what historians thought it necessary to write and what was regarded as officially possible and desirable to write at this stage – or even much later – proved too large.[21]

The 'gap' was between the commitment of the historians to write a history which addressed difficult questions in labour history – including the Communist Party itself – and the Party functionaries, who saw themselves as custodians of the past. Inevitably, the gap widened during 1956 and the group was decimated. A separate discussion had begun on the need for a history of the Communist Party itself. Initially, this was to avoid its history being left to others hostile to the Party (the big fear was a Trotskyist interpretation) but was now fuelled further by the need for clarity over the difficult questions in its recent past. Yet another commission was set up to discuss its potential and once again, Klugmann found himself a key figure in the elaborations. This Party History Commission included mainly full-timers: Robin Page Arnott, Emile Burns, Alan Hutt, Andrew Rothstein and Frank Jackson, plus Eric Hobsbawm and Brian Pearce from the dwindling Historians Group. Hobsbawm and Pearce called for a frank, serious and critical history of the Party, which did not avoid the difficult questions. In any case, if such a history was not commissioned by the Party, they argued, then there were plenty of anti-communists who would address the questions in their own way. The full-timers, however, argued that a better alternative would be a series of essays written by different authors on particular periods, thereby avoiding a more focused and critical investigation into its past.

And then there was Klugmann himself, Hobsbawm's old guru, to whom he and others had turned to for support several times during that tumultuous year.

He sat on the far right-hand corner of the table and said nothing. He knew we were right. If we did not produce a history of our Party, including the problematic bits, they would not go away. The history would simply be written by anti-communist scholars – and indeed within less than two years such a history was written. But he lacked what the great Bismark once called 'Zivilcourage', civilian as distinct from military courage. He knew what was right, but shied away from saying it in public.[22]

After the commission's first meeting, which rejected the arguments of the Historians Group, Brian Pearce left, and Hobsbawm remained an isolated figure, distrusted by the leadership (which expected him to leave); although he retained his Party membership he would shortly withdraw permanently from all official Party work.[23] The commission initially decided on a series of essays on specific periods, which did not elicit any enthusiasm from the historians. On their part the full-time officials thought the historians were pursuing 'delaying tactics'.[24] Then, after a year of procrastination, the commission finally accepted Klugmann's view that 'I do not believe that the work can be done by a large consultative commission'. Instead he proposed that 'a leading comrade be relieved from other duties for the time necessary to do this work'.[25]

The commission at the time felt that the 'leading comrade' would need nine months to a year to do the work. It was decided that Klugmann himself should assume the task, one that would take him the rest of his life and which he would never complete. He had got what he had always wanted: to spend his time writing history fuelled by political commitment. Along the way, though, in the compromises he made, his silences and evasions, he had lost much of his vitality, intellectual credibility and the courage of his convictions. 'He had had the stuffing knocked out of him,' Hobsbawm recalled.[26] In his tribute to Klugmann after his death in 1977, the Party's general secretary, Gordon McLennan, described him as 'eternally young'. In the late 1950s to many of his former comrades at least, he appeared old before his time.

17

A Lost Generation

The late 1950s had been a very difficult time for James Klugmann. He was intellectually broken after his disastrous book *From Trotsky to Tito* and the events of 1956 confirmed the decline in his credibility among his peers. It was a severe loss of personal authority. He lost many friends at this time; among them historians, student contemporaries and those who had seen him as their intellectual leader, even 'guru' in earlier times. He could no longer be trusted as a man of principle; his loyalty to the Party, and all that involved, overrode even his own better judgements. He was also a lonely man. Though he had many acquaintances within the international communist movement and was regarded with affection throughout his own Party, he had few close friends or indeed friends outside the Party, or much social life independent of Party 'socials' and gatherings. His loyalty to the Party, of a familial nature in its intensity and devotion, had by the late 1950s the sense of permanence and the realisation that he had nowhere else to go. Even his career path in the Party seemed to have reached its limits. Over the next few years he would retire from its leading committees. His intellectual credibility had been questioned by former allies, and now his peers in the leadership no longer saw him as the ideal man to deal with the rebuilding of the Party after the crisis of 1956.

He was also losing his own family. His mother and grandmother died within six months of each other in late 1958, and his sister, to whom he remained very close, was in the early stages of the cancer that would kill her in 1965. He was estranged from most of his extended family, never having resolved long-standing political differences and outlooks on life with his two older cousins, Frank and John, who had gone on to work in the family business. An exception was Max Rosenheim, the elder brother of his prep school friend and first political ally Charles (who had died in the war) who was becoming a leading physician and would go on to be a Labour peer.

If he lacked the urgency and conviction of earlier times then Klugmann kept busy, dividing his time between Talbot Road and King Street. His sister and brother-in-law must have been a source of comfort, and despite Kitty's ailing health, his home life offered political reassurance, discussion and reflection on where the Party was going. Maurice Cornforth, his brother-in-law, had serious doubts about the way the Party leadership had handled the dissidents in 1956, and the departures of former friends would have been the subject of much debate. It must have been a period of great personal reflection too; his faith in communism may have remained intact but the justification for his own actions raised fundamental questions about his beliefs – including his long-standing admiration of the Soviet Union.

These doubts, and the growing anti-intellectual climate in the Party, were behind his decision in 1957 to withdraw from the leadership. He would never again be an official spokesman called on to justify the Party's foreign affairs manoeuvres. In the wake of the Party's Special Congress in April 1957, he told the Party's Political Committee that he would no longer take on the joint roles of education and propaganda. As a result, at the Executive Committee Meeting in May 1957 he was removed from the Political Committee. He was replaced by Bill Wainwright, one of the most virulent critics of the intellectuals. From this point on, Klugmann was never completely trusted by the leadership; his star, which had shone so brightly in the late 1940s, when he had the ear of Harry Pollitt, was fading even among the apparatchiks.[1]

He remained on the Executive Committee for another six years, under his revised role in charge of 'Education' and 'Theoretical Work', which at least enabled him to pursue some of his intellectual interests. It was becoming clear that his new work as the Party's official historian would extend beyond the one year initially proposed. Indeed it would take him a full decade to complete the first two volumes, which covered only the Party's first seven years. This work took him to Moscow for preliminary research in 1957, which allowed him to see the Soviet Union without Stalin in a visit where his work in the Comintern archive and other libraries was closely supervised; perhaps for him a reminder of the restrictions imposed on intellectuals by 'actually existing socialism'.

He was also given another task in 1957, one which would absorb much of his time over the last two decades of his life and gradually allow him to rediscover his earlier humanism. One consequence of the exodus of the previous year was the Party's growing concern that it needed to maintain its existing intellectual cohort and provide some competition for the emerging New Left intellectual milieu, one of the outcomes of the schism of 1956. This was the reason for the Party's new 'theoretical and discussion journal', *Marxism Today*, which replaced the *Modern Quarterly* in 1957. Klugmann was initially appointed as assistant editor of the journal, with John Gollan, the Party's general secretary, its editor. This arrangement was itself a neat admission of where his intellectual and political allegiances had taken him – an intellectual who needed the permission of the Party to function effectively. Nevertheless it did allow him more space to think and reflect.

His first reflection, as he took on his new duties, may well have been the stark contrast between the Party's political ambitions, its analysis of British society in the late 1950s, and its general mood and outlook, with that of the New Left. In the spring of 1957, the first edition of *Universities and Left Review*, edited by four Oxford graduates, Stuart Hall, Gabriel Pearson, Raphael ('Ralph') Samuel and Charles Taylor, drew on an impressive line-up of contributors including Eric Hobsbawm, G.D.H. Cole, Isaac Deutscher, Joan Robinson, Basil Davidson and a young David Marquand for their first issue, which claimed a circulation of 8,000 and won positive reviews. Their topics were expansive, with a strong cultural edge on cinema, art criticism and literature, alongside Marxist analysis of class and contemporary capitalism, 'de-Stalinisation', the role of the intellectuals and the future of the Labour Party. Its founding editorial starkly defined the moment of opportunity for the left: 'Universities and Left Review is a calculated risk', it argued. 'The success or failure of this venture depends on the degree of frankness which can be assumed between editors, writers and readers.'

It went on:

> The post-war period was one in which declining political orthodoxies held sway. Every political concept became a weapon in the cold war of ideas, every idea had its label, every person had his place in the political spectrum, every form of political action appeared – in someone's eyes – a polite treason [...]
>
> In these tight compartmentalised worlds, buttressed by bans and proscriptions, suspicions and fears, supported by texts from Lenin and Stalin, mottos from Burke and Bagehot, protected by massive armies with nuclear stockpiles and mutually exclusive military pacts, British socialism suffered moral and intellectual eclipse.[2]

Several public meetings were held in support of the new journal, while its influence spread among activists on the Aldermaston marches against nuclear weapons. A New Left Club was set up which hosted discussions of the key themes twice monthly, initially at a hotel in Bloomsbury, subsequently at the

Partisan Coffee Shop in Soho, founded by Raphael Samuel, the only one of the four editors to have been in the Communist Party and the youngest member of the History Group in 1956.

As Klugmann observed the development of this movement, he must have been reminded of the intellectual promiscuity of the 1930s. His own role in that earlier movement was pivotal; as one of its leading instigators he had sought a critical analysis of a society whose ruling sections were in crisis. Now, in a different period, with capitalism claiming to have resolved its structural defects in the era of consumerism, another generation was speaking out against the inequities and cultural 'contradictions' of contemporary capitalism in new and imaginative ways. From his vantage point, in the shadow of Gollan, he would have been alarmed at the way the Party had become isolated. It seemed to be losing a generation.

Eric Hobsbawm, who was attending the New Left gatherings, confirmed its appeal. Though 'organisationally it is a complete shambles and is virtually certain to go broke', he reported, 'it appears to have a surprisingly firm, and lasting mass basis'. 'ULR [Universities and Left Review] meetings attract the same sort of public as the Left Book Club did in the 1930s; overwhelmingly middle class and intellectual/artistic people, vaguely but strongly rebellious and "progressive".'

He concluded that the Party had been badly informed about the movement and expressed his surprise that he had not come across the Party's youth and student sections – 'whose business it is to keep the Party informed about this kind of thing' – at any of their meetings.[3] The New Left drew in new activists and thinkers – Kenneth Tynan, Lindsay Anderson and John Berger were all regular attenders – in meetings of up to 600 people. It was in marked contrast to the early issues of *Marxism Today*, with ageing Party leaders, tutors at day schools and members of its Cultural Committee among the main contributors.

If *Universities and Left Review* marked the birth of a new generation of left intellectuals, then the *New Reasoner* (which had replaced the *Reasoner*, but was still edited by John Saville and Edward Thompson), just a couple of months later, was a reminder of the quality of the intellectuals who had left the Party. Its editorial made clear its determination to break with the damaging orthodoxies of the past as the British 'Marxist and Communist tradition [was] in need of rediscovery and re-affirmation'. 'It is our hope that we may be able to build some bridge between this tradition and those left socialists who – in the era of Stalin's birthday and the Doctors' Plot – developed their thought altogether outside it.'[4]

Thompson's own article in that first issue, 'Socialist Humanism', addressed the pernicious effects of 'Stalinist ideology': 'The Stalinist today acts or writes in certain ways, not because he is a fool or hypocrite, but because he is the prisoner of false ideas.'[5] For Thompson, Stalinism had 'distorted moral values' and was characterised by economic determinism, mechanistic prisms, anti-intellectualism and class relativism. Stalinist language, Thompson maintained, had replaced personal consciousness, human agency, self-criticism and dissent, with the result that 'creative man is changed into a passive thing'.[6]

Communist Party leaderships, if not the rank-and-file membership – and here he was aiming directly at the CPGB – had been infected by the 'disease of orthodoxy'. Klugmann, as he read these words, would have had much to reflect on. Thompson's reference to Blake, Morris and Thomas More – all heroes of Klugmann's – would also have grated.

Several of the contributors to the *New Reasoner* had been protagonists in the recent split in the CPGB, among them Malcolm MacEwen, Hyman Levy and Peter Fryer. But the split in 1956 was now much more than an internal dispute. The *Universties and Left Review* and the *New Reasoner* would later merge to become the *New Left Review*, and the Party's hold as the exclusive voice of Marxism would be broken.

The contrast in range, scope and depth of analysis was evident in the first issue of *Marxism Today* in October 1957, which carried an article by Harry Pollitt on the fortieth anniversary of the October Revolution and Emile Burns on the theory of crisis. In February, the line-up of reliable Party theorists broadened to include Gollan himself on 'Labour Policy Today', Ron Bellamy on 'Wages, Prices and Inflation' and – less typically – George Thomson, the classicist, on the first English translation of Antonio Gramsci.

Klugmann's first contribution was an article on the new edition of *The British Road to Socialism* in February 1958, a very cautious endorsement of recent Congress resolutions and Executive Committee decisions. Perhaps with the memory of Dorothy Thompson's passing comment still fresh in his mind, he went some way to point out the importance of the British conditions: 'Each country will have its own, its specific road to socialism [...] but whilst the *forms* change the *essence* remains the same' (emphasis in original).

Marxism Today did not attempt anything like the expansive political and cultural analysis of the New Left. In fact, while it had much to say about international questions, on colonialism, US imperialism and China – Klugmann keeping faith with the Chinese Communist Party later than most of the Party leadership – its analysis of social and cultural change in Britain was weak. Hobsbawm's recognition that the New Left was making real gains among the young radical middle classes and intellectuals, with direct links to the Aldermaston marches, did not have much impact on the Party's analysis. Indeed, as the New Left grew in influence, the Party became more insular and dismissive of its potential. Arnold Kettle, one of Klugmann's closest friends and comrades since the 1930s, was particularly venomous in his denunciation of the New Left radicals: 'It is a characteristic [...] of petty-bourgeois ideology that it is at once critical – up to a certain point – of capitalism and yet limited in its range by bourgeois preconceptions.'[7]

In Kettle's view, bourgeois preconceptions apparently included not only 'tone, language and perceptions', but the habits of meeting in coffee bars and reading sociology. Kettle was particularly irked by the criticism of the Soviet Union and the apparent omission of the need for a Communist Party.

Klugmann may have publicly shared this criticism but he must have been uncomfortable with the breach with such significant intellectuals as Thompson, Saville and others. In fact the Party was politically isolated in other ways. In the late 1950s it opposed unilateral nuclear disarmament on the grounds that it was divisive and such questions were better left to negotiations between the superpowers. This position was expressed through the British Peace Committee, which the Party dominated and which was briefly a rival to the fast-growing Campaign for Nuclear Disarmament (CND), until it became apparent that CND was gaining a powerful foothold in the left, which precipitated a change of line in 1959.[8] The Party was also very slow to recognise the importance of pop and rock culture, which it continued to view as emblematic of American cultural imperialism (or at least another example of the commodification of mass culture) until its own youth section, the Young Communist League, started to invite rock stars to its festivals from the mid-1960s. On a more positive front, the Party consolidated its strength in the trade union movement into the early 1960s – albeit having to survive a major corruption scandal in the Electricians' Union – and this was how it was able partially to rebuild its base. From the mid-1960s, under the leadership of industrial organiser Bert Ramelson, it would begin to regain significant influence and exert more political pressure on the TUC and Labour Party over the next decade.

Klugmann's role at *Marxism Today* brought a renewed direction and purpose to his work. From July 1960, an 'Editorial Comments' section at the front of the journal was included as an experiment, with Klugmann adapting suggestions from readers as well as his own pronouncements on a broad range of subjects. He gradually brought his personal stamp to the editorial commentary, where his deep interest in world events, expansive reading and interest in books was evident to his readership. The first Editorial Comments gives a flavour of its miscellaneous offerings, with short notes on Richard Crossman's critique of Marx, R.M. Titmuss's new book *The Irresponsible Society* and an item on the nationalised industries. Over the following years, readers would be offered an eclectic mix of comments on Italian neo-realist cinema, the power of advertising, the work of Hemingway and Sillitoe, his admiration for the BBC arts programme *Monitor* – essential Sunday-night viewing in Talbot Road – as well as general political observations.

Klugmann was gradually recovering his earlier optimism and once more turned to the younger generation. Invited back to his own university to talk to Cambridge communists, he predicted that the 1960s would be a revolutionary decade, quite different from the preceding one. 'It was very prescient', Conrad Wood, one of the organisers, recalled later.[9] In December 1961 he went to Paris to attend 'a week of Marxist thought' under the title of 'Marxism and Humanism' at the Centre d'études et de récherches Marxistes (Centre of Marxist Study and Research). He was clearly inspired by this event, which drew 20,000 people, including around 6,000 for a discussion on Marxism and philosophy involving Jean-Paul Sartre, held at the old Left Bank meeting place Mutualité, which revived memories of his time there in the 1930s. Then Marxism had been a strong influence among professors, while some of the student body had gone over to fascism. 'Now', he noted, 'a great renaissance of Marxist thought is taking place, with particular strength amongst the French students.'[10]

Released from the responsibilities of Party leadership, he began to rediscover some of the core values which first attracted him to communism at Gresham's. He was delighted with his old schoolfriend Benjamin Britten's *War Requiem*, which he heard at Westminster Abbey at the end of 1962. This 'hauntingly beautiful and profoundly disturbing work' portrayed 'not only the vileness of war, but the comradeship of man'. Britten's 'imaginative music is full of deep feeling, sorrow and anger'. His Editorial Comments included warm praise too for Giuseppe Tomasi di Lampedusa's novel *The Leopard*, commending the 'subtlety of its political and human insight'.[11]

His rediscovery of humanism revived rather than diminished his Marxism. He was dismissive of those who, at the beginning of the 1960s, pronounced Marxism dead and buried in the face of the capitalist boom period. Professor

Stuart Hampshire – whom he had tried to recruit to Soviet intelligence with the help of Anthony Blunt in Paris in 1937 – was among those who claimed Marxism was finished, bringing a strong reaction from his former acquaintance.

An obituary of Marxism was published recently in the New Statesman. This was written by a fairly eminent philosopher, Professor Hampshire, who handsomely acknowledged that Marx had made some contribution to human thought but went on to say that Marxism is now dead. A few wreaths were laid at the graveside in subsequent correspondence.

Yet, he pointed out: 'Marxism seems to thrive on "dying" and the more it is "buried" by enthusiastic reactionaries the wider its influence seems to become.'[12]

Nevertheless, it was becoming clear to him, as he took over the sole editorship of *Marxism Today* in 1962, that the Communist Party no longer had a monopoly on Marxism. Eric Hobsbawm's comment three years later neatly summed up the predicament facing Party intellectuals in that period.

We had to learn to live with the fact that the Marxist intellectuals who were in the Communist Party were only a part – and not as in the past the overwhelming majority – of the intellectuals who called themselves Marxists. In fact today, it is impossible to make the simple statement on which many of us were brought up; there is one, and only one 'correct' Marxism and it is to be found in Communist Parties.[13]

The Party had to win back some of the lost generation who had turned to radical politics in the early 1960s. This was the thinking behind 'The Challenge of Marxism' series, the best of a number of *Marxism Today* public forums, which attracted reasonable audiences. Klugmann once again enthused over the mix of 'students [who] were able to argue with their teachers, amateurs with professionals, Marxists with non-Marxists, and enough complex problems of aesthetics raised to occupy the most erudite Marxist for many years to come'. *Marxism Today* cautiously began to seek a wider base in the Party and by mid-1963, under Klugmann's editorship, was able to report 'slowly rising sales in recent months'.

Though his work as editor of *Marxism Today* was a growing commitment, he continued to be in demand as a tutor, and an unexpected teaching opportunity arose in 1964. This offered him the chance to experience once again the excitement of teaching students at a moment of radical political change. Klugmann had known Kwame Nkrumah as a student activist in the 1930s, and then again after the war, when Nkrumah was helping to organise the Pan-African Congress in Manchester. Back in Ghana, Nkrumah had played a leading part in the anti-colonial movement before becoming prime minister in 1952 and had overseen the transition to independence from British rule in 1957. As a Marxist doing battle with British colonialism, Nkrumah received support from the British Communist Party, and some of its intellectuals had been encouraged to contribute to the newly socialist Ghana. In 1964, in its mission to train future party and state leaders through a series of intensive classes, the Kwame Nkrumah Ideological Institute was set up, and Klugmann was invited to be one of its first visiting lecturers. He was 'highly honoured' to be asked, and he took a Ghana Airlines flight the following January, prepared to deliver an eight-week lecture course on such topics as materialism, dialectics, religion, African history, class struggle and neo-colonialism.

He arrived in Ghana in the midst of a 'fierce political battle' within the ruling party over the direction and pace of socialist advance, and not without a little chaos and confusion in the arrangements. The institute was based in Winneba, some 40 miles along the coast from Accra. He was put up in a bungalow and met the other 20 or so staff colleagues, which included Poles, Czechs and East Germans as well as Ghanaians. After much waiting around ('for the first four to five days it was impossible to get any discussion on what I was to do'[14]), he finally got the chance to meet the institute's director and they agreed a revised schedule of general politics lectures for second-year students and classes on socialism and general politics in French for a group of Congolese students. The two-hour lectures were to be followed by two-hour discussion periods – a 'marathon', as he later put it – and the titles give some indication of the developing political crisis in Ghana: 'What Socialism is and what it is not'; 'The Lower and Higher Stages of Socialism'; 'The Role of the Vanguard Socialist Party'; 'Stages of the National Liberation Movement'; 'What Are the Problems of Transforming an Anti-Imperialist Movement into a Vanguard Socialist Party?'

Nevertheless, Klugmann was in his element, partly reliving his earlier experiences in Cairo with the Croatian miners at the villa by Mena House, and his subsequent Party education classes. In addition to the formal classes, he organised what he called 'a host of personal discussions and group discussions and most afternoons and evenings when I got to know the students I had from two to twelve students discussing every subject under the sun'. He found the

Congolese inexperienced and without much political education or access to literature in French, but 'thirsting for the most elementary knowledge about socialism'. Given that the teachers from Eastern Europe had language difficulties and taught in more formal modes, his own inimitable lecturing style proved very popular.

He found the Ghanaians

gay, passionate, excitable, affectionate, bubbling over with life and excitement. They roar with laughter at jokes, clap each other on the back, hiss the villain when you are describing imperialism, exclaim with horror when you describe things like concentration camps. And though they treated my grey hairs with complete respect, you got a wonderful relationship in the course of lectures. They love to shout and interrupt and are not at all charitable to their fellow students, whom they tend to hiss, shout down [...] My first discussion with the whole 135 was utter bedlam.

On his departure, he received 'an uproarious send-off, with speeches and gifts', testament to the new friendships, not least with the Congolese, who were grateful they could talk to him in French. He found the whole experience inspiring and rewarding. The director 'requested strongly that I should return for the first term of the next academic year, (ie October–December 1965), for a course of general lectures and also to prepare the general textbook', he told Party leaders.

Just before he was due to depart, he received an invitation to see President Kwame Nkrumah, who had just returned from a ten-day 'fasting and meditation' break. Over a 40-minute discussion, 'as warm as could be', in which Nkrumah repeated the invitation for him to return to lecture and complete the textbook, they discussed the current political situation, including 'one or two theoretical problems' on which Klugmann would report back verbally to the British Communist Party leaders. These 'theoretical problems', which amounted to differences over strategies for socialism and Nkrumah's own leadership, would not be resolved, however. In fact Nkrumah's time was coming to an end – he would be ousted by a coup the following year – and with it went another of Klugmann's socialist dreams.

10 At one of many Communist Party education schools. Klugmann is on the right, towards the back

11 A good Jesuit? James Klugmann
shortly before he died

12 *James Klugmann* by Renzo Galeotti

18

Late Spring

On Klugmann's return from Ghana, his life took another turn with a big change in his personal circumstances, one initially tinged with profound sadness. His sister Kitty, for so long a confidante and comrade, a lasting intellectual influence and an ally in the early family battles over communism, died in April 1965 after a long battle with breast cancer. She was just 57. Tributes poured in to him and Maurice, remembering a comrade who was 'so full of vitality', with 'a great sense of humour bubbling through', as a fighter and tireless worker for the Party, latterly in the London District offices, on social welfare issues. Telegrams and letters arrived at the house and notices appeared in the *Daily Worker*. Kay Beauchamp, who had taught her at Kingsley School, reminded James that Kitty had told her that it was her lessons on India that influenced her decision to become a communist. Bert Ramelson told him that Kitty's work for the Party was the kind 'which attracts no plaudits from the multitude, no public limelight but it is nevertheless the steel framework of the revolutionary movement, without which we would never rise higher than a propagandist group'. He went on:

> I appreciate how close you were. Brother and sister tied together with joined ideals and work and concern at each other's health, so the blow is the heavier. She gave all she could to the movement, which was the breath of her life.[1]

At her funeral at Golders Green Crematorium, Bill Alexander described her 'devoted and loyal activity to further the aims of the Party . In all, Maurice and James received some 75 letters of condolence, with Maurice putting joint thanks on their behalf in the *Daily Worker*. Some of those closest to Klugmann offered support to help him cope in the short-term, but in his replies he was able to say that after so much painful suffering her death came as a 'release'.

Among the letters they received was a warm message of condolence from his cousin Max Rosenheim – later Baron Rosenheim of Camden – the leading physician who had treated Kitty at University College Hospital (UCH).

Rosenheim and his mother Martha were two family members with whom James and Kitty had kept in touch, and Max had known for a while that she would not pull through. Max described Kitty as 'a wonderfully brave person'. Klugmann, in his reply, let his cousin know that 'for years she had been expressing her gratitude to Maurice and myself for all that you did to help her, and in general we are tremendously grateful to the UCH'.[2]

These warm messages from family and friends must have brought some relief to Klugmann. Kitty had been ill since 1957 and there had been many pressures on him and his brother-in-law in a household that continued to be dominated by the needs of the Party. He was not particularly domesticated and not always able to keep up with household chores, which tested the patience of Cornforth, while there was barely enough room for his books. In fact, three years before Kitty died, Klugmann had had to move out of Talbot Road after the floor started collapsing under the weight of his books. He had to store some of his volumes with the Seiferts nearby, until he found larger accommodation.[3]

Though his finances were by now very tight, mainly reliant on his small Party wage, he had some money left from his mother's will which helped the purchase of a large four-storey house in Chelsham Road, Clapham. This, however, was not merely a change of environment for Klugmann, but the beginning of a new phase in his life, in which he would become an integral part of two families. This arrangement would suit him politically as well as domestically, for he became an unofficial mentor to two of the leading reform-minded communists who were inspired by the youth and student movements of the 1960s. They sought an alternative model of communism to that of the Soviet Union – what would later be called 'Eurocommunism' – and this resonated with Klugmann's own rethinking. His new domestic arrangements went a long way to reviving the youthful appetite for politics (even if ill-health restricted his mobility) which had first drawn him to the left in the 1930s.

Pete Carter was a building worker from Birmingham in his early twenties when he went to work as a Young Communist League organiser at the Party's King Street offices in 1962. On his first day he arrived at the Party's warren of cubby holes early at 8.30. At about 10 a.m. the occupant of the office next door, which had an adjoining window, arrived.

My first impression of him was that he was pulling faces at me through the window. And making all sorts of gestures with his hands. As I gradually got to know him I realised that he was a very lonely person and as a result he was

very, very sociable. And he liked to relate his wit and his humour onto whoever
would suffer it.[4]

Carter had moved to London with his young family and was looking for
somewhere to live; Klugmann was able to offer him the top floor of his house.
It took Klugmann a long time to move his books from Highgate and he had to
do up the house to accommodate them all. Carter remembers the books arriving
by lorry ('juggernauts', he called them) over several days. 'It was absolutely
incredible. You couldn't go anywhere in the house where you wouldn't stumble
over books.' Books narrowed the staircases, were stacked up in the bathroom
and toilet and lined up in all the rooms. His own bed was surrounded by books
and bookcases.

He had found a new family, and a regular domestic routine ensued. In the
morning he would go upstairs for an early cup of tea with the Carters and either
continue working at home or travel later by the 88 bus into the King Street
offices. Pete Carter and his wife Norma were often away on Party duties and so
their two young children would be left under Klugmann's wing. He would take
them shopping or on visits to Clapham Common, and they got to love him as a
'surrogate father'. He was now spending more time writing at home and would
communicate to the children in the upstairs flat through a box hauled up and
down by a piece of string. In it would be messages, or sweets and presents signed
'From Pat the Pigeon'. 'We had our own internal communications system,' Mike
Carter remembered. 'He would leave letters and notes for us, signed "Pat."' 'If
we wanted some sweets, he would say, "ask Pat." [...] He would be downstairs
writing and would tell us, "Pat the pigeon will look after you".'[5] There was great
affection for him and he became part of the family, though it quickly became
clear that he himself needed looking after, and he would go upstairs for meals
and get help with domestic chores. He had a small cooker and fridge and the
Carters would sometimes smell food wafting through the floorboards at night, as
his long-standing difficulties of sleeping properly continued.

By the mid-1960s he had also found a new political outlet for his revived
socialist humanism in the form of the Marxist–Christian Dialogue. This became
a public forum for ideas on the humanitarian questions of the day, notably peace
and social justice, solutions for tackling poverty and hunger, opposition to racism
and the search for common ethical values. Initially inspired by the overtures
of Pope John XXIII towards the Italian Communist Party in Italy, it grew as
a movement in other parts of Europe, resulting in a three-day gathering in

Salzburg in May 1965, of Marxists and Christians from Italy, France, Yugoslavia, Belgium and Austria. Klugmann had shown a keen interest in this development and played the pivotal role in opening up the dialogue in Britain. Early *Marxism Today* forum discussions had involved some Christians in debate and in March 1966 he published an article by John Lewis, a former Unitarian minister and Christian communist, on the 'Dialogue of Christianity and Marxism'. The *Marxism Today* editorial board then made the decision to send Lewis's article to several Christian denominations, inviting them to participate. 'To our extreme pleasure', Klugmann informed his readers, 'the invitation met with a warm response, some accepting, others, too busy, wishing us well, and no-one at all opposing or rejecting.'[6]

Over the next 18 months the journal published 12 contributions in response to Lewis's initial article – nine by Christians, and three by Marxists – with Lewis replying to the discussion. The contributors from the Christian side included notable leaders and scholars, among them D.M. MacKinnon, Professor of Divinity at Cambridge; Adam Fox, canon of Westminster Cathedral; Thomas Curbishley, ex-master of Campion Hall; the well-known broadcaster and Quaker William Barton and Adrian Cunningham, one of the authors of the 'Slant Manifesto' produced by the Catholic left. One of the leading participants was Paul Oestreicher, who would become Klugmann's main collaborator in the dialogue, while it was also welcomed by the British Council of Churches.

However, the Marxist–Christian Dialogue went beyond a series of articles, and several public meetings, conventions and conferences were organised, with Klugmann normally the leading speaker from the Marxist side. In October 1966, the first Teilhard de Chardin Association conference attracted some 700 contributors at St Pancras Town Hall in London, including Catholics, Christians and Communist Party branches. Two months later the Student Christian Movement, at its annual conference, brought 400 Christians and Marxists together under the 'Man Unmasked' theme. In February 1967, the Marx Memorial Library was 'filled to the brim' (as Klugmann put it) for a debate on Marxism and religion, while the following month young communists and young Christians debated 'How to Change the World?' at a gathering in Coventry. Marxism and Christianity was the theme of the 1967 International Youth Festival at Skegness in May, organised by the Young Communist League. In the same month, Klugmann shared a platform with the Bishop of Barking and Paul Oestreicher in debating Marxism and Christianity to an 'intense, critical but friendly' audience of Catholics, Protestants and Marxists. In June, *Marxism*

Today co-organised a '10-a-sider' weekend discussion on 'Man, Society and Moral Responsibility' with the Quaker, Peace and International Relations Committee. This was surpassed, however, by the '15-a-sider' in October on the topics of 'Human Dignity' and 'Man and Society' held at the Royal Foundation of St Katherine's of Stepney in east London, the long-time home of Father Groser, the Catholic Christian socialist.[7]

The next three months saw an intense round of activity where Klugmann was briefly in the public eye. Among the national press, *The Times* took most interest, while two edited book publications were already on the way. In November, he and Paul Oestreicher took part in a three-part late-night television discussion, 'Dialogue with Doubt', held over consecutive nights and chaired by Christopher Chataway.[8] He had thrown himself into this venture with great hope and energy and was convinced in his own mind of the dialogue's potential. 'When I – an atheist and materialist – discuss with a Christian, the last thing that we mutually wish to conceal is *his* belief or *my* unbelief in God.' The dialogue was 'not a manoeuvre for an impossible synthesis', but an opportunity to explore deep human values, the 'concern for man, our desire to improve and radically change the world'. The search was for a 'mutual vision of a world of brotherhood without barriers of class, race or nation, where exploitation of man by man is ended'.[9]

On Klugmann's part, this was clearly a return to his strongest humanism, which rekindled earlier alliances formed in the international student and anti-fascist movements, where Blaho Hruby, by now an eminent Protestant minister, was one of his closest comrades. It was a chance to explore a future communist society away from the dominating spectre of the Soviet Union, on which he now held more private doubts. The question 'what kind of revolution?' was foremost in the discussion and for Klugmann was one which enabled him to look again at his own communist faith. Can love be combined with hatred? Is violence necessary for social change? 'Can wars ever be justified? Can man be truly human?'[10]

Paul Oestreicher got to know Klugmann well as a friend in this period. He was impressed by Klugmann's 'refreshing clarity' and 'pretty sharp mind', 'who would take you up if imprecise'. Klugmann, he felt, 'never reverted to Party jargon', and was 'free of dogmatic atheism'. As well as the formal dialogue meetings, in which Oestreicher and Klugmann shared several platforms, the two men also met informally both at King Street and at Klugmann's house in Clapham. Oestreicher was taken with his friend's simple lifestyle and his 'impressive humanism'.

I saw James as a Communist Franciscan. You had the feeling that this guy shares what he's got with anyone who needs it. What's mine is yours. My most significant memory of James was in his own home. It left a deep impression on me of a house almost entirely filled with books. This place is open to anyone who wants to come. You had the feeling he never really locked the front door.

Oestreicher recalled that Klugmann 'was not shy of going to churches, which reflected the mood of the period'. In fact, there was a church at the back of the Clapham house which he visited regularly to update them on news of the dialogue.

Oestreicher felt the dialogue gave Klugmann an important cathartic release from some of the dark periods of the past, of his Cold War duplicity:

He was part of the story, but by that time it was not a story he could be unambiguously proud of. Now he was doing some personal reparation. It was quite clear he looked back on that period as a very dark time. It took him out of those very difficult areas which probably weighed on his conscience.

Oestreicher retained hopes that socialism in Eastern Europe 'might turn into something positive' and for him and Klugmann much hope was invested in Czechoslovakia's Prague Spring, which was set in motion by the election of Alexander Dubcek as the Communist Party's first secretary in January 1968. It lasted until August of that year, when Soviet troops were sent in to 'normalise' the country. Dubcek's 'Action Programme' promised political liberalisation through greater freedom of the press, fewer restrictions on travel, an opening up of the economy to encourage greater consumerism, more autonomy to the Slovakians and the introduction of new democratic reforms which would eventually lead to a multi-party system. The reforms had the support of Czech writers and artists, though its critique of the past was carefully couched in the language of socialism. For Klugmann, this was the high point of communist humanism, and Dubcek's belief that communist society should release a fuller embodiment of human and democratic values was a perfect endorsement of what he had been arguing in the dialogue. His own Party, however, while welcoming the turn, hesitated in typical fashion as Soviet unease increased. After failed negotiations, Soviet and Warsaw Pact troops invaded the Czech capital on the night of 20–1 August. At news of the invasion, the British Communist Party's Executive Committee condemned the 'intervention', which elicited the opposition of two of its elderly intellectuals, Rajani Palme Dutt and Andrew Rothstein, in addition to a small faction who would later break away. Though this was hardly a strong endorsement, the decision was crucial in maintaining the support of the younger Eurocommunists who sought alternatives to the Soviet model. For those, like Klugmann, however, the defeat of the Prague Spring was very serious, questioning whether the system they had put their trust in would ever be reformed. For Paul Oestreicher, Klugmann's friend and ally in the dialogue, it was the 'tipping point', and the Marxist–Christian Dialogue never recaptured its earlier energy and direction.[11]

In Clapham, Klugmann, expecting the worst for Dubcek, warned Pete Carter at an early point in the Prague Spring: 'He won't last long, you know.' He knew Soviet troops would move in eventually; he had seen too much of it before. His differences with the leadership were increasing, and while he never put this into print or sought confrontation, his private doubts mounted and he passed on his concerns to Pete Carter. Carter was by now a leading figure in a radicalised Young Communist League which had embraced the cultural energies of the 1960s often beyond what the Party could tolerate – or even understand – and he often found himself in conflict with the leadership. On one occasion after the YCL had proposed the legalisation of drugs, Carter was called in along with other leaders to explain their actions and told if they did not desist they would be asked to leave. Carter pulled out a couple of toy tanks from under the table and in jest attempted a mock execution of John Gollan, the Party general secretary and Bill Alexander his assistant. They were not amused.

When Klugmann was told about it, he laughed. 'He enjoyed it,' Carter recalled. Now outside the leadership, Klugmann began to relive his politics through Carter and his younger comrades, supporting their direct action when they stormed the Rhodesian Embassy, or on anti-Vietnam War campaigns. 'He would glorify in our exploits.'[12] He would come forward with ideas and ways of supporting their campaigns, often – according to Carter – inspiring some of their initiatives. For example, he supported the 'Trend' communism campaign, the YCL's own political take on the 1960s counter-culture, which had been launched at the Skegness 'Trend' Festival in 1967, where Klugmann was one of the keynote speakers. At this festival, he delivered what was by now one of his stock lectures on 'the nature of communist society'. Tom Bell, later YCL general secretary, saw Klugmann in action here for the first time:

> I go into this room and it was packed. Choc-a-bloc. There was a little bloke down the front holding up his trousers every two minutes. He had the audience in the palm of his hand which I had never seen before.

Klugmann set out an inspiring vision of communism, according to Bell, rooted in the William Morris tradition of *The News from Nowhere*; a classless society of abundance. His speaking style demystified complex theories, explained ideas in simple terms and used humour to great effect. His gentle questioning and cajoling of the audience, with his slight lisp and often-breathless delivery, ending sentences with 'you see?', 'you understand?' appealed to the younger audience. It made him 'less ominous, more human and more vulnerable', according to Bell.[13]

His enthusiasm for the exploits of the YCL was indicative of a more open attitude to others on the left and he contributed to some of the early discussions of the May Day Manifesto group, largely made up of former 'first New Left' intellectuals. His own copy of the initial draft of the manifesto was heavily annotated with margin comments, some of which were encouraging – 'good' next to the section on the 'capitulation' of the Wilson government, and 'very good' on its analysis of the media, for example. In other places he was irritated by the 'very weak' points on the militancy of the shop stewards, by the absence of any mention of the Party's role, or some acknowledgement of the achievements of socialism.

Nevertheless he welcomed the opportunity to debate with others on the left, corresponded with the authors and visited Raymond Williams, one of the May Day Manifesto's main writers, in Cambridge in July 1967 to discuss its ideas. He was also more encouraging to older dissidents within his own party, notably the historian Monty Johnstone, a long-standing critic of the Party's Stalinism, with whom he would spend hours discussing aspects of the history of communism and Marxist theory. His openness was now in marked contrast to the orthodox communist tradition, which had remained in entrenched positions, represented by Rajani Palme Dutt, the Stalinist intellectual with whom he had long held differences. These now increased in their rival attitudes to the radical politics of the 1960s as the Party's more critical line on Moscow developed. He had consulted Dutt on his history of the Communist Party, but there were big differences between him and the apparatchik he now referred to at home in Clapham as 'Palme-Dotty'.[14]

However, his optimism was tempered by old fears. One day in 1966, the house in Clapham was surrounded by reporters, with Klugmann retreating behind the sofa. A *Sunday Times* 'Insight' team was investigating the Philby case, as was the *Observer*, which was also planning to publish extracts from the memoirs of Philby's third wife, Eleanor. Klugmann's concern at the implications of Philby's public exposure as the 'third man' was not unfounded. Up to that point there had been limited public discussion of the activities of the Cambridge communist group and their significance for the spy circle. Philby and Anthony Blunt, who had secretly confessed to MI5 in 1964 after being named by Michael Straight, had both protected their comrade from further investigation. These new investigations were to be more thorough. Moreover, Klugmann had never discussed the espionage question with Carter, so the arrival of reporters came as a shock. 'My wife was there and the kids. I said to James, "What's going on here, mate?"'

Klugmann did not respond to press enquiries at this time. However, there was worse news to follow. Klugmann's former close friend and comrade Bernard Floud, after an earlier career in the Civil Service at the Board of Trade, had been elected Labour MP for the London seat of Acton in 1964. Following his re-election in the 1966 general election, Labour prime minister Harold Wilson made it clear that he was thinking of offering Floud a ministerial appointment, which would require MI5 clearance. MI5 sent Wilson a briefing on Floud which revealed his earlier communist connections and the prevailing view of some MI5 officers that there may have been an Oxford 'spy' ring, a suspicion partly fuelled by information given by Jenifer Fischer Williams to the Security Services about Floud's links with 'Otto' (Arnold Deutsch). The chief reason, for their suspicion, however, was the visit Floud had made with Klugmann to China in 1938, as MI5's D3 (Peter Wright) made clear in March 1966:

> The case for suspecting that Floud may have worked for the Russians as a talent spotter when an undergraduate rests on his early association with James Klugmann – who is known to have so acted – and certain analogies between the two men's pre-war careers. It seems highly probable that what Klugmann was doing at Cambridge was echoed by Floud at Oxford. Floud's direction of Jenifer Fischer Williams [...] lends credence to this hypothesis.[15]

In his subsequent MI5 interrogation, which commenced in August 1966 and was carried out by 'Derek Hammond' and Peter Wright, in central London, in an operation code-named 'Roast Potato' (and recorded and monitored simultaneously at MI5 offices), Floud was asked about his communist allegiances, his friendships at Oxford, in the World Student Association and in the Civil Service. His interrogators found him to be 'uneasy, evasive and less than frank'[16] and concerned about the implications of his past communist activities on his ministerial ambitions. The interviews were interrupted in January 1967, following the death of his wife Ailsa after a long illness. When they resumed in March, the intensity of the interviews increased and Floud was made aware of the information provided by Jenifer Fischer Williams, who had admitted being recruited to the Communist Party by him, and to meeting 'Otto' while acting as a secret communist in the civil service. Wright recalled in his book *Spycatcher* that Floud was 'very agitated' when confronted with this information, though he did not 'break'. At the last interview MI5 informed Floud that his unwillingness to discuss his precise communist allegiances meant that he was seen as a 'full security risk' and they would not authorise security clearance. On 10 October, more than six months after his final interrogation, Floud took his own life. Depression at his wife's death and despair at his thwarted ministerial career were thought by his family to be the reasons for his suicide. As Christopher Andrew has concluded, there was no evidence to suggest Floud was an NKVD agent or had communist contacts after 1952.[17]

It was his link to Klugmann, however, that brought Floud to MI5's attention, and news of Floud's suicide must have come as a bombshell to his old friend. After all, he had been friend and part mentor to Floud – who was three years his junior at Gresham's School and his co-organiser in the communist student movement – with whom he had shared one of his most profound political awakenings and finest moments on the student delegation to China. Did he feel in any way responsible for introducing Floud to the international communist movement?

On the same day that Floud took his own life, Klugmann's picture appeared over an article on the Marxist–Christian Dialogue on page 2 of *The Times*. Asked at the press conference if the dialogue had been a success, he is quoted as replying: 'I would say eminently so.'[18] Yet, for all his renewed optimism, it seemed that he could not escape the past. He had already been unsettled by the Philby investigation, and in the aftermath of the 'third man' inquiry there was growing suspicion of a 'fourth' and 'fifth' man.

His earlier espionage activities were catching up with him. In the aftermath of the defection of Burgess and Maclean in 1951, John Cairncross, Klugmann's former friend and recruit to the NKVD, had come under suspicion. This was initially because a letter in Cairncross's handwriting had been found among Burgess's belongings at the time of his disappearance. The interviews then were inconclusive. Cairncross moved first to Rome, as *Economist* correspondent, then undertook short spells of translating and editing work in Geneva, Bangkok and Karachi. Eventually, he landed an academic post, on the recommendation of his former professor at the Sorbonne, Raymond Picard, in Cleveland, Ohio, in 1964. However, just two months after taking up his appointment, he received another visit from MI5's Arthur Martin as well as one from the FBI.

On this visit, Martin, helped by information from Blunt – who had, by now, confessed, though this was not made public for another 12 years – and the ongoing investigations into Philby's disappearance in 1963, succeeded in extracting a confession from Cairncross about his own espionage. After being pressed on the circumstances of his recruitment in 1937 Cairncross named Klugmann and 'Otto' as his recruiters, before going on to admit passing Enigma decrypts detailing German battle orders to the Soviets and removing other secret documents while at the Foreign Office. Cairncross was told that the matter was treated 'very seriously', had been discussed by the British cabinet, and he should be in no doubt that there would be big headlines if the news got out. It was made clear that as things stood he would be arrested if he returned to Britain, with the prospect of a long sentence, something which was confirmed to him by the FBI. However, Martin told him that his confession would not be made public on the understanding that he would not return to England permanently. The involvement of the FBI meant that Cairncross was obliged to leave the US only a couple of months after arriving; although relieved that no further action was to be taken, he later revealed that his confession 'was a gesture of despair whereby I was accepting ruin, since I was prepared to lose everything'.[19]

After leaving the US, Cairncross returned to Rome, working for the Food and Agriculture Organisation, and soon received another visit from Arthur Martin, this time accompanied by Peter Wright. In a break from their questions on the details of his own espionage, Martin asked him about his attitude to his former friend, and

> whether I was not angry with Klugmann for the sneaky part he played in effecting my recruitment to the KGB back in 1937. Would I be willing to testify against him if the possibility arose of bringing him to trial? I replied that I would have no hesitation in bearing witness against him. This question was taken a step further by Peter Wright, and the possibility of complete immunity was held out, plus the continuation of complete confidentiality and the freedom to visit England if I succeeded in pinning down Klugmann as one of the architects of my involvement with the KGB.[20]

MI5 asked him to arrange a meeting with Klugmann, with the hope of inducing an admission that would lead to trial and more information on the Cambridge spy circle. Cairncross set up a lunch meeting at a London hotel in 1967, some 30 years since they had last met. After both had eaten well – 'I had been carefully advised by MI5 to wait until he had been wined and dined before trying to extract a confession from him' – and had left the restaurant, he broached the difficult topic. Klugmann, whom Cairncross had found 'nervous' and 'concerned' during the meeting,

Declared in an obvious falsehood, that he did not know anything about the Russian agent present at the Regent's Park meeting. When in a final appeal, I reminded him of our common opposition to Nazism, he simply dwelt on the importance of the communist movement among the students at Cambridge at that time, and all I could extract from him was the admission that he had been asked by various friends or acquaintances to come forward and report his activities to MI5. However, he felt no obligation to do so and it was clear that my approach had been a failure.[21]

19

Hopes and Fears

By the late 1960s James Klugmann had gone a considerable way in restoring his faith in the communist ideal. The Marxist–Christian dialogue, which continued into the 1970s, won him new friends and had taken him beyond the confines of the Party. He was still receiving regular invitations from Methodists, Catholics and Quakers, and was a regular guest of the Bloomsbury Baptists in Shaftesbury Avenue and the Dominican Friars at Blackfriars in Oxford. Invitations continued to come in, even if the dialogue's most radical edge on the communist side had been blunted by the defeat of the Prague Spring.

Through the dialogue's meetings and publications, Klugmann had begun to re-articulate his vision of communism. The dialogue helped to cement his deeper humanist beliefs, ones he had first formed as a young man at Gresham's under Frank McEachran's influence. It was there, in one of his first political speeches in the school's Debating Society, that he pronounced 'modern man' 'had lost his sense of values and was treating soap and machinery as ends in themselves, instead of as means to a fuller and more satisfying experience'.

His short book published by the Communist Party in 1970, *The Future of Man*, embodied these ideas, rooted in the belief that once again there was a marked conflict between the capacity for realising individual potential and dominant economic interests. It was his best writing for decades, released from the constraints of orthodoxy and drawing inspiration from his earlier experiences: 'We are moving, in the seventies, into a period of stormy change in man's knowledge, society, thought. Never has the great contradiction been so clear between what is and what could be.'[1]

On the one hand, there was a 'nightmare vision' characterised by 'a vast supermarket society, canned and commercialised, with standardised mass-produced man helplessly, inextricably, tied up within it, estranged, alienated, helpless, hardly human'.[2] On the other, he argued, returning to the early writings of Karl Marx, there was a real prospect of hope: hope that the great scientific advances could be used to eradicate poverty, and draw on the 'vast inexhaustible potential of all human beings' to further man's development.[3] The previous year he had been invited to give a talk on 'The Marxist Hope' at the annual conference of the Society for the Study of Theology in Birmingham, which had taken as its theme 'The Christian Hope'. 'It seemed to me,' he wrote, 'as I reflected on the subject, that Marxists were people of great hope.'[4] He recalled the hunger marchers arriving in Cambridge. They may have come from depressed areas, but they themselves 'were not depressed, were confident, full of hope'.[5] Also 'full of hope' were those in the international youth and student movements, and the Yugoslav Partisans fighting fascism underground. Then there was his inspirational student delegation to China.

> I think back to my months in China in 1938. The Japanese were invading. China was ruled by a small, rich, powerful clique, corrupt and brutal, utterly dehumanized [...] Chinese communists leading the national liberation struggle and in the liberated areas, were already showing how life and man could be changed.[6]

His vision of communism, set out with a renewed clarity in his writing, was now at odds with what he knew about the Soviet Union. The freshness of his writing also sat uneasily with his own official account of the Party's early history, the first two volumes of which had been published in 1968–9 by Lawrence and Wishart. This had been more than a decade in preparation; a long commitment which must have felt a chore, as well as a duty, one which had borne him ill-health, stress and the feeling that one of its main purposes was to protect the heritage of the Party. In his preface to *The History of the Communist Party of Great Britain, Volume 1: Formation and Early Years 1919–1924*, he admits that it is 'an openly partisan history'. This was to be expected, but the preface is also defensive and almost apologetic in the admission that 'much of [the work] was done in the course of and alongside other political responsibilities'. He was not interested in polemical discussions with the work of other historians. Henry Pelling, whose earlier history 'did not seem to me serious', or Leslie Macfarlane's admittedly more serious book on the earlier years, which had been published shortly before, were both given short shrift.[7]

Undoubtedly, the first two volumes were extensive and well researched; the detailed notes and papers in his own library – including some taken from Comintern archives in Moscow collected during his 1957 trip – are testament to that, and he drew on new material in providing an important account of the formation of the Party in 1920. Yet, as a work of history it suffers from the long years he served as a loyal functionary, dependent on the endorsement of his peers and leaders. His drafts were commented on by the full range of in-house Party historians, but not by the impressive generation of Marxists who formed the Historians Group. Thus Robin Page-Arnot supplied 78 pages of notes and comments on the draft, a resumé of six sections was received from Palme Dutt and a 19-page summary from Andrew Rothstein. Frank Jackson, a carpenter-turned-Party librarian, commended the final product, telling him: 'James, you have created a classic.'[8] Within the Party, there was warm praise too, following a well-attended launch of the book in Holborn, and the first volume sold reasonably well (at the price of 63 shillings); 1,000 copies were purchased quickly within the Party's education sections.

However, the wider reception was quite different. 'I didn't see the review in "Union Voice",' Klugmann told Edmund Frow, 'but it is probably just as well. It certainly couldn't have been worse than the one in the *Times Literary Supplement*.'[9] The *Times Literary Supplement* review had been by Professor Eric Hobsbawm, his old friend from the 1930s, who had remained in the Party but distant enough to maintain a critical engagement. In Hobsbawm's view, Klugmann did not seriously address any of the main problems of British communist history, namely the Comintern' s view of the British Party; why the CPGB made little headway in the 1920s and the nature of its support, including its minimal influence among intellectuals prior to the 1930s. 'Unfortunately,' Hobsbawm wrote, 'he is paralyzed by the impossibility of being both a good historian and a loyal functionary.'[10] While his research did provide some fresh material on early Party activists, he had essentially written a textbook for Party militants.

A more hostile review was delivered by Peter Fryer, with whom Klugmann had earlier fallen out over Tito and Hungary. Fryer, by now a Trotskyist who had long given up on the Communist Party, did not miss the opportunity to remind readers that Klugmann had never offered any public self-criticism of *From Trotsky to Tito*. He was vitriolic and scathing in his denunciation of the 'impudent volumes', which 'conceal' and 'distort' and barely told half the story. 'Klugmann writes in the emphatic, repetitive, itemising style so familiar to those who have ever sat at his unstraying feet during one of his lectures, with their headings, sub-headings, and sub-sub-headings neatly ticked off on his fingers.' This was harsh and indicative of previous hostile encounters, but it was difficult to disagree with his description of Klugmann throughout as the 'Official Historian'.[11]

What would have hurt Klugmann most as he reflected on the book's reception was Hobsbawm's view that despite hours looking through the Comintern and other archives he had, in the end, 'wasted much of his time'.[12] Ironically, Donald Maclean, in exile in Moscow since his disappearance with Guy Burgess in 1951, had just published *British Foreign Policy Since Suez*, which was free of orthodox communist language. In fact Maclean had sounded out his old friend about a publisher – Klugmann was on the Lawrence and Wishart board – but was turned down for fear of negative publicity.[13] The book's eventual publication by Hodder and Stoughton indicated that Maclean, from his base in the Moscow Research Institute, was able to put enough material together for a reasonable historical account that showed little evidence of Cold War assumptions.

All this would have been on Klugmann's mind as he began the third volume on the period after 1927, that is to say, one of the most controversial in the Party's history, which included the sectarian 'Class Against Class' era. Initially, he thought it would take him a couple of years, but despite compiling the usual list of headings and sections, journals to be consulted and individuals to be contacted, not much writing had been completed by the time he boarded the plane to Moscow to begin the research. The recently published Lawrence and Wishart edition of Gramsci's *Prison Notebooks*, with its sophisticated analysis of ideology, power and the role of intellectuals, was stimulating reading material for his trip, though hardly ideal preparation for what awaited him in Moscow. As he trawled through the Comintern archives, a depressing picture emerged of his own Party's duplicity in delivering the Moscow line and the contrast between its view of 'actually existing socialism' and realities of life inside the Soviet Union in that period. 'I can imagine that you must be unearthing facts that you will find rather depressing. I can only say it was much more depressing to live through them than to discover this in articles etc,' Jack Cohen, who had studied at the Lenin School and lived in Moscow in the late 1920s and early 1930s, told him.[14]

Cohen, his old colleague in the education department, who was now helping with his historical research, was looking after *Marxism Today* in Klugmann's absence. Betty Reid, the Party's national organiser, had accompanied Klugmann to Moscow for a Fraternal Workers' Parties Conference in November but had returned earlier. Reid, the long-standing partner of John Lewis, was one of Klugmann's closest Party friends, and his regular lunch companion at King Street. She was alarmed on arriving back in London to find that Klugmann had become ill in Moscow. Ill-health was now a growing problem, asthma and other breathing difficulties made it difficult for him to get about and he was overweight. Pills of various sorts were keeping him going but she felt his voracious appetite was not doing his health any good. The documents he found in the Comintern archives would not have helped either. His previous illnesses had often been stress-related – in the agonising weeks of duress which accompanied the Tito–Stalin split, for example. Now, confronted with the evidence of his Party's knowledge of Soviet repression in the 1930s, the pressure got the better of him once again. 'You do seem to be working extremely hard,' Cohen wrote to him just before Christmas, 'and you may find as a result of all your intense labours you will need another rest of 4 or 5 months to get over it. So take it easy if you can.'[15]

In fact, after spending Christmas in Moscow, Klugmann found himself in hospital by early January, where he was to spend the next seven weeks. Cohen, Reid and his other friends became very worried. Enquirers were told his illness would keep him in Moscow until the end of March. At home, his own affairs needed some attention, with outstanding tax demands related to his previous house and the need to find new tenants for the upstairs flat of his current one, after the Carters had returned to the Midlands. There were also concerns over Party and *Marxism Today* finances, and Jack Cohen, who did not have Klugmann's editorial aptitude, was reporting some difficulties, while doing his best to keep his friend supplied with essentials on his release from hospital. Cohen and Betty Reid arranged for a 'shipload of light literature' to be sent. By the end of mid-March, Cohen was reporting 'one or two disasters' and Reid was missing her lunches, though had better news on his new tenants.[16]

Klugmann eventually returned in May 1972, to learn that his old boss in the Propaganda Section, Emile Burns, had passed away; another Party Congress had endorsed the more reform-minded line ('the Duttites being smote hip and thigh [...] and their knavish tricks frustrated', his friend Hymie Fagan told him[17]) and the Party had appointed a new student organiser in an attempt to win over the new militants on campus.

In fact, the new student organiser, Dave Cook, was also Klugmann's new tenant, who had moved into the upstairs flat in Chelsham Road. Cook had moved from Yorkshire, where he had been the Young Communist League organiser. He could not have had a more apt landlord. Klugmann, after all, had been a student leader in the 1930s and knew very well what was needed to galvanise broad support, 'propagandise' the political message and inspire a generation of student militants.

The 1970s was a very different era, but there were again signs of economic crisis, industrial struggle and a growing interest in Marxism, and there were new social movements like feminism, which could help revitalise the Party.

There was some hope that the Party could play a crucial role in the new politics. This was very much Klugmann's terrain, and even though he was from an earlier generation there was much he could do to help Cook. Under Cook's leadership, the communist students grew from a moribund base – the communist student organisation had appeared weak and conservative at the time of *les événements* of 1968 – to become the fastest growing section of the Party. It reached a peak of 1,000 members in 1973 and was instrumental in the new broad left alliance which took over the leadership of the National Union of Students. Cook's own influential pamphlet *Students* (1973) was ground-breaking in arguing for new alliances between the left and new social movements. It also made the case that students should be seen as a distinctive mass group, whose position was being transformed by social and economic change. This analysis, in which Cook identified a distinctive ideological role for students, had strong connections with Klugmann's political insight, some 40 years earlier. Cook's Party pamphlet clearly reflected hours of fruitful debate and discussion at Chelsham Road.

The political strategy Cook advocated for the students would become the basis for a later political challenge by Eurocommunists to the leadership. But Cook's input in transforming the Party's student base, aided by Klugmann and others, went beyond political alliances and embraced the new developments in Marxism. Much was achieved through the Communist University of London (CUL), an annual summer gathering of students, thinkers, intellectuals and activists to discuss new developments in Marxism. From its modest origins in 1969, it grew to become a cutting-edge forum for left intellectuals, which reflected the Party's more open attitude towards the New Left and others. Speakers at the week-long events – on topics such as architecture, history, science and art and culture, the role of the state and the ideas of Antonio Gramsci – included Paul Hirst, Stuart Hall, Raphael Samuel, Raymond Williams and Ralph Miliband. The CUL embraced Klugmann's 'creative Marxism' and the role of the communist student as an intellectual – something that had inspired him in Cambridge.

His belief that the Party had to open up to new Marxist theories and the wider left now penetrated the pages of *Marxism Today*, when in 1972, Louis Althusser, the French structuralist Marxist, who was gaining a large following, participated in a debate with John Lewis. In the January and February 1972 editions, Lewis wrote a humanist critique of Althusser's theory – 'The Althusser Case' – which described the latter as a dogmatist and anti-humanist. Grahame Locke, a postgraduate researcher and Communist Party member, who was then studying in Paris, showed the article to Althusser, who had never heard of Lewis. Althusser let him know, however, that he would like the opportunity to respond to Lewis's critique, an offer which Locke raised with Klugmann. He welcomed the suggestion, with his own recent experience of participating in debates with French Marxists fresh in the memory. 'He didn't have the slightest difficulty. On the contrary, he was very interested, eager to help, genuinely interested. He didn't respond as a humanist who didn't like this stuff.' Nor, according to Locke, did Klugmann feel the need to 'refer to anybody at the top' before commissioning the article.[18]

Althusser's two *Marxism Today* articles, 'Reply to John Lewis', appeared in the October and November editions and were indicative of Klugmann's enthusiasm for new developments in Marxism. His house in Clapham was now open to a range of acquaintances on the New Left, while he was always pleased to share the best Armagnac with older comrades from the French Communist Party. In the pages of *Marxism Today* and the packed rooms of the CUL, Klugmann enjoyed the debates on Althusser and Gramsci and the burgeoning interest in the Italian Communist Party, which was riding high in the polls under its popular leader Enrico Berlinguer. This sustained his appetite for teaching, and he found himself once again in the position of mentoring young radical converts.

A short series of talks at West Lewisham Young Communist League, in one of the most radical Eurocommunist districts, provides more insight into the clarity of his teaching style, and one of his lifelong projects to convert young people to communism. In these gentle conversational lectures, structured by neat sub-headings and in the engaging style of an adult education tutor who is aware of the different levels of knowledge of his students, but concerned not to patronise, he set out to demystify Marxist terminology and apply it to the contemporary situation in Britain. It was a style of light probing, with clear definitions of Marxist concepts, erudite explanations with lucid, often humorous, embellishments and insightful historical detail, often culminating in his gentle enquiry: 'do you see?', 'do you understand?', 'you follow?'.

In his 'Reformism and the State' lecture, for example, he started by defining the key term – 'a word you meet a great deal in the Communist Party and the League [...] a word called reformism'. He then grounded the idea in an accessible potted historical account of the various Labour governments, looking for the common patterns behind their demise – invariably described as 'fiascos' and 'failures'. Then, after a long pause, he led up to the explanation for these defeats, his voice lowered – 'Why?'

After the war, in the London District, there were 100 lads and lasses and we were talking about this 'Why' [...]Why did Ernie [Bevin] do it? Because he's a bastard? [*giggles from the young audience*]. [...]

They say when you're drowning your past flashes in a second before your eyes [...] the list of reformist leaders [...]

No, it isn't all due to the personal deficiencies of right-wing leaders, and their fiascos and failures [...] But the *outlook* of the leaders [...] the outlook, the philosophy, the ideas; in other words, it is *reformism* that's the real cause behind it.[19]

The so-called 'neutral', reformist state was a bit like a bicycle, waiting at the kerbside to be ridden by Tory and Labour MPs alike, with a smooth journey guaranteed as long as the rider keeps to the safe and narrow roads, but the likelihood of being dismantled if he veers to the left.

At times, he referred back to his own experiences at Cambridge, in China or Yugoslavia to make a point, often drawing laughter when he reminisced about his own mild acts of rebellion, in refusing to have his hair cut or wearing Oxford 'bags' at university. With his soft voice and quick wit, he also exercised a quiet authority and an almost pastoral concern for the welfare of his young audience as they began their journey as communists.

In his second lecture, 'Revolution', he returned to the difference between a rebel and a revolutionary, a transition he had made earlier at Cambridge. Again, he starts with a question: 'What is Revolution?' We must begin, he told his audience, by 'what it isn't'. He warned them not to be taken in by media image of 'blood, hatred, lust, killing, murder, death'. Nor, he argued, moving on to the 'ultra left', was it 'a banner, a shout, a declaration'. Rather, he told them, it was a shift in power, taking many different forms in different countries and situations, when young people go beyond merely rejecting the system by wearing their hair long, or by challenging conventions of sex or culture, or merely opposing some aspects of capitalism, and they reach the point 'when they know what they are *for*'. The 'task' of the Young Communist League, he told his audience, many of them a similar age, if not class background, to his former recruits at Cambridge, was to 'take them further': 'You feel their way around their rebellion, to convert rebels into revolutionaries.' There was 'no future in being a hippie, no future in being a rebel'. 'He had a talent spotting eye,' Conrad Wood remembered.[20]

In passing on his experience as the talent spotter of the Cambridge student movement, he told the next generation that they must 'start at the point where real men and women are starting', whether it was poetry, love or art. 'One aspect of the life of a real revolutionary' was 'not being arrogant and to start modestly, patiently helping the organisation'. That, he concluded, lowering his voice, 'is one side of being a revolutionary'.

'The other side of being a real revolutionary', his voice raised as he spoke to the Lewisham Young Communists, 'is to explain the need for revolution, to build a revolution and trying to give a vision of where we are going to.'[21]

The Lewisham lectures gave an insight into Klugmann's teaching style, but the other side to being a communist intellectual was also evident. These were the intellectual constraints and the political ends to which each lesson was directed. Though there were occasional references to Greek drama or French history, the stock lectures were constrained in a tight explanatory framework which did not do justice to his intellectual range.

Moreover, as the new generation of intellectuals and activists he had supported and influenced sought a new Eurocommunist direction, he was found wanting. He was sympathetic to the 'young Turks', but this did not extend to a public criticism of the leadership; while he welcomed the Eurocommunist directions of the Italian, French and Spanish Communist Parties, there were few signs that he would openly support any political challenge to the current CPGB leadership.

Martin Jacques, one of the leading Eurocommunists who would succeed Klugmann as editor of *Marxism Today* and later transform the journal into a 'magazine' of the left, described him in this period as 'extraordinarily timid', as a man who 'would never step out of line and take anyone on'.[22] Pete Carter, for all the affection he held for his friend and landlord, agreed: 'After a while I found that James was planting the bullets for me to fire. He had terrible differences with the leadership, but he would never say anything to them.'[23]

A group of Eurocommunist economists, Bill Warren, Dave Purdy, Mike Prior and Pat Devine, had begun to clash with Bert Ramelson, the Party's industrial organiser (and an old comrade of Klugmann's), on the Party's Economics Committee and in the Party press. By the mid-1970s, Ramelson was a key player in the big industrial disputes, at the time of the three-day week and the case of the imprisonment of the shop stewards known as the Pentonville Five, and his organisational work on the trade union advisories had been very successful in building alliances in the trade union movement which had won him the admiration of Jack Jones and Hugh Scanlon, the most prominent left-wing trade union leaders of the decade. The Party's industrial department was its most influential section and Ramelson, to whom the Party leadership deferred, had some autonomy in pursuing his strategy. Ramelson was a Spanish Civil War veteran and popular Party organiser, a figure of prestige and authority. However, his alliance with Jones and Scanlon broke down following the Labour government's adoption of the Social Contract. The young Turks on the Economics Committee, chaired by Ramelson, had put together a critique of his strategy, which they regarded as 'economistic' and 'sectionalist'. Influenced by the ideas of Antonio Gramsci, they set out their alternative position in a series of articles, initially in *Marxism Today*, and encouraged by Klugmann. However, as the debate continued, and the diverging political strategies became apparent, he returned to a more familiar stance, consulting Ramelson before publishing critical pieces and then only publishing them with Ramelson 'rejoinders', ensuring that the Party had the final word.[24]

20

A Good Jesuit

In 1973, the BBC Radio 4 presenter Rita Dando visited James Klugmann at Chelsham Road to discuss his love of book-collecting. In 'It Takes All Sorts – James Klugmann', Dando provided an insight into the private world of this unusual 'journalist, author, lecturer, debator and collector', with his 'round, scholarly face and spectacles'.[1] With 'just enough room to sit down' in front of the electric fire in his living room – the only warm room in the house – he told her he first became interested in book-collecting at Cambridge. After getting involved in left-wing politics and studying the history, philosophy and 'outlook' of the movement, he quickly realised that the working-class movement's own history was not easily available and started searching for 'working-class literature'. This soon included not only books but 'pamphlets, leaflets, pottery, visual material, snuff-boxes, articles and pictures'. His passion took him to second-hand bookshops, but also junk shops, where he would search behind old wash basins for tatty and 'dog-eared' leaflets, occasionally finding gems like the ballads of 1794 on the futility of war, written on tiny scraps of paper to elude the recruiting sergeants ('You'll be shot at for sixpence a day. You'll never grow old when you're shot at for sixpence a day'). He would visit mystic bookshops for the early socialist writings of Annie Besant; even the Eastbourne establishments of 'retired Colonels' were happy to give away socialist material. The best thing a book collector can do, he told Dando, is to 'go where you least expect it'. Dando was impressed with his collection and his passion for books; 'history does come alive' she observed, as she made her way through the shelves and piles of books and pamphlets, occasionally interrupted by Lester Cook, the three year old he was baby-sitting. 'If there was such a disease of Bibliophilia, fear of books in an enclosed space, Mr Klugmann's home wouldn't be for you', Dando remarked, noting the books growing out of the bathroom and along the staircase. 'I don't think one has to share Mr Klugmann's political views', she added, a trifle condescendingly, 'to appreciate the collection'.

Yet, Klugmann told Dando, 'I would hate to be remembered by my collection. I regard it as a most insignificant part of my life.' What had saved him from going the way of other 'obsessive' book collectors, he told her, was his political commitment. His collection was a life's commitment to the history and struggles of the working-class movement. 'The history of the movement always inspires and helps to develop the movement in its present struggles.'

Moreover, he was happy to connect his own interest in book collecting with one of his illustrious predecessors. 'It is always nice to have authority for one's vices,' he had suggested in earlier *Marxism Today* Editorial Comments:

> Incorrigible collectors of books will be glad to learn that Karl Marx, asked in 1865 what was his favourite pastime, replied: 'bookworming' [...] Even in his hardest most poverty-stricken days, books still found their way on to his shelves, and, as with all bookworms, there were never till his dying days shelves enough.[2]

Klugmann did not want to be remembered for his book collection, but for his contribution to the international communist movement for which he had made many sacrifices. Yet as he considered the past once again during the final few months of his life, he must have wondered if it had all been worth it. His Party was in a critical state. It was losing its industrial influence, had little electoral base and seemed to be heading towards more inner conflict. While the Eurocommunists were directing their energies towards a new edition of *The British Road to Socialism*, the programme he had initially helped bring to fruition, many of his own generation were looking inwards once more.

Following his retirement as general secretary in 1975, John Gollan revisited the events of the 20th Congress of the Soviet Union in 1956 and its repercussions for the CPGB, in two articles for *Marxism Today*, accompanied by what would be a farewell speaking tour, as he was by then seriously ill. Gollan had little new to say on the subject, arguing unconvincingly that the events of 20 years before had 'acted as a catalyst in carrying forward vital developments already emerging in the Soviet Union' and that 'subsequent developments had been profoundly progressive'.[3]

Gollan, a working-class communist leader who had risen through the Party to succeed Harry Pollitt as general secretary, was an old comrade of Klugmann's but lacked the latter's analytical brain and lucid exposition. As editor of *Marxism Today*, Klugmann had the unenviable task of presenting an uninspiring contribution in a positive light, as well as trying to produce a stimulating discussion from the 93 follow-up contributions he received through the post. It was not the number of responses to Gollan's articles that concerned him but the wildly diverging views, which provided more evidence that his Party was splitting. Some thought Gollan had gone too far, while many of the Party faithful took comfort from his words and believed that lessons had been learned. The most vehement criticism came from the Eurocommunists, who argued that there had been 'no advance in analysis' in the Party's attitude to Stalinism and the Soviet Union since the fateful Congress 20 years before.[4] The lack of self-criticism on Gollan's part also implicated Klugmann himself. After all, he was the person who took responsibility for one of its darkest moments in the Tito–Stalin split. That, and the feeling that the ruptures in his Party were widening, would have left him with a bleak impression of the future.

He was still a figure of affection in the Party and an inspiring speaker who could hold an audience. Yet he was in deteriorating health and short of money. Despite his prosperous family background, a life spent working for the Communist Party had brought him financial insecurity – as it did for many others. In any case, among his 'unworldly' characteristics was a disdain for money or much interest in material possessions. Friends remembered him regularly setting off with a basket and a shopping list, only to return with a bag full of books and a tin of baked beans. Brian Simon, Margot Heinemann and other friends supported him through the 'Klugmann Trust', set up in the early 1970s. This was intended to provide for any emergencies, house repairs and general maintenance which he accepted with gratitude, humour and affection.

'Dear Margot,' he wrote on 17 April after he had received the 1974 instalment,

very many thanks to you and all those who have made it possible. Don't worry, the future of the Building Society is secure, and I am not (alas) off to a Bolshevik beano in the Bahamas. It is a very big relief to feel that the cash is there in the case of emergencies with house or health.

After the 1976 instalment, he was equally grateful, though more downbeat about health and home.

6.4.76

Dear Margot,

This is just to acknowledge with very best thanks to the comrades concerned, the safe receipt of the cheque for £331.25. Now that the sun is peeping out I am beginning to feel a little better but it has been a difficult winter. Hope to see you sometime. All the very best, Love, James.

Ill-health was now a big problem for him. His asthma and weight made it difficult to climb stairs and his visits to King Street, which could be a 40-minute bus journey, were less frequent. When he was in the office, he spent most of his time in a little room at the top of the building. He still enjoyed his visits to districts and branches to give talks, though was finding the travelling more difficult. He was also lonely. His surrogate families continued to provide some security, but he had little life outside the Party. One friendship in the last part of his life was important to him. The artist Renzo Galeotti had done some work for *Rinascita*, the Italian Communist Party's theoretical magazine, and his style very much appealed to Klugmann, who was looking for images for *Marxism Today*. Once a month Galeotti would drive to Clapham to pick up Klugmann and take him back to Kingston, where his wife would cook Sunday lunch. His appetite had not diminished; he was a '*buona forchetta*', according to Galeotti, and could easily eat anything and everything, with Mrs Galeotti's roast beef and Yorkshire pudding his particular favourite. He and Galeotti would discuss art, and Klugmann would tell him about his earlier appreciation of German expressionism, Mexican murals and the influence of Anthony Blunt. Galeotti also admired Klugmann's 'very beautiful collection' of pre-Victorian pottery, which he kept alongside his prints and political cartoons. Klugmann was kind to Galeotti's young son Mark, bringing him a dusty copy of H.G. Wells's *War of the Worlds* and, according to Galeotti, inspired him to later apply to Cambridge. Galeotti remembered Klugmann for his humanity and as 'a very honest' and 'open person' who had been 'very neglected by the Party in later years'. According to Galeotti, Klugmann felt he had been 'used' by the Party, which was something that 'stuck in his throat'.[5]

He had been used by the Party. He had been instructed by its leadership to introduce John Cairncross to the Soviet spy Arnold Deutsch. The Party told him – undoubtedly under pressure from Moscow – to denounce Tito, his former friend and ally. Then, after he had sacrificed much of his remaining intellectual integrity to serve loyally in its leadership, edit its newspaper and educate its members, he was seemingly dispensed with by the early 1960s. Lacking the courage he had displayed in the 1930s and 1940s, it was a long road back to regaining any kind of intellectual integrity.

By the beginning of 1977 he had already decided that he no longer wanted to carry on editing *Marxism Today*. The Gollan debate had taken quite a bit out of him and he had little energy for the emerging conflict in the Party over the new edition of *The British Road to Socialism*, which was to be published that autumn. He also had the next volume of the Party history to consider and he saw release from his editorial duties as essential in freeing up more time for his research.

He had been editing *Marxism Today* for most of its 20-year existence, and looking back on his time as editor, he took some pride in its contribution to Marxist theory. Despite 'reformism' retaining its 'dominating influence' on the British working-class movement, he noted the 'important advance of Marxism' over the previous 20 years, evident in research, projects, PhD theses, the Party's specialist groups and in the Communist University of London. If his vision of the journal was a world away from the magazine it would later become under his successor, Martin Jacques, then his time as editor was widely admired by the Party readership.[6]

There were the occasional comforts to be drawn from reminders of past endeavours during the seminal decade of the 1930s. One of the roles he fulfilled in the latter part of his life was as chairman of the board of the Party publishers Lawrence and Wishart. He never missed these monthly meetings and the chance to talk about forthcoming editions of Marx and Engels 'classics' or the prospect of commissioning new books on working-class history. He took pleasure in republishing Lewis Jones's two working-class novels set in the Welsh mining valleys in the 1930s that he himself had visited soon after joining the Party. Jones, a communist organiser for the NUWM, led several of the hunger marches of those years, and the books evoked important memories for Klugmann.[7]

He also enthused about one of the Communist Party's more creative initiatives of his last months, the 'People's Jubilee', which was organised as an alternative to the bigger spectacle. The 'People's Jubilee' attracted 11,000 people to Alexandra Palace, one of the biggest public events it had organised since the war. He found it 'a glad, heart-warming, moving gathering' which evoked the secular humanism and republicanism of the Popular Front.

> The People's Jubilee captured the mood of the people as an alternative and *People's* Jubilee. Positive (and not just the disgruntled 'stuff the jubilee'), angry and critical, yet full of humour, with a feeling for the different sort of Britain which, with courage, struggle and unity, could be built.[8]

In a contribution to a collection of essays on the 1930s, co-organised by his closest friend since that time, Margot Heinemann, he revisited his Cambridge days, the sense of 'impending doom' of British capitalism and the feeling of revolution in the air during what he called a 'decade of commitment'.[9] It brought with it the certainty that this was a decisive historical juncture and that stark political choices were there to be made. His own choice was to become a professional revolutionary and commit his life to the Party. As his successor as editor of *Marxism Today* put it:

> It was a hard life. The reward was that you were on the side of the movement that would transform the world and liberate. You were certain. This was the security. History was on your side. That's what gave people the courage to do it.[10]

However, he had another occasion to revisit that decade. Andrew Boyle, the journalist and biographer, had got in touch over his new book on the Cambridge spies. In 1951, on the disappearance of Burgess and Maclean, and during the 1960s as the Philby story broke, Klugmann had refused to meet MI5 officers or journalists investigating the Cambridge spy circle. Now, late in life, he agreed to meet Boyle. Boyle's friend Dick White, who had come across Klugmann during his time as the head of both MI5 and MI6, was pleasantly surprised: 'We could never have done that, or begun to get any closer.'[11] Klugmann would not have relished meeting Boyle, and indeed the encounter brought him some stress, as the Cooks found when he returned home. He met Boyle on an early August evening at a pub in Bedford Street, Covent Garden, round the corner from the Party's King Street offices. Boyle's notes reveal a wide-ranging discussion over an hour and a half, with Klugmann opening up on some of his early life while remaining evasive on other aspects. Boyle asked him about Donald Maclean, whom Klugmann admitted knowing. He told Boyle: 'I dislike and resent what Maclean, Burgess and Philby did', but would not be drawn further. ('I openly mentioned DM and GB but he didn't rise,' Boyle noted.) The discussion then moved on to his reasons for becoming a communist at Gresham's (including the influence of Frank McEachran), and his thrill at being involved in left-wing politics in Cambridge and Paris. It was a 'splendid time', he told Boyle. 'The young can't begin to understand our sense of exhilaration and adventurous freedom.' He told Boyle of his wartime role with Fitzroy Maclean, his confrontation with the 'insufferable' Evelyn Waugh and his sadness at the death of Frank Thompson. On the espionage question, he would not be pushed, however, despite Boyle's gentle pressing ('"I know what you're thinking I'm thinking that you're thinking I'm thinking" etc.', Boyle commented in his notebook). By the end of the discussion, Boyle concluded

that Klugmann 'has been a good Jesuit. V. good at teaching young people [...]
True spirit of the missionary'.[12]

Klugmann had been open with Boyle and, although he did not go into his
own espionage activity, it was clear that he wanted to convince him of the
extraordinary political situation of the 1930s. Boyle, for his part, largely took
his words in good faith. His book *The Climate of Treason*, which exposed Anthony
Blunt and prompted Margaret Thatcher's announcement in parliament of the
former's status as a spy, was not published until after Klugmann's death. In fact
Klugmann died three weeks after the Boyle interview.

These questions were on his mind. At the end of May, ITV had shown *Philby,
Burgess and Maclean*, one of the first dramatisations of the circumstances surrounding
the exposure of the three Cambridge spies. This 78-minute drama depicted the
pressures the three faced as the net closed in. It opened with Konstantin Volkov's
claim in 1945 – less than a month after MI5 recorded Klugmann's debriefing to
Bob Stewart – that there were two Soviet agents at the Foreign Office and one who
was leading counter-espionage in MI6. It moved swiftly on to the news emerging in
the US that there might be another Soviet spy working for the foreign office, code
name 'Homer', who of course was Donald Maclean. The drama included Maclean's
nervous breakdown in Cairo and gave attention to the pressures and torments he
felt as fear of his exposure increased. Inevitably, much attention focused on the
circumstances of his and Burgess's disappearance, including a gripping portrayal
of the anguish felt by Maclean in the days running up to his departure. As the
Maclean character confided to Burgess: 'There's no one you can tell. Talk to.
Discuss the most passionately important thing in your life. I've sometimes felt the
sheer loneliness and lack of human contact was cracking my head open.'

If Klugmann had seen this short, gripping drama, which lacked the frills of
some of the later ones, then it would have brought back the memories of ten
years before when he was confronted by Cairncross. After learning that Boyle
was in search of the fourth or fifth man, he must have felt the past catching up
with him again. 'Curious how it keeps coming back to Cambridge', the Skardon
character remarked to Philby in the film.

The leading characters in Raymond Williams's novel *Loyalties* share the
experiences of several of the Cambridge communists, notably conflicts of loyalty,
secrecy, the different responsibilities assumed by open communists and above all
the difficulty in explaining choices made in the 1930s to the later generation.
We do not know how much Williams took from his 1967 meeting with the
real intellectual talent spotter of that group, but the conflicts of loyalties faced

by Norman Braose, his sister and their comrades were similar to the ones felt by Klugmann and his Cambridge cohort. He did not, of course, share all of them. He was and remained an open communist. His direct espionage role was mainly confined to nine months in the late 1930s. He did not endanger the lives of British agents, as had Kim Philby, the head of counter-espionage at MI6 and the only one of the Cambridge spies to be feted in Moscow. He did not, like his schoolfriend Donald Maclean, pass information on the development of the atomic bomb to Moscow, and he was not required to publicly renounce his beliefs, as Guy Burgess had done so dramatically. The double lives they had led, which in Burgess's case ended miserably and prematurely in Moscow, would have been beyond Klugmann's capabilities. His personality as well as his politics would not have permitted it.

Hugh Trevor-Roper, who worked with Kim Philby in MI6, described how he was left 'perplexed' by the latter's character.

> He was, I believed, an intellectual; and yet he never seemed willing to discuss any intellectual subject. How one longed, in those drab, mechanical days, to escape from routine work and routine postures and to discuss ideas! And yet Philby, who seemed so intellectual, so sophisticated in his outlook, who was so different from most of our colleagues, and whose casual, convivial conversation I found so congenial, never allowed himself to be engaged.[13]

Klugmann was very different. He liked nothing more than to engage in intellectual conversation, something he did throughout his life in many different contexts with anybody who would listen. Indeed, his role as intellectual mentor to Maclean, Burgess, Blunt, Michael Straight and others is crucial to understanding the political rationale for young men in their early twenties considering working for the Comintern. The predicaments they then found themselves in, from which they were unwilling or unable to extract themselves, were not ultimately down to him.

Perhaps the member of the Cambridge circle who provides the best comparison with Klugmann is John Cairncross, his former friend who was the victim of his only direct contribution to Soviet espionage. Both were deeply affected by that moment; for Cairncross, of course, the consequences were far more severe. Brilliant linguists with a deep interest in French history and literature, they both had strong intellectual ambitions. Cairncross never joined the Party, but he made the bigger sacrifice for what he considered a just cause. Klugmann, the Party intellectual, was not driven into exile, but he ironically was the more compromised and constrained in his intellectual endeavours. He never reached the heights Cairncross attained, as an established expert on Molière and a noted translator of French literary works.

In the end, Klugmann's most serious conflicts of loyalties were with his own conscience and intellectual integrity. As his old comrade Malcolm MacEwen, who fell out with him in 1956, recalled:

> He stood both for all that was best in the Party – unselfishness, disregard for making money, lack of personal ambition, devotion to the cause and a keen intelligence – and for one of its most fatal defects: carrying loyalty to the point where it silenced his conscience and blunted his good sense.[14]

His sacrifices and devotion to the Party came at some personal cost – even his sexuality seems to have been repressed from an early age because of damage he perceived it would cause the Party. He chose a life in the Party ahead of an academic career of the type enjoyed by the likes of Eric Hobsbawm and Christopher Hill, both of whom had prospered despite the attentions, reports and scaremongering by MI5 in their early formative years in the Cold War era.[15] Close friends like Arnold Kettle, Margot Heinemann and Brian Simon also made successful academic careers. For perhaps the brightest intellectual of his generation there were mountains of articles for the Party press, an unfinished history of the Party that avoided contentious areas, shorter pamphlets and his Editorial Comments in *Marxism Today*. For the Party faithful his legacy was evident in his enormous library, which took several years to reassemble after his death. Much of it would go to the Marx Memorial Library. In 1983, 100 years after Marx's death, A.L. Morton, the founding spirit of the Communist Party Historians Group, opened the Klugmann Room.

Klugmann's last edition of *Marxism Today* was the September 1977 issue, which marked 20 years of the journal and would bring to an end his 30 years of full-time work for the Party. His health deteriorated rapidly and he was taken ill shortly after giving up the editorship and died on 14 September, just as the October edition was going into production. The official cause of death was a heart attack, brought on by his bronchial and asthmatic condition. Martin Jacques felt 'James died because there was no life after this for him'.[16] His death was sudden and came as a shock to those closest to him. Henry Cook was probably the last person close to him to see him alive, visiting him in hospital the day before he died. He knew what had happened as soon as his mother took the call. Mike

Carter recalled that when the news of Klugmann's death reached his family back in Birmingham, it was 'the only time I saw my dad cry. He was inconsolable.'

At his funeral, at Golders Green Crematorium on 20 September, his coffin was draped in the Party's Executive Committee banner. Arnold Kettle described how Klugmann and his comrade John Cornford had articulated an 'entirely new conception of the universities as fortresses against Fascism'. 'His life speaks for itself,' he told the hundreds of mourners who had stood in silent tribute as the coffin passed. Gordon McLennan, the Party's general secretary, told them that 'James was eternally young. No one in Britain in the past 40 years had done more than our comrade to explain and win understanding of the world-changing ideas of Marxism.'

'Homage to Klugmann Teacher of Genius' was the *Morning Star* headline. Tributes poured in from comrades around the world. Pete Carter urged today's intellectuals to 'follow the example of James Klugmann, learn from him, try to develop a humanity and modesty, and above all learn from his ability to explain complex ideas in a way everyone can understand'. Louis Althusser and Etienne Balibar were among those who sent a condolence message to the *Morning Star*. They may not always have been in agreement but they appreciated that his opening to them 'reached across frontiers for the cause of communism'.

Although he had gone prematurely grey in his late twenties, there was some truth that Klugmann was 'eternally young' in his unrelenting optimism that the next generation could be won to revolutionary ideas – something he practised in his teaching, talent spotting and many conversational missions throughout his life. Nevertheless the mourners arriving at Golders Green may have been bemused by the giant white swan and crowds of young people which greeted them as they waited to say goodbye to their popular intellectual. Marc Bolan, rock icon of the 1970s and a true figure of eternal youth who had died two weeks short of his thirtieth birthday, had been cremated the previous day.

James Klugmann's life didn't 'speak for itself'. Those who knew him in later years found it extraordinary that this owl-like, donnish, avuncular, bespectacled and eccentric Billy Bunter could have parachuted in to Yugoslavia or shared Mao's base camp at a height of revolutionary agitation.[17] But those were not the only mysteries. An idea for a book on his life, enthusiastically discussed by Jack Cohen, Brian Simon and others, was dropped when they were unable to decide how the Yugoslavia question would be handled.[18] More significantly, if unsurprisingly, there was no mention of espionage and the extended commitments it produced, the sacrifices it demanded and the divided loyalties it depended upon.

Notes

Prologue

1 E. Hobsbawm, *Interesting Times* (London: Allen Lane, 2002), p. 123.

1 Hampstead: Bourgeois Beginings

1 M. Holroyd, *Lytton Strachey: A Biography* (London: Penguin Books, 1971), p. 340.
2 Ibid., p. 376.
3 Ibid., p. 407.
4 In the unpublished memoirs of Harry Hodson, a former pupil at Gresham's School, who unfortunately got Klugmann muddled up with his elder cousin. Klugmann's own surname was frequently spelled with a single 'n' throughout his life.
5 Linda Rene-Martin (née Rittenberg), 'Kingsley School Remembered', private document passed to the author.
6 Ibid., and Linda Rene-Martin interview with the author.
7 L. Susan Stebbing, *Thinking to Some Purpose* (London: Pelican, 1939), p. 10.
8 Ibid., p. 30.
9 L. Susan Stebbing, *Logic in Practice*, cited in S. Chapman, *Susan Stebbing and the Language of Common Sense* (Basingstoke: Palgrave Macmillan, 2013), pp. 104–5.
10 Linda Rene-Martin interview with the author.
11 The history of the school is documented in P. Heazell (ed.), *One Hundred Years in Hampstead: The Story of the Hall School* (London: privately printed, 1989).
12 Ibid., p. 57.
13 Unlikely as it may seem, he even showed 'good promise' on the football field, according to a Junior School report of January 1922, in The Hall School Archive, The Hall School, Hampstead. However, at Gresham's he was never a keen sportsman.
14 *The Hall Magazine*, April 1925, p. 23.
15 *The Upper Sixth Former*, September 1926, The Hall School Archive. Poem reprinted by permission of The Hall School.
16 'Editorial', *The Hall Magazine*, September 1926.
17 *The Upper Sixth Former*, September 1926, The Hall School Archive.
18 Mark Wathen, letter to Roderick Bailey, 28 May 2004.
19 'Headmaster's Report', *The Hall Magazine*, July 1926, p. 179.
20 The Hall School Archive.

2 Outsider at Gresham's

1 B. Simon Papers, Institute of Education, University of London, 3im/4/5/2/9.

2 Ibid.

3 For a fuller discussion of how Gresham's fitted the Simon family's liberal ethos, see G. McCulloch and T. Woodin, 'Learning a Liberal Education: The Case of the Simon Family', *Oxford Review of Education* xxxvi/2 (2010), pp. 187–201.

4 Ibid., p. 195.

5 R. Cecil, *A Divided Life: A Personal Portrait of the Spy Donala Maclean* (New York: William Morrow, 1989), p. 13.

6 W.H. Auden, 'Honour: Gresham's School Holt', in G. Greene (ed.), *The Old School* (Oxford: Oxford University Press, 1984; first published 1934), p. 2.

7 The 2013 film *Peace and Conflict*, part dramatized documentary, directed by Tony Britten (no relation) addressed this aspect of Britten's life.

8 J. Bridgen, 'Frank McEachran 1900–1975: An Unrecognised Influence on W.H. Auden', in K. Bucknell and N. Jenkins (eds), *W.H. Auden, The Map of All my Youth: Early Works, Friends and Influences* (Oxford: Clarendon Press, 1990), p. 117.

9 Bridgen, 'Frank McEachran', p. 117.

10 F. McEachran, *The Unity of Europe* (n.p.: Search Publishing Co., 1932), p. 3.

11 Andrew Boyle, 'Notes of Andrew Boyle Interview with James Klugmann', 23 August 1977, Cambridge University Library, Add. 9429/1G/425(i).

12 James Klugmann interview cited in A. Boyle, *The Climate of Treason* (London: Hutchinson, 1979), p. 59.

13 Auden, 'Honour: Gresham's School Holt', p. 8.

14 Ibid.

15 Quoted in McCulloch and Woodin, 'Learning a Liberal Education', p. 197.

16 P. Kildea, *Benjamin Britten: A Life in the Twentieth Century* (London: Allen Lane, 2013), p. 51.

17 Cecil, *A Divided Life*, p. 15.

18 Debating Society Minutes, 11 October 1930, *The Gresham* 18/10/1930, Gresham College Archive.

19 *The Grasshopper*, Gresham College Archive.

20 Ibid.

21 Cecil, *A Divided Life*, p. 17.

3 A Cambridge Communist

1 T.E.B. Howarth, *Cambridge Between the Wars* (London: Collins, 1978), p. 142.

2 Ibid., p. 148.

3 G. Freeman, *Alma Mater: Memories of Girton College 1926–1929* (Cambridge: Mistress and Fellows of Girton College, 1990), Girton College Archive, Cambridge.

4 K. Raine, *Autobiographies* (London: Skoob Books, 1991), p. 128.

5 *Girton College Review*, Easter and Michaelmas 1930, Girton College Archive.

6 Kitty Klugmann letter to Miss Major, mistress of Girton College, 15 April 1931, Girton College Archive.

7 Maurice Cornforth, in C. Haden Guest (ed.), *David Guest: A Scientist Fights for Freedom, A Memoir* (London: Lawrence and Wishart, 1939), p. 95.

8 Cornforth, in ibid., pp. 95–6.

9 Cited in R. Monk, *Ludwig Wittgenstein: The Duty of Genius* (London: Penguin Books, 1991), p. 343.

10 See the recollections of Guest in Haden Guest, *David Guest: A Scientist Fights for Freedom*.

11 Cornforth, in ibid., p. 97.

12 P. Seale and M. McConville, *Philby: The Long Road to Moscow* (London: Hamish Hamilton, 1973), p. 32.

13 A. Boyle, *The Climate of Treason* (London: Hutchinson, 1979), p. 69.

14 N. Montserrat, *Life is a Four Letter Word*, vol. 1, quoted in Seale and McConville, *Philby*, p. 19 (Montserrat was a Trinity College student 1929–32).

15 Klugmann recounted this story to Stephen Sedley; Stephen Sedley interview with the author.

16 J. McNeish, *The Sixth Man: The Extraordinary Life of Paddy Costello* (London: Quartet Books, 2008), p. 34.

17 V. Kiernan, 'On Treason', *London Review of Books* ix/12, 25 June 1987.

18 M. Straight, *After Long Silence* (New York: W.W. Norton, 1983), pp. 66–7.

19 J. Klugmann, 'Introduction: The Crisis in the Thirties, a View from the Left', in J. Clark et al. (eds), *Culture and Crisis in Britain in the 30s* (London: Lawrence and Wishart, 1979), p. 15.

20 The minutes of CUSS meetings held between 1928 and 1935 were withheld by MI5 after it received them in 1972, but were made available to Christopher Andrew for his authorised history. See C. Andrew, *The Defence of the Realm: The Authorized History of MI5* (London: Allen Lane, 2009), pp. 172–3. Seale and McConville, *Philby*, pp. 27–8, also discuss them, based mainly on correspondence with Jim Lees.

21 M.P. Ashley and C.T. Saunders, *Red Oxford* (Oxford: Oxford University Labour Club, 2nd edition, 1933), p. 43.

22 Frank Strauss Meyer, in detailed evidence given to the FBI in May 1952. He was the October Club's founding president. The FBI passed this material to MI5 and it is available at The National Archives, London (TNA), KV 2/3501.

23 M.Y. Lang, 'The Growth of the Student Movement', in Haden Guest, *David Guest: A Scientist Fights for Freedom*, p. 90; Boyle, *The Climate of Treason*, p. 75.

24 References to this meeting can be found in Boyle, *The Climate of Treason*, pp. 75–6 and B. Page, D. Leitch and P. Knightley, *Philby: The Spy Who Betrayed a Generation* (London: Sphere Books, 1977), p. 70.

4 Organising the Movement

1 Frank Strauss Meyer, TNA, KV 2/3501.

2 Ibid.

3 Ibid.

4 *Student Vanguard* i/1, November 1932.

5 Frederick Lawton, 'The Decline of the Union', *Cambridge Review*, 30 October 1931. He noted that in Michaelmas 1931 'only 350 freshmen had joined the union compared to 600 the previous year'.

6 *Cambridge Review*, 20 May 1932.

7 Ibid.

8 J. Klugmann, 'Introduction: The Crisis in the Thirties, a View from the Left', in J. Clark et al. (eds), *Culture and Crisis in Britain in the 30s* (London: Lawrence and Wishart, 1979), p. 20.

9 Ibid., p. 18.

10 Ibid., p. 28.

11 G. Orwell, *The Road to Wigan Pier* (London: Penguin Books, 2014), p. 105.

12 M.Y. Lang, 'The Growth of the Student Movement', in C. Haden Guest (ed.), *David Guest: A Scientist Fights for Freedom, A Memoir* (London: Lawrence and Wishart, 1939), pp. 91–2.

13 Kenneth Sinclair-Loutit, 'Very Little Luggage', unpublished memoir, pp. 32–3.

14 'D.G.', 'Fascism: A Blind Alley', *Trinity College Magazine*, May 1933, p. 20.

15 Ibid., p. 21.

16 V. Kiernan, 'Recollections', in Pat Sloan (ed.), *John Cornford: A Memoir* (Dunfermline: Borderline Press, 1938), p. 121 (emphasis in the original).

17 *Cambridge Review*, 10 November 1933.

18 'Students Jailed for Fighting War', *Student Vanguard*, ii/1, October 1933.

19 A nationwide poll on whether Britain should remain part of the League of Nations and to judge if there was support for disarmament through international agreement.

20 Sloan, *John Cornford*, p. 100.

21 Ibid., pp. 101–2.

22 They included Alan Turing, then a student at King's but not politically aligned. He had been outside the Tivoli Cinema fracas and noted in his diary on 12 November, 'There was a very successful A(nti) W(ar) demonstration yesterday'. Quoted in Andrew Hodges, *Alan Turing: The Enigma* (London: Vintage Books, 2012), p. 87.

23 'Editorial', *Cambridge Review*, 17 November 1933.

24 T. Driberg, *Guy Burgess: A Portrait with Background* (London: Weidenfeld and Nicolson, 1956), p. 18.

5 Mentor and Talent Spotter

1 Anthony Blunt, 'Biographical Memoir', British Library, MS 88902/1, p. 17.

2 James Klugmann interview with Andrew Boyle, cited in A. Boyle, *The Climate of Treason* (London: Hutchinson, 1979), p. 72.

3   Margot Heinemann, undated letter (but early 1934) to family. Heinemann Papers, Goldsmith's College, London, Box A4.

4   N. Wood, *Communism and British Intellectuals* (London: Victor Gollancz, 1959), p. 86.

5   'Cambridge Socialism', in Pat Sloan (ed.), *John Cornford: A Memoir* (Dunfermline: Borderline Press, 1938), p. 105.

6   *Student Vanguard*, December 1933. The October Club continued to hold meetings at Ruskin College, which did not come under the jurisdiction of the university.

7   These included Margot Heinemann, who said the experience 'made you feel you had to stand up and be counted'. Heinemann interview with Conrad Wood, Imperial War Museums (IWM), 9239/5/1 1986.

8   'Cambridge Socialism', in Sloan, *John Cornford*, pp. 104–5.

9   P. Kingsford, *The Hunger Marchers in Britain 1920–1940* (London: Lawrence and Wishart, 1982), p. 184.

10 Margot Heinemann interview with Conrad Wood, IWM, 9239/5/1-2 1986.

11 J. Klugmann, 'Introduction: The Crisis in the Thirties, a View from the Left', in J. Clark et al. (eds), *Culture and Crisis in Britain in the 30s* (London: Lawrence and Wishart, 1979), p. 29.

12 Ibid., p. 29.

13 *Communist Review*, September 1932 (emphasis in the original).

14 Rajani Palme Dutt, in *Labour Monthly*, October 1933; N. Branson, *History of the Communist Party of Great Britain 1927–1941*, London: Lawrence and Wishart, 1985), p. 200.

15 Sloan, *John Cornford*, p. 171.

16 George Kitson Clark letter to James Klugmann, 17 June 1934, Klugmann Archive, Marx Memorial Library, London.

17 Margot Heinemann interview with Conrad Wood, IWM, 9239/5/2 1986.

18 C. Rycroft, 'Memoirs of an Old Bolshevik', in Peter Fuller (ed.), *Psychoanalysis and Beyond* (London: Hogarth Press, 1991), p. 207.

19 Ibid., pp. 207–8.

20 Ibid., p. 210.

21 Ibid.

22 Ibid., p. 211.

23 Kenneth Sinclair-Loutit, 'Very Little Luggage', unpublished memoir, p. 34.

6 The Making of a Communist Intellectual

1   J. Klugmann, 'Introduction: The Crisis in the Thirties, a View from the Left', in J. Clark et al. (eds), *Culture and Crisis in Britain in the 30s* (London: Lawrence and Wishart, 1979), p. 34.

2   E. Hobsbawm, *Interesting Times* (London: Allen Lane, 2002), p. 113.

3   James Klugmann, 'Revolution', talk to West Lewisham Young Communist League, December 1973, British Library, Archive Recordings, Sound Recording 1973.12, C613/06/01.

4   J. Cairncross, *The Enigma Spy: An Autobiography* (London: Century Random House, 1997), p. 42.

5   Anthony Blunt, 'Biographical Memoir', British Library, MS 88902/1.

6   A. Blunt, 'From Bloomsbury to Marxism', *Studio International* (1973), quoted in M. Carter, *Anthony Blunt: His Lives* (London: Macmillan, 2001), p. 122.

7   M. Straight, *After Long Silence* (New York: W.W. Norton, 1983), p. 57.

8   Ibid.

9   Ibid., p. 58.

10 Ibid., pp. 59, 60.

11 Ibid., p. 61.

12 Eva Tas Archive, International Institute of Social History, Amsterdam (IISH), File 1. Eva Tas was a Dutch anti-fascist and participant at the RME Congresses.

13 Ibid.

14 Ibid.

15 Ibid.

16 K. Morgan, *Against War and Fascism* (Manchester: Manchester University Press, 1989), p. 33.

17 George Kitson Clark letter to James Klugmann, 31 July 1935, Klugmann Archive, Marx Memorial Library.

18 Quoted in K. Ingram, *Rebel: The Short Life of Esmond Romilly* (New York: E.P. Dutton, 1986), p. 61. Michael Barratt Brown interview with the author.

19 Klugmann, 'Introduction: Crisis in the Thirties', p. 17.

20 N. Wood, *Communism and British Intellectuals* (London: Victor Gollancz, 1959), p. 217.

7 Working for the Comintern

1   E. Hobsbawm, *Interesting Times* (London: Allen Lane, 2002), p. 122.

2   K. Morgan et al. (eds), *Communists and British Society 1920–1991* (London: Rivers Oram Press, 2007), p. 122.

3   For a useful summary of Mornet's position in English see R. Chartier, *The Cultural Origins of the French Revolution* (Durham, NC: Duke University Press, 1991), pp. 1–8.

4   Letter from J.T. Saunders, secretary of Board of Research Studies to James Klugmann, 5 December 1935, Klugmann Archive, Marx Memorial Library.

5   Letter from J. Browne, Rosenheim, Ross and Rosenheim, to J. Klugmann ('Dear Norman'), 20 January 1936, Klugmann Archive, Marx Memorial Library.

6   S. McMeekin, *The Red Millionaire: A Political Biography of Willi Münzenberg* (New Haven, CT: Yale University Press, 2003), p. 265.

7   E. Mortimer, *The Rise of the French Communist Party 1920–1947* (London: Faber and Faber, 1984), p. 191.

8   Ibid., p. 193.

9   J. Miles, *The Nine Lives of Otto Katz* (London: Bantam Books, 2010).

10 Hobsbawm, *Interesting Times*, p. 122.

11 Eva Tas Archive, IISH, RME File 5.

12 Eva Tas Archive, IISH, RME File 6. Tas herself was the Dutch delegate at this meeting.
13 J. Klugmann, *La Voix des Étudiants*, February 1936, p. 17, Eva Tas Archive, IISH, File 5.
14 J. Klugmann, *La Voix des Étudiants*, January 1936, p. 13, Eva Tas Archive, IISH, File 5.
15 J. Danos and M. Gibelin, *June 36: Class Struggles and the Popular Front in France* (London: Bookmarks, 1986), p. 44.
16 Ibid.
17 J Klugmann, 'Introduction: The Crisis in the Thirties, a View from the Left', in J. Clark et al. (eds), *Culture and Crisis in Britain in the 30s* (London: Lawrence and Wishart, 1979).
18 Manès Sperber, the Austrian-French novelist, then living in Paris and active in the anti-fascist movement, in *Au-delà de l'Oubli*, quoted in J. Jackson, *The Popular Front in France; Defending Democracy 1934–1938* (Cambridge: Cambridge University Press, 1988), p. 287.
19 Hobsbawm, *Interesting Times*, p. 124.
20 D. Healey, *The Time of my Life* (London: Penguin, 1990), p. 38.
21 S. Samuels, 'The Left Book Club', *Journal of Contemporary History* i/ 2 (1966), p. 65.
22 Ibid., p. 68.
23 Ibid., p. 67.
24 Ibid., p. 73.
25 Ibid., p. 78.
26 Margot Heinemann letter to family (undated), Heinemann Papers Box A4, Goldsmith's College, London.
27 In Cornford's own words in a letter to Margot Heinemann, in P. Stansky and W. Abrahams, *Journey to the Frontier* (London: Constable and Co., 1966), p. 332.
28 John Cornford to Margot Heinemann, in Stansky and Abrahams, *Journey to the Frontier*, p. 316.
29 J. Sommerfield, *May Day* (London: Lawrence and Wishart, 1984; first published 1936), p. 84.
30 *Bulletin d'Information*, 10 March 1936, Eva Tas Archive, IISH, RME File 7.
31 M. Straight, *After Long Silence* (New York: W.W. Norton, 1983), p. 98.
32 Ibid., p. 99.

8 The Professional Revolutionary

1 Paris International Exhibition brochure, Eva Tas Archive, IISH, File 9.
2 K. Schlogel, *Moscow 1937* (Cambridge: Polity, 2012), p. 199.
3 Ibid.
4 Ibid.
5 Ibid.
6 Ibid., p. 201.
7 TNA, KV 2/788/1/6.

8 R. Cecil, *A Divided Life: A Personal Portrait of the Spy Donala Maclean* (New York: William Morrow, 1989), p. 56.

9 TNA, KV 2/788.

10 Ibid.

11 Ibid.

12 MI5 notes, TNA, KV 2/788.

13 Ibid.

14 T. Buchanan, *East Wind: China and the British Left 1925–1976* (Oxford: Oxford University Press, 2012).

15 *China Forum* i/15, 28 May 1938.

16 This was the figure Klugmann cited in his report to the Third RME Congress in 1939, Eva Tas Archive, IISH, File 15.

17 'Address to the World Student Delegation by Wang Ming', 'Chinese Communist Leaders Speak to the World Student Delegation', published by the Information Committee, Eva Tas Archive, IISH, File 13.

18 Klugmann later recounted his experiences – 'I have visited anti-illiteracy classes in many a cave' – in a letter to Leslie Limage in response to his suggesting an article on adult literacy programmes in Vietnam, 20 July 1976, Klugmann Archive, Marx Memorial Library.

19 All quotes from 'Interview Between Mao Tse Tung and the Delegates of the World Student Association (July 12 1938) Questions by Miss Molly Yard, James Klugmann, Bernard Floud and Grant Lathe', published by the Information Committee, Eva Tas Archive, IISH, File 13.

20 Activities included Cambridge students placing 'Boycott Japanese goods' placards in shops and a 'house to house' plebiscite in Oxford calling on students to take up a boycott.

21 Report of Executive Bureau of RME Paris, 23 October 1938, Eva Tas Archive, IISH, File 14.

22 Eva Tas Archive, IISH, File 14.

23 This statement is unsigned but accompanies other material with Klugmann's signature.

24 Eva Tas Archive, IISH, File 15.

25 Eva Tas Archive, IISH, File 16.

9 The Spy Circle

1 James Klugmann conversation with Bob Stewart, King Street, August 1945, TNA, KV 2/791.

2 N. West and O. Tsarev, *The Crown Jewels* (London: HarperCollins, 1999), p. 347.

3 G. Borovik, *The Philby Files*, ed. Philip Knightley (London: Warner Books, 1995), p. 12. Borovik recorded 'unprecedentedly open conversations' and 'did not clear (the) manuscript with anyone' (p. xvi).

4   D. Burke, *The Lawn Road Flats: Spies, Writers and Artists* (Martlesham: Boydell Press, 2014), p. 2.
5   Kim Philby, in Borovik, *The Philby Files*, p. 30.
6   Philby, in ibid., p 46.
7   Ibid.
8   R. Cecil, *A Divided Life: A Personal Portrait of the Spy Donald Maclean* (New York: William Morrow, 1989), p. 35.
9   Borovik, *The Philby Files*, p. 49.
10 Anthony Blunt, 'Biographical Memoir', British Library, MS 88902/1, p. 25.
11 Maurice Dobb to Guy Burgess, 2 January 1936. The correspondence can be found in Dobb's MI5 file, TNA, KV 2/1759.
12 Maurice Dobb to Guy Burgess, undated, TNA, KV 2/1759.
13 Blunt, 'Biographical Memoir', p. 22.
14 Ibid., p. 24.
15 Ibid.
16 Ibid., p. 29.
17 M. Carter, *Anthony Blunt: His Lives* (London: Macmillan, 2001).
18 Brian Simon, interview with Miranda Carter, ibid., p. 191.
19 M. Straight, *After Long Silence* (New York: W.W. Norton, 1983), p. 67.
20 Ibid., p. 71.
21 Ibid.
22 Ibid., p. 72.

10 The Reluctant Spy

1   C. Pincher, *Their Trade is Treachery* (London: Sidgwick and Jackson, 1981), p. 127.
2   M. Straight, *After Long Silence* (New York: W.W. Norton, 1983), p. 73.
3   Ibid., pp. 101–2.
4   M. Carter, *Anthony Blunt: His Lives* (London: Macmillan, 2001), p. 185.
5   J. Cairncross, *The Enigma Spy: An Autobiography* (London: Century Random House, 1997), p. 46.
6   N. West and O. Tsarev, *The Crown Jewels* (London: HarperCollins, 1999), p. 206.
7   Ibid.
8   Y. Modin, *My Five Cambridge Friends* (London: Headline, 1994), p. 106.
9   Cairncross, *The Enigma Spy*, pp. 61–2.
10 Ibid., p. 62.
11 Anthony Blunt, 'Biographical Memoir', British Library, MS 88902/1, p. 26.
12 E. Hobsbawm, *Interesting Times* (London: Allen Lane, 2002), p. 102.
13 Eric Hobsbawm, interview with the author.
14 Ibid.
15 James Klugmann interview with Bob Stewart, King Street, August 1945, TNA, KV 2/791.
16 V. Kiernan, 'On Treason', *London Review of Books* ix/12, 25 June 1987.

17 Ibid.
18 N. West, *MASK: MI5's Penetration of the Communist Party of Great Britain* (London: Routledge, 2005).
19 D. Hyde, *I Believed* (London: William Heinemann, 1951), p. 146.
20 Ibid., p. 147.
21 West and Tsarev, *The Crown Jewels*, p. 206.
22 Ben Nicholson, unpublished diaries. I am grateful to Andrew Lownie for this reference, and to Ben Nicholson's daughter, who gave permission for him to share it with me.
23 P. Wright, *Spycatcher* (New York: Viking Penguin, 1987), pp. 248–9.
24 West and Tsarev, *The Crown Jewels*, p. 207.
25 Ibid.
26 J. Hart, *Ask Me No More: An Autobiography* (London: Peter Halban, 1998), p. 70.
27 Ibid., p. 72.
28 See West and Tsarev, *The Crown Jewels*, pp. 274–6 for a discussion of Scott and the planned Oxford ring.
29 *The History of the London Rezidentura*, vol. 1, p. 151, cited in West and Tsarev, *The Crown Jewels*, p. 207.
30 TNA, KV 2/791.

11 A Communist Goes to War

1 TNA, KV 2/791.
2 Ernest Simon, letter to James Klugmann, 13 November 1939, Klugmann Archive, Marx Memorial Library. Sarah Benton correspondence with the author.
3 James Klugmann, letter to George Kitson Clark, 2 February 1941 and George Kitson Clark, letter to James Klugmann, 4 Feburary 1941, Kitson Clark Archive, Trinity College, Cambridge.
4 Bob Stewart debriefing, 8 August 1945, TNA, KV 2/791.
5 Ibid.
6 TNA, HS9/1645.
7 TNA, KV/2/788.
8 Many of the agents he used were communists with Yugoslav roots, and some had fought in the Spanish Civil War.
9 Bob Stewart debriefing, 8 August 1945, TNA, KV 2/791.
10 Ibid.
11 Ibid.
12 TNA, KV2/788/2/8, Keble himself, who was regarded by senior SOE colleagues as an ambitious officer, was intent on generating as many Balkan missions as he could, both to confront the enemy and to consolidate his own power base and secure his place in history. This would have suited Klugmann's own motives for seeking more Yugoslav missions.
13 R. Bailey, 'Communist in SOE: Explaining James Klugmann's Recruitment and Retention', *Intelligence and National Security* xx/1 (2005), pp. 92–3.

14 F. Maclean, *Eastern Approaches* (London: Cape, 1949), p. 281; M.R.D. Foot, *SOE: The Special Operations Executive 1940–1946* (London: BBC, 1984).

15 B. Davidson, *Special Operations Europe: Scenes from the Anti-Nazi War* (London: Grafton Books, 1987), p. 113.

16 Ibid., pp. 131–2.

17 Michael Barratt Brown, interview with the author.

18 Bob Stewart interview, TNA, KV 2/791.

19 J. Earle, *From Nile to Danube: A Wartime Memoir* (Ljubljana: Mladika, 2010), p. 71.

20 Ibid., p. 72.

21 Bob Stewart debriefing, 8 August 1945, TNA, KV 2/791.

12 Comrade or Conspirator

1 *Spectator*, 31 July 1999 and subsequent letters 14 August 1999, 21 August 1999, 28 August 1999 and 11 September 1999.

2 This also appeared as 'The Freedom of the Press' in *Times Literary Supplement*, 15 September 1972.

3 Major Archie Jack interview, 18 March 1989, IWM 10640.

4 D. Martin, *The Web of Disinformation* (New York: Harcourt Brace Jovanovich, 1990).

5 M. Lees, *The Rape of Serbia* (New York: Harcourt Brace Jovanovich, 1990), p. 32.

6 Ibid., pp. 39–40.

7 Ibid., p. 33.

8 P.J. Conradi, *A Very English Hero: The Making of Frank Thompson* (London: Bloomsbury, 2012), p. 359.

9 Ibid., p. 296.

10 S. Johnson, *Agents Extraordinary* (London: Robert Hale, 1975), p. 30.

11 P.J. Conradi, *Iris Murdoch: A Life* (London: Harper Collins, 2001). p. 183.

12 E.P. Thompson, *Beyond the Frontier* (London: Merlin Press, 1997).

13 Lees, *The Rape of Serbia*, p. 53.

14 Kenneth Sinclair-Loutit, 'Very Little Luggage', unpublished memoir. Conradi, *A Very English Hero*, p. 393.

15 R. Bailey, *Forgotten Voices of the Secret War: An Inside History of Special Operations During the Second World War* (London: Ebury Press, 2008), p. 169.

16 Ibid., p. 171.

17 Ibid., p. 173.

18 Basil Davidson interview, 14 November 1988, IWM, 10505.

19 R. Bailey, 'Communist in SOE: Explaining James Klugmann's Recruitment and Retention', *Intelligence and National Security* xx/1 (2005).

20 Quoted in D. Lane Patey, *The Life of Evelyn Waugh: A Critical Biography* (Oxford: Blackwell, 1998), p. 410, fn. 65.

21 M. Barratt Brown, *Seekers: A Twentieth Century Life* (Nottingham: Spokesman, 2013), p. 98.

22 J. Earle, *From Nile to Danube: A Wartime Memoir* (Ljubljana: Mladika, 2010), pp. 203–4.

23 The Klugmann connection with Waugh's two novels has been briefly discussed in Lane Patey, *The Life of Evelyn Waugh*, p. 410.

24 E. Waugh, *Unconditional Surrender* (London: Penguin, 1964), p. 155.

25 Ibid., p. 163.

26 Ibid., p. 165.

27 Ibid., p. 166.

28 E. Waugh, *Love Among the Ruins* (London: Chapman and Hall, 1953).

29 As he told Andrew Boyle in his 1977 interview; Boyle's 'Notes from the Interview with James Klugmann', Cambridge University Library, Add. 9429/IG/425(i).

30 Intercepted letter from Lieutenant Meredith, quoting Klugmann, to Betty Wallace, TNA, KV/2/788

31 James Klugmann to Bob Stewart, TNA, KV 2/791. Further details of Klugmann's time in Belgrade with UNRRA are held at the School for Slavonic and East European Studies, London, KLU/1/1 to KLU/7/4.

32 TNA, KV 2/788.

33 Ibid.

34 TNA, KV 2/791.

35 M. Carter, *Anthony Blunt: His Lives* (London: Macmillan, 2001), p. 319.

13 Great Expectations

1 Colonel Valentine Vivian to Roger Hollis, 22 October 1946, TNA, KV 2/788.

2 Kim Philby to Roger Hollis, 20 June 1946, TNA, KV 2/791.

3 C.A. Simkins memo, 4 March 1947, TNA, KV 2/791.

4 Vivian to Hollis, 22 October 1946, TNA KV 2/788.

5 James Klugmann, 'Notes on Yugoslavia', TNA, KV 2/788.

6 Ibid.

7 See Harry Pollitt to Maurice Thorez, 12 October 1946, TNA, KV 2/789.

8 James Klugmann, letter to Agit Prop Department, Communist Party of France, 20 October 1946, TNA, KV 2/789.

9 The Garibaldi restaurant was part of the Mazzini-Garibaldi Club for Italian workers. Special Branch had an officer present at the meeting who reported back to MI5, along with the observation that 'Klugmann has become to be recognised as the Party's expert on American affairs and it was obvious from his speech that he has wide contacts in that country'. TNA, KV 2/789.

10 Phone conversation, King Street (incoming), James Klugmann and Margot Heinemann, 6 November 1946, TNA, KV 2/789.

11 Details of his talks are in the Klugmann Papers at the CPGB Archive at the People's History Museum in Manchester. A collection of Klugmann's handwritten speaker notes, complete with subtitles and bullet points are held at CP/IND/KLUG/02.

12 International Committee, 11 July 1947, Klugmann's notes of meeting, CPGB Archive, CP/IND/KLUG/02.

13 The Fabian Society debate was held in Watford on 18 February 1948, CPGB Archive, CP/IND/KLUG/02.
14 31 July 1947, TNA, KV 2/789.
15 K. Cornforth, 'British Road to Socialism', *Communist Review*, April 1947.
16 Harry Pollitt, letter to James Klugmann, 4 June 1947, CPGB Archive, CP/IND/KLUG/12/02.
17 TNA, KV 2/789.
18 He would expand this argument in the Communist Party booklet *Wall Street's Drive to War* (London: Communist Party, 1950).
19 Edward Upward's *The Rotten Elements* (London: Quartet, 1979), the second volume of a trilogy based on life in the Communist Party, deals with the inner party conflicts over this question.
20 TNA, KV 2/2335.
21 A. Koestler, *The Invisible Writing* (London: Vintage, 2005), pp. 286–7.
22 MI5 notes of Greenlees's report, 24 October 1947, TNA, KV 2/789.

14 Cold War Intellectual

1 James Klugmann to Robin Page Arnott, 14 September 1947, TNA, KV 2/789.
2 Margot Heinemann to Kitty Cornforth, MI5 phone check (incoming) Talbot Road, 24 October 1947, TNA, KV 2/789.
3 J. Klugmann, 'The Petkov Pattern', *World News and Views*, 11 October 1947.
4 Ibid.
5 Ibid.
6 Ibid.
7 Ibid.
8 *World News and Views*, 3 July 1948.
9 *World News and Views*, 17 July 1948.
10 'Yugoslavia and the Cominform Declaration', Belsize Branch, 21 July 1948, CPGB Archive, CP/IND/KLUG/02.
11 J. Klugmann, 'From Social Democracy to "Democratic Socialism", Part II', *Communist Review*, January 1949.
12 G. Eley, *Forging Democracy: The History of the Left in Europe* (Oxford: Oxford University Press, 2002), p. 309.
13 V. Kiernan, 'The Unrewarded End', *London Review of Books* xx/18, 17 September 1998.
14 TNA, KV 2/789. The intelligence report notes, with more than a hint of sarcasm, that 'it seems surprising that communists should find it necessary to treat such a crisis in a bourgeois manner'.
15 A. Potts, *Zilliacus: A Life for Peace and Socialism* (London: Merlin Press, 2002), p. 120.
16 Special Branch attended this meeting and gave a written report to MI5, 23 January 1950, TNA, KV 2/789.
17 Incoming call to King Street, 14 April 1950, TNA, KV 2/789.
18 Kiernan, 'The Unrewarded End'.

19 All quotes taken from Hansard, 29 March 1950.
20 MI5 notes on meeting with Egorov, 14 April 1950, TNA, KV 2/789.
21 James Klugmann, 'Who are the Traitors?', Muswell Hill Communist Party, 9 May 1950, CPGB Archive, CP/IND/KLUG/02.
22 Phone check, King Street, 14 April 1948, TNA, KV 2/789.
23 A. Macleod, *The Death of Uncle Joe* (London: Merlin Press, 1997), p. 26. Macleod recalls that she later bumped into Haldane on the London Underground and, after remarking that his 'old friends wish that you would get in touch with them', 'Haldane gave me a look of absolute horror. I realised for the first time what he had been through', ibid., p. 27.
24 Phone conversation, 22 January 1951, phone check on Talbot Road, TNA, KV 2/790.
25 J. Klugmann, *From Trotsky to Tito* (London: Lawrence and Wishart, 1951), p. 9.
26 Ibid., p. 11.
27 Ibid., p. 39 (emphasis in original).
28 Ibid., p. 40.

15 Trials and Tribulations

1 K. Morgan, *Harry Pollitt* (Manchester: Manchester University Press, 1993), p. 123.
2 Jeff Skelley, interview with the author.
3 These discussions in the afternoon of 13 June 1950 were picked up by the MI5 microphone in King Street, TNA, KV 2/1777.
4 James Klugmann, 'Studying History of Communist Movement', talk to Recent History Group, 28 February 1950, CPGB Archive, CP/IND/KLUG/02.
5 Krivitsky published an account of his activities in the NKVD, see *I Was Stalin's Agent* (London: Hamish Hamilton, 1939) and testified before House Un-American Activities in October 1939.
6 Guy Liddell diaries, 29 May 1951, TNA, KV 4/473.
7 G. Rees, *A Chapter of Accidents* (London: Chatto and Windus, 1972), p. 135.
8 A. Martin memo, 8 June 1951, TNA, KV 2/790.
9 Guy Liddell diaries, 12 June 1951, TNA, KV 4/473.
10 Guy Liddell diaries, 26 June 1951, TNA, KV 4/473.
11 Joan Bellamy, interview with the author. She had heard it from Donald Maclean in Moscow.
12 Jeff Skelley, interview with the author.
13 V. Kiernan, 'The Unrewarded End', *London Review of Books* xx'18, 17 September 1998.
14 J. Klugmann, 'Lessons from the Prague Trial', *Communist Review*, March 1953.
15 H. Srebrnik, *London Jews and British Communism* (Edgware: Valentine Mitchell, 1995), p. 61.
16 R. Samuel, *The Lost World of British Communism* (London: Verso, 2006), p. 167.
17 K. Morgan et al. (eds), *Communists and British Society 1920–1991* (London: Rivers Oram Press, 2007).
18 These would include Klugmann's friend Chimen Abramsky, who left in 1957. For the

effect it had on him, see S. Abramsky, *The House of Twenty Thousand Books* (London: Peter Halban, 2014).

19 H. Pollitt, *In Memory of Joseph Stalin and Klement Gottwald* (London: CPGB, 1953), St Anthony's College Archives, Oxford, PAM1656.

20 A. Macleod, *The Death of Uncle Joe* (London: Merlin Press, 1997), p. 46.

21 Morgan, *Harry Pollitt*, p. 172.

22 J. Saville, 'The 20th Congress and the British Communist Party', *Socialist Register* xiii (1976).

16 The Party Functionary: 1956 and After

1 This and the ensuing correspondence between Klugmann and Thompson as well as the details of the Halifax motion can be found in the CPGB Archive, CP/CENT/ORG/98/04.

2 CPGB Archive, CP/CENT/ORG/98/04.

3 A. Macleod, *The Death of Uncle Joe* (London: Merlin Press, 1997), p. 74.

4 CPGB Archive, CP/CENT/ORG/98/04.

5 CPGB Archive, CP/IND/KLUG/06.

6 E.P. Thompson, letter to Bert Ramelson, 28 May 1956, CPGB Archive, CP/CENT/ORG/98/04.

7 J. Saville, 'The 20th Congress and the British Communist Party', *Socialist Register* xiii (1976), p. 6.

8 Ibid., p. 7.

9 E.P. Thompson reports on this meeting in a letter to 'Howard' (almost certainly Howard Hill, the Sheffield Borough secretary), 20 August 1956, CPGB Archive, CP/CENT/ORG/98/04.

10 He later published a fuller version elsewhere.

11 Macleod, *The Death of Uncle Joe*, p. 144.

12 Saville, 'The 20th Congress and the British Communist Party', p. 15.

13 This was confirmed by Dorothy Thompson in correspondence with Peter J. Conradi, 18 August 2009.

14 Dorothy Thompson correspondence with Peter J. Conradi, 16 August 2009.

15 M. MacEwen, 'The Day the Party Had to Stop', *Socialist Register* xiii (1976), p. 30.

16 Christopher Hill, draft paper on 'methods of election', quoted in ibid., p. 32.

17 MacEwen, 'The Day the Party Had to Stop', p. 32.

18 Ibid.

19 E. Hobsbawm, 'The Historians Group of the Communist Party' in M. Cornforth (ed.), *Rebels and their Causes* (London: Lawrence and Wishart, 1978), p. 26.

20 Ibid., p. 29.

21 Ibid.

22 E. Hobsbawm, *Interesting Times* (London: Allen Lane, 2002), p. 209.

23 Eric Hobsbawm's MI5 file, released in 2014, makes clear the extent of hostility towards him from the Party leadership in the aftermath of 1956, TNA, KV 2/3985.

See also G. Andrews, 'Eric Hobsbawm and MI5', *Open Democracy*, 20 November 2014. Available at www.opendemocracy.net/geoff-andrews/eric-hobsbawm-and-mi5 (accessed 24 March 2015) and F. Stonor Saunders, 'Stuck on the Flypaper', *London Review of Books*, 9 April 2015.

24 F. Jackson, report on Party History Commission, 1 August 1957, CPGB Archive, CP/IND/KLUG/02/06.

25 James Klugmann, report on Party History Commission to Political Committee, 2 January 1958, CPGB Archive, CP/IND/KLUG/02.

26 Hobsbawm, *Interesting Times*, p. 124.

17 A Lost Generation

1 Executive Committee Minutes, 11–12 May 1957, CPGB Archive, CP/CENT/EC/04/07.

2 Editorial, *Universities and Left Review,* i/1 (Spring 1957).

3 E. Hobsbawm, 'Some Notes about the *Universities and Left Review*', report to Executive Committee Meeting, 10–11 May 1958, CPGB Archive, CP/CENT/EC/05/08.

4 Editorial, *New Reasoner*, Summer 1957.

5 E.P. Thompson, 'Socialist Humanism', *New Reasoner*, Summer 1957, p. 108.

6 Ibid., p. 114.

7 A. Kettle, 'How New is the New Left?', *Marxism Today*, October 1960.

8 W. Thompson, *The Good Old Cause* (London: Pluto Press, 1992), pp. 116–17.

9 Conrad Wood, interview with the author.

10 'Editorial Comments', *Marxism Today*, March 1962.

11 'Editorial Comments', *Marxism Today*, February 1963 and May 1963.

12 'Editorial Comments', *Marxism Today*, April 1963.

13 E. Hobsbawm 'The Dialogue on Marxism', *Marxism Today*, February 1966. This was based on a talk given at the Marx Memorial Library on 31 October 1965.

14 Details of his Ghana visit and his report can be found in Klugmann Archive, Marx Memorial Library.

18 Late Spring

1 'Kitty Cornforth Obituaries', Klugmann Archive, Marx Memorial Library.

2 Max Rosenheim to James Klugmann, 20 April 1965, and Klugmann's reply, 24 May 1965, Klugmann Archive, Marx Memorial Library.

3 Michael Seifert, interview with the author.

4 Pete Carter, interview with the author.

5 Mike Carter, interview with the author.

6 J. Klugmann, 'Preface', in J. Klugmann (ed.), *Dialogue of Christianity and Marxism* (London: Lawrence and Wishart, 1968).

7 Ibid.

8 The series was shown on the Rediffusion ITV channel on 7, 8 and 9 November 1967.

9 Klugmann, 'Preface', in Klugmann, *Dialogue of Christianity and Marxism*, pp. viii–ix.

10 Ibid., p. ix.
11 Paul Oestreicher, interview with the author.
12 Pete Carter, interview with the author.
13 Tom Bell, interview with the author.
14 Klugmann Archive, Marx Memorial Library.
15 C. Andrew, *The Defence of the Realm: The Authorized History of MI5* (London: Allen Lane, 2009), p. 539.
16 'Hammond', quoted in ibid., p. 539.
17 Ibid., p. 540.
18 *The Times*, 10 October 1967.
19 J. Cairncross, *The Enigma Spy: An Autobiography* (London: Century Random House, 1997), p. 142.
20 Ibid., pp. 145–6.
21 Ibid., pp. 146–7.

19 Hopes and Fears

1 J. Klugmann, *The Future of Man* (London: Communist Party, 1970), p. 1.
2 Ibid.
3 Ibid., p. 2.
4 Ibid., p. 21.
5 Ibid., pp. 21–2.
6 Ibid., p. 9.
7 J. Klugmann, 'Preface', in J. Klugmann, *The History of the Communist Party of Great Britain, Volume 1: Formation and Early Years 1919–1924* (London: Lawrence and Wishart, 1968).
8 Frank Jackson to James Klugmann (undated), CPGB Archive, CP/IND/KLUG/11/08.
9 James Klugmann to Edmund Frow, 21 October 1968, CPGB Archive, CP/IND/KLUG/03/01.
10 An extended version of the article appeared as 'Problems of Communist History', in E. Hobsbawm, *Revolutionaries* (London: Meridian, 1973), p. 8.
11 P. Fryer, 'Blimps and Little Red Flags', *Encounter* xxxiii, October 1969.
12 Hobsbawm, *Revolutionaries*, p. 9.
13 Jeff Skelley, former director of Lawrence and Wishart, confirmed this in interview with the author. He emphasised that Klugmann rejected it before it was discussed at board level.
14 Jack Cohen to James Klugmann (undated), Klugmann Archive, Marx Memorial Library.
15 Jack Cohen to James Klugmann, 14 December 1971, Klugmann Archive, Marx Memorial Library.
16 Klugmann Archive, Marx Memorial Library.
17 Hymie Fagan to James Klugmann, 8 December 1971, Klugmann Archive, Marx Memorial Library.

18 Grahame Locke, interview with the author.

19 Recordings of the two lectures to the West Lewisham Branch of the Young Communist League in autumn and December 1973 are in the British Library Sound Archive, C613/05 and C613/06.

20 Conrad Wood, interview with the author.

21 British Library, C613/06.

22 Martin Jacques, interview with the author.

23 Pete Carter, interview with the author.

24 Conrad Wood, interview with the author

20 A Good Jesuit

1 A recording of the programme is held at the Marx Memorial Library. All quotations from it here are from my transcript.

2 J. Klugmann, 'Editorial Comments', *Marxism Today*, January 1968.

3 J. Gollan, 'Socialist Democracy – Some Problems: The 20th Congress of the Communist Party of the Soviet Union in Retrospect', *Marxism Today*, January 1976.

4 See Pat Devine's contribution among others, CPGB Archive, CP/IND/KLUG/12/08.

5 Renzo Galeotti, interview with the author.

6 J. Klugmann, '20 Years of *Marxism Today*', *Marxism Today*, September 1977.

7 The two books were *Cwmardy* and *We Live*. Andreas Michaelides (former CPGB treasurer), interview with the author.

8 J. Klugmann, 'Editorial Comments', *Marxism Today*, August 1977.

9 J. Klugmann, 'Introduction: The Crisis of the Thirties: A View from the Left', in J. Clark et al. (eds), *Culture and Crisis in Britain in the 30s* (London: Lawrence and Wishart, 1979).

10 Martin Jacques, interview with the author.

11 T. Bower, *The Perfect English Spy: Dick White and the Secret War 1935–1990* (London: Heinemann, 1995), p. 376.

12 Boyle's 'Notes from the Interview with James Klugmann', Cambridge University Library, Add. 9429/IG/425(i).

13 H. Trevor-Roper, 'The Philby Affair', in E. Harrison, *The Secret World* (London: I.B.Tauris, 2014), p. 81.

14 M. MacEwen, *The Greening of a Red* (London: Pluto Press, 1991), p. 196.

15 Hill's MI5 file was released along with Hobsbawm's in 2014. See G. Andrews, 'Eric Hobsbawm and MI5', *Open Democracy*, 20 November 2014. Available at www.opendemocracy.net/geoff-andrews/eric-hobsbawm-and-mi5 (accessed 24 March 2015).

16 Martin Jacques, interview with the author.

17 Michael Seifert, Jane Bernal and Pete Carter, interviews with the author.

18 'Someone should do the Yugoslavia period – who?' Brian Simon to Jack Cohen, 7 October 1977, Brian Simon Papers, Institute of Education, University of London, OR/SIM/3/1.

Select Bibliography

Abramsky, S., *The House of Twenty Thousand Books* (London: Peter Halban, 2014).

Andrew, C., *The Defence of the Realm: The Authorized History of MI5* (London: Allen Lane, 2009).

Andrew, C. and V. Mitrokhin, *The Sword and the Shield* (New York: Basic Books, 1999).

Andrews, G., *Endgames and New Times: The Final Years of British Communism* (London: Lawrence and Wishart, 2004).

Auden, W.H., 'Honour: Gresham's School, Holt', in G. Greene (ed.), *The Old School* (Oxford: Oxford University Press, 1984; first published 1934).

Bailey, R., 'Communist in SOE: Explaining James Klugmann's Recruitment and Retention', *Intelligence and National Security* xx/1 (2005).

—— *Forgotten Voices of the Secret War: An Inside History of Special Operations During the Second World War* (London: Ebury Press, 2008).

Barratt Brown, M., *Seekers: A Twentieth Century Life* (Nottingham: Spokesman, 2013).

Borovik, G., *The Philby Files*, ed. P. Knightley (London: Warner Books, 1995).

Boyle, A., *The Climate of Treason* (London: Hutchinson, 1979).

Bridgen, J., 'Frank McEachran 1900–1975: An Unrecognised Influence on W.H. Auden', in K. Bucknell and N. Jenkins (eds), *W.H. Auden, The Map of All my Youth: Early Works, Friends and Influences* (Oxford: Clarendon Press, 1990).

Bower, T., *The Perfect English Spy: Dick White and the Secret War 1935–1990* (London: Heinemann, 1995).

Branson, N., *History of the Communist Party of Great Britain 1927–1941* (London: Lawrence and Wishart, 1985).

—— *History of the Communist Party of Great Britain 1941–1951* (London: Lawrence and Wishart, 1997).

Buchanan, T., *The Spanish Civil War and the British Labour Movement* (Cambridge: Cambridge University Press, 1991).

—— *East Wind: China and the British Left 1925–1976* (Oxford: Oxford University Press, 2012).

Burke, D., *The Lawn Road Flats: Spies, Writers and Artists* (Martlesham: Boydell Press, 2014).

Cairncross, J., *The Enigma Spy: An Autobiography* (London: Century Random House 1997).

Callaghan, J., *Cold War, Crisis and Conflict: The CPGB 1951–68* (London: Lawrence and Wishart, 2003).

Carter, M., *Anthony Blunt: His Lives* (London: Macmillan, 2001).

Cecil, R., *A Divided Life: A Personal Portrait of the Spy Donald Maclean* (New York: William Morrow, 1989).

Chapman, S., *Susan Stebbing and the Language of Common Sense* (Basingstoke: Palgrave Macmillan, 2013).

Clark, J. et al. (eds), *Culture and Crisis in Britain in the 30s* (London: Lawrence and Wishart, 1979).

Conradi, P.J., *Iris Murdoch: A Life* (London, Harper Collins, 2001).

—— *A Very English Hero: The Making of Frank Thompson* (London: Bloomsbury, 2012).

Danos, J. and M. Gibelin, *June 36: Class Struggles and the Popular Front in France* (London: Bookmarks, 1986).

Davidson, B., *Special Operations Europe: Scenes from the Anti-Nazi War* (London: Grafton Books, 1987).

Driberg, T., *Guy Burgess: A Portrait with Background* (London: Weidenfeld and Nicolson, 1956).

Earle, J., *From Nile to Danube: A Wartime Memoir* (Ljubljiana: Mladika, 2010).

Eley, G., *Forging Democracy: The History of the Left in Europe* (Oxford: Oxford University Press, 2002).

Haden Guest, C., *David Guest: A Scientist Fights for Freedom* (London: Lawrence and Wishart, 1939).

Hart, J., *Ask Me No More: An Autobiography* (London: Peter Halban, 1998).

Healey, D., *The Time of my Life* (London: Penguin, 1990).

Hobsbawm, E., *Revolutionaries* (London: Meridian, 1973).

—— 'The Historians Group of the Communist Party', in M. Cornforth (ed.), *Rebels and their Causes* (London: Lawrence and Wishart 1978).

—— *Interesting Times* (London: Allen Lane, 2002).

Holroyd, M., *Lytton Strachey: A Biography* (London: Penguin Books, 1971).

Howarth, T.E.B., *Cambridge Between the Wars* (London: Collins, 1978).

Hyde, D., *I Believed* (London: William Heinemann, 1951).

Ingram, K., *Rebel: The Short Life of Esmond Romilly* (London: Weidenfeld and Nicholson, 1985).

Jackson, J., *The Popular Front in France; Defending Democracy 1934–1938* (Cambridge: Cambridge University Press, 1988).

Johnson, S., *Agents Extraordinary* (London: Robert Hale, 1975).

Kiernan, V., 'On Treason', *London Review of Books* ix/12 (25 June 1987).

—— 'The Unrewarded End', *London Review of Books* xx/18 (17 September 1998).

Kildea, P., *Benjamin Britten: A Life in the Twentieth Century* (London: Allen Lane, 2013).

Kingsford, P., *The Hunger Marchers in Britain 1920–1940* (London: Lawrence and Wishart, 1982).

Klugmann, J., *Wall Street's Drive to War* (London: Communist Party, 1950).

—— *From Trotsky to Tito* (London: Lawrence and Wishart, 1951).

—— (ed.), *Dialogue of Christianity and Marxism* (London: Lawrence and Wishart, 1968).

—— *The History of the Communist Party of Great Britain, Vol. 1: Formation and Early Years 1919–1924* (London: Lawrence and Wishart, 1968).

—— *The History of the Communist Party of Great Britain, Vol. 2: The General Strike 1925–1926* (London: Lawrence and Wishart, 1969).

—— *The Future of Man* (London: Communist Party, 1970).

Koestler, A., *The Invisible Writing* (London: Vintage, 2005).

Krivitsky, W., *I Was Stalin's Agent* (London: Hamish Hamilton, 1939).

Lane Patey, D., *The Life of Evelyn Waugh: A Critical Biography* (Oxford: Blackwell, 1998).

Lees, M., *The Rape of Serbia* (New York: Harcourt Brace Jovanovitch, 1990).

McCulloch, G. and T. Woodin, 'Learning a Liberal Education: The Case of the Simon Family', *Oxford Review of Education* xxxvi/2 (2010).

McEachran, F., *The Unity of Europe* (n.p.: Search Publishing Co., 1932).

MacEwen, M., 'The Day the Party Had to Stop', *Socialist Register* xiii (1976).

——, *The Greening of a Red* (London: Pluto Press, 1991).

Macintyre, B., *A Spy Among Friends* (London: Bloomsbury, 2014).

Maclean, F., *Eastern Approaches* (London: Cape, 1949).

Macleod, A., *The Death of Uncle Joe* (London: Merlin Press, 1997).

McMeekin, S., *The Red Milllionaire: A Political Biography of Willi Münzenberg* (New Haven, CT: Yale University Press, 2003).

McNeish, J., *The Sixth Man: The Extraordinary Life of Paddy Costello* (London: Quartet Books, 2008).

Martin, D., *The Web of Disinformation* (New York: Harcourt Brace Jovanovitch, 1990).

Miles, J., *The Nine Lives of Otto Katz* (London: Bantam Books, 2010).

Modin, Y., *My Five Cambridge Friends* (London: Headline, 1994).

Monk, R., *Ludwig Wittgenstein: The Duty of Genius* (London: Penguin Books, 1991) .

Morgan, K., *Against War and Fascism* (Manchester: Manchester University Press, 1989).

—— *Harry Pollitt* (Manchester: Manchester University Press, 1993).

Morgan, K. et al. (eds), *Communists and British Society 1920–1991* (London: Rivers Oram Press, 2007).

Mortimer, E., *The Rise of the French Communist Party 1920–1947* (London: Faber and Faber, 1984).

Orwell, G., *The Road to Wigan Pier* (London: Penguin Books, 2014; first published 1937).

Page, B., D. Leitch and P. Knightley, *Philby: The Spy Who Betrayed a Generation* (London: Sphere Books, 1977).

Philby, K., *My Silent War* (London: MacGibbon and Kee, 1968).

Pincher, C., *Their Trade is Treachery* (London: Sidgwick and Jackson, 1981).

Potts, A., *Zilliacus: A Life for Peace and Socialism* (London: Merlin Press, 2002).

Raine, K., *Autobiographies* (London: Skoob Books, 1991).

Rees, G., *A Chapter of Accidents* (London: Chatto and Windus, 1972).

Rycroft, C., 'Memoirs of an Old Bolshevik', in P. Fuller (ed.), *Psychoanalysis and Beyond* (London: Hogarth Press, 1991).

Samuel, R., *The Lost World of British Communism* (London: Verso, 2006).

Samuels, S., 'The Left Book Club', *Journal of Contemporary History* i/2 (1966).

Schlogel, K., *Moscow 1937* (Cambridge: Polity, 2012).

Seale, P. and M. McConville, *Philby: The Long Road to Moscow* (London: Hamish Hamilton, 1973).

Sommerfield, J., *May Day* (London: Lawrence and Wishart, 1984).

Srebnik, H., *London Jews and British Communism* (Edgware: Valentine Mitchell, 1995).

Stebbing, L.S., *Thinking to Some Purpose* (London: Pelican, 1939).

Straight, M., *After Long Silence* (New York: W.W. Norton, 1983).

Thompson, E.P., *Beyond the Frontier* (London: Merlin Press, 1997).

Thompson, W., *The Good Old Cause* (London: Pluto Press, 1992).

Toynbee, P., *Friends Apart* (London: Sidgwick and Jackson 1954).

Upward, E., *The Rotten Elements* (London: Quartet, 1979).

Waugh, E., *Love Among the Ruins* (London: Chapman and Hall, 1953)

—— *Unconditional Surrender* (London: Penguin, 1964).

West, N., *MASK: MI5's Penetration of the Communist Party of Great Britain* (London: Routledge, 2005).

West, N. and O. Tsarev, *The Crown Jewels* (London: HarperCollins, 1999).

Wood, N., *Communism and British Intellectuals* (London: Victor Gollancz, 1959).

Wright, P., *Spycatcher* (New York: Viking Penguin, 1987).

Index